R. ACWORTH · THE PHILOSOPHY OF
JOHN NORRIS OF BEMERTON

STUDIEN UND MATERIALIEN
ZUR GESCHICHTE DER PHILOSOPHIE

Begründet von Heinz Heimsoeth und Giorgio Tonelli

Herausgegeben von Yvon Belaval und Gerhard Funke

Kleine Reihe
Band 6

RICHARD ACWORTH
THE PHILOSOPHY OF
JOHN NORRIS OF BEMERTON

1979

GEORG OLMS VERLAG HILDESHEIM · NEW YORK

RICHARD ACWORTH

THE PHILOSOPHY OF
JOHN NORRIS OF BEMERTON
(1657 – 1712)

1979

GEORG OLMS VERLAG HILDESHEIM · NEW YORK

© Copyright 1979 by Georg Olms, Hildesheim
Alle Rechte vorbehalten
Printed in Germany
Druck: Aku, Bamberg
ISBN 3 487 06884 2

IN MEMORY OF MY PARENTS

CONTENTS

Preface   IX
Chapter   I: Life and work   1
Chapter   II: Earliest writings, 1682-1684   21
Chapter III: The root of liberty (1685)
               and Norris's correspondence
               with Henry More   41
Chapter   IV: The miscellanies of 1687   55
Chapter   V: The ideal world: God and human
               thought   89
Chapter   VI: The theory of love   154
Chapter VII: The practical teaching of
               Norris   184
Chapter VIII: Reason and faith   212
Chapter   IX: Essence and substance, and
               the immorality of the soul   230
Chapter   X: Controversies with Locke and
               with the Quakers   251
Chapter   XI: Conclusion   285
Notes   311
Bibliography   370

PREFACE

Norris is a little known figure in the history of English thought. While his poetry has never been entirely neglected and his significance in literary history is recognised, his philosophical and religious thought has been largely forgotten and he is known, if at all, only as a late follower of the Cambridge Platonists, a critic of Locke, and an admirer of Malebranche. It is true that he was not a philosopher of the first rank; but his works continued to be read for a century after his death, and he is, I believe, a figure of considerable interest in his own right. In this study, the attempt is made to present his thought as clearly as possible, in close reliance on his own works. The presentation is intended to be primarily historical, since it is essential to know what his views were before their permanent significance can be assessed. If he is treated in comparative isolation, this reflects the fact that he was a somewhat isolated figure in his own lifetime, influenced more by his reading of Greek, medieval and French philosophers than by discussion with his English contemporaries. Nevertheless it is hoped that his involvement in contemporary controversies has also been fully documented.

In this book, the main themes of Norris's writings are examined in turn. The reader who seeks a fuller account of the contents of each of Norris's books individually is refered to my French thesis, "La Philosophie de John Norris (1657-1712)", where each book is treated separately.

My thanks are due to many people: to Professors Henri Gouhier and Ferdinand Alquié of the Sorbonne, above all; to many individual people and institutions who are mentioned in the footnotes; and to the libraries of the following libraries in particular:

Cambridge University Library; Sion College Library, London; Niedersächsische Landesbibliothek, Hannover; Universitäts- bibliothek der Karl-Marx-Universität, Leipzig; in addition to those mentioned in the French thesis.

Derby, January 1979

CHAPTER I LIFE AND WORK

John Norris was born at Collingbourne Kingston, Wiltshire,
on 2 January 1657, and was baptised ten days later.[1] His father,
also called John, was vicar of this parish at the time, but in the
list of incumbents he is labelled as "intruder" because his pre-
decessor had been deprived as a royalist. On the restoration of
the monarchy in 1660 the elder Norris lost his living, but he quickly found another and became vicar of Aldbourne in the same diocese
of Salisbury, where he remained till his death in 1682. It was here
that Norris passed his childhood with his parents, his two brothers,
and his sister.[2] But the family's connection with Collingbourne
Kingston was not lost: the elder Norris had bought an estate there
which was divided at his death amongst his children, and throughout his life our Norris owned lands in his native parish which he in
turn left to his eldest son.

The elder Norris seems to have been a Calvinist in theology,[3]
but he was no separatist. He seems to have been one of those mod-
erates who felt that the external constitution of the Church was a
matter of insufficient importance to justify any schism or separation
from the national Church. This is the point of view which he expressed in his posthumous Discourse concerning the Pretended Religious
Assembling in Private Conventicles, published by his son in 1685.
Norris's own position on this matter was not fundamentally different
from that of his father, though he was more strongly devoted to epis-
copacy than his father had been. Although Norris early abandoned
the Calvinism in which he had been brought up, he seems to have
been profoundly influenced by the religious seriousness of his home
background. He speaks of his father with affection and respect in

the preface to his edition of his posthumous book.

At the age of thirteen Norris went to Winchester College. There still exists in the College archives a letter from George Morley, Bishop of Winchester, to the College authorities, dated 9 September 1671, recommending that Norris, who was already at the College, should be made a "childe" or scholar. "Having received a very good character of John Norris a youth in your schoole as to his proficiency since his coming thither, and the progresse he is likely, if continued there, to make in learning; I have thought fit to write to you in his behalfe, and to desire you to admit him Childe of your Colledge at your next election, if you find him (as I am informed you will) well qualified and very capable of your favour in this particular, to which he is very earnestly recommended by your Visitor and very loving freind...."[4] This recommendation was acted on, and Norris became a "childe" of Winchester. The curriculum at Winchester at this period, as indeed a century later, was exclusively classical;[5] there was nothing of the mathematics which had so strongly impressed the young Descartes at the Jesuit College of La Flèche fifty years earlier. Later in life Norris strongly criticised this purely classical education, but he tells us at the same time that he had followed it with enthusiasm, and all his writings give evidence of his good knowledge of Greek and Latin literature.

In 1676 Norris entered Exeter College, Oxford, as a "sojourner" or commoner. The choice of Exter College was probably due to the fact that his elder brother Samuel had been a Fellow there since 1663. Norris seems to have given himself wholeheartedly to academic life and studies, and it was at Oxford that his intellectual development chiefly took place and that his own ideas began to be formed. The course which he must have followed began with classical grammar, rhetoric, and logic, and went on to moral and meta-

2

physical philosophy. The philosophy that was taught was Aristotelian, and it appears from Norris's own writings that the manuals in use consisted largely of the works of seventeenth century Protestant Scholastics, such as those of Burgersdictus in logic and of Scheibler in metaphysics, [6] though the works of the great Scholastics and of Aristotle himself were also read to some extent. One had to follow the courses and take part in scholastic disputations, but examinations scarcely existed and a keen student could devote a large part of his time to private reading. [7]

Although in his Reflections upon the Conduct of Human Life Norris sharply criticised the practice of scholastic disputation as a mere intellectual sleight of hand (a criticism that he later to a great extent withdrew in the preface to the Second Part of his Theory of the Ideal or Intelligible World), it is clear from all his writings that he acquired both a mastery of and a high esteem for the scholastic method. Nevertheless Aristotelian and Scholastic philosophy did not form the centre of his interests. Norris's interest was centred on Platonic philosophy, from Plato, Plotinus, and Hierocles to Ficinus and Henry More, and it is clear that he read widely in this field. It is not possible to say to what extent these studies date from Norris's time at Exeter College and to what extent from after 1680, when he took the degree of Bachelor of Arts and became a Fellow of All Souls, but it is certain that by that time he had already acquired a good reputation for classical and philosophical learning.

In 1680 All Souls was at a turning point in its history. Since the middle of the sixteenth century an abuse had been growing in the election of Fellows. Retiring Fellows often had a young relative or friend whom they wished to have as their successor, and candidates recommended in this way were invariably successful at the annual elections, regardless of their intellectual standing. The abuse reached its peak after the Restoration, when certain retiring Fellows simply nominated the candidates who offered them the largest sums of money. Finally, in 1680-1, Jeames (Warden 1665-1687), in agreement with Archbishop Sancroft the Visitor, took energetic measures to curb this scandalous practice. For two successive years he used his veto to prevent the election of all candidates who were supported by retiring Fellows; and since this rendered the elections void the Visitor had the right under the statutes to fill up the vacant places. After two years the opposition of the Fellows was broken, and ordinary elections could be resumed without abuse. Norris was one of the Fellows nominated by Archbishop Sancroft during this crisis.

Sancroft, it is clear, took his duty of nominating the new Fellows of All Souls seriously. He obtained specimens of the work of the candidates, together with short notes of what was otherwise known about them. There still exists in the Bodleian Library a Latin exercise on the theme Ferrum tuetur principem melius fides signed by "Jo.Norris e Coll Exon", which is one of these specimens and to which the following note has been added: "A very excellent Scholar and one who spoke verses in the Theater with very great applause, a very good Grecian and philosopher, and a young Batchelour of Arts, he had his duration at Winchester School and is a Wiltshireman and a Clergyman's second son."[8]

Although Norris was a Fellow for only nine years, he always retained a great affection for All Souls. As late as 1701, in the preface to the First Part of his Theory of the Ideal ... World, he spoke of the time "When I had the honour to be one of the Fellows of All Souls College, which may God ever bless and prosper." Conversely, when the Codrington Library was built in the middle

4

Fellows of the past, a fine bust of Norris was set up there. In a sermon preached before the Fellows and published in 1691 under the title of a Discourse concerning the Excellence of Praise and Thanksgiving, Norris declared that the life of a Fellow combined the advantages of the "active" and "contemplative" lives. "Here you have solitude, retirement, and leisure, and so may serve God without distraction and without disturbance ... And as you here enjoy all the advantages of serving God in the way of a contemplative life, so secondly you have here all the advantages of fitting your selves to serve both him and the public in an active life, whenever you shall be called to it. For ... you have all the advantages of learning that books and conversation, and leisure to make the best use and improvement of both, can possibly afford."[9] There is no doubt that, in his later life as a country parson, Norris was to miss the tranquillity for study, thought, and writing that he had known at All Souls.

In 1684 Norris received the degree of Master of Arts and was ordained priest. The first of his published sermons, the important Discourse upon Romans 12, 3, usually referred to by Norris as The Root of Liberty, was preached before the University in the church of St. Peter's in the East during the following Lent.[10] But even the first years of his stay at All Souls were filled with literary activity. These writings, which will be examined in the following chapter, are our main source of knowledge for the development of his personality, interests, and ideas during these years, for few references to him during his life at Oxford survive. Hearne indeed tells us that he "had always the character of an ingenious, sober, and industrious man",[11] while Anthony Wood, speaking of the pub-

lication of his <u>Tractatus adversus Reprobationis Absolutae De-</u>
<u>cretum</u>, calls him "a conceited youngster".[12] This criticism by
the censorious Wood probably signifies only that the young Norris
was sure of his own views and had no hesitation in contradicting
those of others. In his Oxford days Norris was indeed pushing and
self-confident; it was only later that he became a notably fair and
polite controversialist, and that his own philosophy led him to be
careful to affirm nothing as certainly true but what he clearly saw
to be so. But the self-confidence of the early Norris was only the
concomitant of his originality and intellectual independence. By
1687, when he published his <u>Miscellanies</u>, the essential lines of
his thought were already clear.

    Norris's last two years at Oxford saw the publication of <u>The</u>
<u>Theory and Regulation of Love</u> (1688) and <u>Reason and Religion</u>
(1689). These two works developed themes which he had already
broached in his earlier writings, but <u>The Theory and Regulation</u>
<u>of Love</u> contained his first references to the works of Malebranche,
while <u>Reason and Religion</u> showed strong evidence of his influence.
There is thus every reason to believe that these last years at Oxford
marked the beginning of Norris's study of Malebranche, which was
to have such a notable influence on his later works. The development of Norris's philosophy is probably best understood if his
early writings, culminating in the <u>Miscellanies</u> of 1687 which always remained one of his most popular works, are considered on
their own, and accordingly this is the plan that has been followed in
this book.

    In 1689 Norris married and left Oxford. It is not known whether
the desire to marry was the principal reason which led him to leave
the university, but probably this desire was linked with the wish
that he had often expressed to move into the country. Very little is

known about his wife, Elizabeth, whom he named as executrix of
his will in 1706 and who survived him. The Norrises had three
sons and a daughter, named John, Edward, Elizabeth, and Thomas,
of whom John and Edward were later ordained, while Elizabeth
married a clergyman. [13] Norris's love for his children, and the
care that he took of their upbringing, can be seen from the little
book which he wrote for their use: Spiritual Counsel; or, the Father's Advice to his Children (1694). His love for and confidence
in his wife can be seen from his will, so that all the indications
that we have suggest that the Norrises were a united, serious-
minded, and profoundly Christian family.

On leaving Oxford in 1689, Norris was appointed rector of
Newton St. Loe in the diocese of Bath and Wells. It is not known
how he came in contact with the patron of this living, Joseph Langton, a rich Bristol merchant who had bought the manor of Newton
St. Loe, which lies between Bristol and Bath, in 1666 and who lived
there, a Justice of the Peace and respected local figure, until his
death in 1720. [14] Soon after his arrival in the diocese Norris was
called on to preach the Visitation Sermon before Bishop Ken and
the assembled clergy in Bath Abbey on 30 July 1689, and his sermon,
in which he denounced the evil of non-residence, bore witness to
his high ideal of the pastoral ministry. But although Norris, in his
letter dedicating Discourses upon the Beatitudes (1690) to Langton,
expressed his gratitude to him for the retreat which he now enjoyed,
it does not seem that he was altogether happy at Newton St. Loe.
In his "Letter to the Reader" introducing the same volume of sermons, he expresses the fear that he will not be able to do, where
he is, all the good that he might have done in a different situation:
his sermons are not very well received in his parish, and that, he
declares, is why he publishes so many books and sermons, hoping

to do elsewhere in this way the good that he cannot do at home.
Fresh from Oxford, Norris doubtless found that his rural congre-
gation hardly appreciated his learned and profound sermons. But
he was right in thinking that they would be better received elsewhere. The Discourses upon the Beatitudes attained their fifteenth
edition in 1728, and were followed in 1691 by a second volume of
sermons, entitled Practical Discourses upon Several Divine Subjects.

The two and a half years that Norris spent at Newton St. Loe
were a period of intense literary activity for him. In addition to
the two volumes of sermons already mentioned, he also published
Reflections upon the Conduct of Human Life in 1690, a second and
much enlarged edition of which appeared in the following year. These
years also marked the beginning of Norris's involvement in three
controversies. As soon as Locke's Essay concerning Human Understanding appeared in 1690, a friend asked Norris his opinion of it,
and later that same year Norris published his Cursory Reflections
upon a Book called, an Essay concerning Human Understanding as
an appendix to his Discourses concerning the Beatitudes. Le Clerc
replied to Norris's criticism in his Bibliothèque Choisie, and his
reply was translated and published in the Athenian Gazette. Norris
in turn replied to this hostile criticism of his Cursory Reflections,
but Locke himself did not enter the controversy at this stage, perhaps because he and Norris had a mutual friend in Lady Masham.[15]

It was also at Newton St. Loe that Norris came into contact
with the Quakers. Passages in Reflections upon the Conduct of
Human Life led certain Quakers to think that Norris's theory of
knowledge resembled their own view of "the light within". A notable
Quaker named Richard Vickris lived near Newton St. Loe and was
a friend of Joseph Langton; it was through him that Norris came to
know the Quakers and the Quakers interested themselves in him.

There followed a sometimes sharp but interesting controversy, in which Norris traced the precise differences between his system and that of the Quakers.[16]

It was at this period too that Norris became involved in a controversy with the Nonconformists. In the course of his sermon on the text "Blessed are the Peacemakers" (the seventh of the Discourses upon the Beatitudes) he accused the Dissenters of the sin in schism, a charge that was particularly resented on account of the recent passing of the Toleration Act of 1689. Norris replied to their complaints in The Charge of Schism Continued (1691), an originally anonymous work which in the course of time drew two replies from the Nonconformist side. Norris always remained in sympathy with the High Church party, as the anonymous pamphlet The Distinction of High Church and Low Church, which he seems to have written in 1705, testifies, but his views on secular and ecclesiastical politics had little or no connection with the rest of his thought. They are briefly summarised in an appendix to this chapter.

Throughout this time Norris was in friendly contact with Locke's friend Lady Masham, despite a misunderstanding on the subject of her supposed blindness, and in the spring of 1692 he received a strong testimony of the esteem that she and Locke had for him. Norris was presented to the benefice of Bemerton, near Salisbury, by the Earl of Pembroke to whom Locke had dedicated his Essay concerning Human Understanding; and, as he learned not long after, he owed this presentation to Locke's recommendation. Later in the same year, however, the good relations of Norris and Locke were broken by a personal quarrel which was destined to embitter all their later dealings with each other. Norris and Locke would in any case have been philosophical adversaries, but the asperity of their references to each other after 1692 (more particularly of Locke's references to Norris) had its source in a private quarrel. [17]

Bemerton is today a suburb of Salisbury. Opposite the little church stands the rectory, built by George Herbert who was rector of Bemerton from 1630 till 1633, where the Norrises lived. The lawns of the rectory go down to the Nadder, a chalk stream full of trout which joins the Avon at Salisbury, and the whole gives a picture of almost idyllic peace. Norris remained at Bemerton till his death, holding the prebend of Stanton in addition to his parish. But despite Bemerton's appearance of peace, Norris found some difficulty in combining his parochial duties with his literary work. Moreover, the position of Bemerton close to the main road from London to Exeter meant that he was often visited by friends who were travelling past. One of these visitors was Lady Mary Chudleigh,of Ashton,near Exeter, herself a poetical and philosophical authoress, and it is to her that we owe the only description of Norris's appearance that we possess. In a letter to Elizabeth Thomas, the "Corinna" who corresponded with Norris without ever meeting him in person, Lady Chudleigh wrote: "He is a little man of a pale complexion, but he has a great deal of sweetness and good humour in his face, attended with an extraordinary modesty and a more than common air of humility; there seems to be a reservedness in his temper, but when you are acquainted with him you will find it only the result of thoughtfulness. In a word he is a man whose conversation is very agreeable as well as instructive,..." [18]

Although Lady Masham passed from friendship to hostility, Norris never lacked friends and admirers among the learned ladies of his time. More important from our point of view than either Lady Chudleigh or "Corinna" was Mary Astell. Not only did Mary Astell

correspond with Norris on the subject of the love of God, a correspondence that was published in 1695 under the title of <u>Letters
concerning the Love of God</u>, but she also became a capable defender
of his views in the controversies which did not cease to surround
him.[19]

A certain shadow was cast over Norris's life at Bemerton
by the hostility of his bishop, Gilbert Burnet, a strong Whig who
was determined to refuse him any further preferment in his diocese.[20] But Norris still had contacts at Oxford,[21] and his literary
output was considerable. A third volume of sermons appeared in
1693, a fourth in 1698. It was in one of the sermons in the third
volume, <u>A Discourse concerning the Measure of Divine Love</u>, that
Norris first enunciated his mature teaching on the love of God,
teaching which was explained and amplified in his correspondence
with Mary Astell. Besides this important correspondence, two
other exchanges of letters with Norris during his time at Bemerton
have also been published. In 1693 a young lawyer named William
Melmoth wrote to ask his advice on the morality of taking the oath
of allegiance to William and Mary; about 1696 Elizabeth Thomas
("Corinna") introduced herself to Norris by sending him an ode she
had written in his honour, and asked his advice for the direction of
her studies. These letters throw some light on Norris's thought,
but their main interest is that they show that his reputation in the
country was growing.

It was not, however, until 1697 that Norris wrote the first
full length book of his Bemerton period: <u>An Account of Reason and
Faith</u>. In this, one of his most successful works, he intervened in
the controversy with the Socinians and Deists, putting his position
with great clarity and arguing in a serious and courteous manner,
so that his book became of lasting value. Then in 1701 appeared

the First Part of his principal metaphysical work, An Essay towards the Theory of the Ideal or Intelligible World, which was
followed in 1704 by the Second Part of the same book. Norris had
been intending to write such a book since his last years at Oxford,
but had put the project aside for many years. The First Part of
his Theory treats of the Intelligible World in itself, and its teaching is to a large extent a restatement and explanation of theories
advanced in his early writings; the Second Part deals with man's
knowledge of this Intelligible World, and its teaching owes much
to that of Malebranche.

Many of Norris's works were widely popular and often reprinted, but this was not the case with the Theory. Nevertheless
its publication did not go unnoticed. "Corinna" repeated to Norris
the comments that she heard about it,[22] while its sometimes sen-
tentious style became the object of a satirical parody.[23] Henry
Needler on the other hand welcomed it with great enthusiasm[24],
as did Leibniz's English correspondent Thomas Burnet and his
namesake the author of Theoria Telluris Sacra.[25] Leibniz replied
to Burnet in a somewhat noncommittal way;[26] his considered judgement after reading the book would probably have been similar to
that expressed in the review of the Second Part of the Theory which
appeared in the Leipzig Acta Eruditorum, a review which was generally sympathetic but which suggested that Norris would have
profited from reading Leibniz's Meditationes de Cognitione, Veri-
tate, et Ideis.[27] Other reactions to Norris's Theory will be examined later in this book.[28]

Although Norris's Theory was not altogether a success, it
did not mark the end of his literary projects. The Miscellanies
fully retained their early popularity, but since the time of their
publication Norris had changed his views on some of the questions

that they treated. Accordingly he completely revised the Miscellanies for the fourth edition, which appeared in 1706. But Norris
also planned to write a series of works on the Christian virtues.
The first volume of this series, A Practical Treatise concerning
Humility, appeared in 1707, but before he could write a second
his interest wad distracted by the controversy on the immortality
of the soul. Norris intervened in this controversy with two works,
both occasioned by the writings of Henry Dodwell. In 1708 he published A Philosophical Discourse concerning the Natural Immortality of the Soul, and in the following year he replied to Dodwell's
answer to this Discourse in A Letter to Mr. Dodwell concerning
the Immortality of the Soul of Man. These two works were always
subsequently printed together. They are both polite in tone and
clear in their reasoning, and must be regarded as a useful contribution to the debate on the soul.

After this more metaphysical interlude, Norris returned to
his plan of writing a series of "practical" studies of the virtues.
But he now declared that the completion of this project would be
too much for one of his poor health: instead he would write on only
one fundamental virtue. A Treatise concerning Christian Prudence
was published in 1710, and it was destined to be the last of Norris's
works. His health had not been good during the last years of his
life, and he died at the beginning of February, 1712, and was buried
on 5 February at Bemerton. A memorial tablet on the north wall of
the church there recalls his memory in the words:

> H(ic) S(epultus) E(st)
> JOHANNES NORRIS
> Parochiae hujus Rector
> Ubi annos 20 bene Latuit
> Curae Pastorali et Literis vacans:

Quo in Recessu Sibi posuit

Late jam p(er) Orbem sparsa

Ingenii paris ac Pietatis

Monumenta

Obijt Ano $\quad$ Dni 1711 $\quad$ 29
AEtatis 54

That Norris lived in obscurity is true: at Bemerton he was
far from the centres of the intellectual life of his time. But it is
also true that his works were already widely scattered through
the world. Leibniz discussed him in his letters, and the Acta
Eruditorum published reviews of two of his works. And in England itself many of his writings long retained their popularity. An
Accound of Reason and Faith was republished as late as 1790 in
a fourteenth edition, while some of his shorter essays were reprinted even more often. The Theory of the Ideal or Intelligible
World, it is true, was not so generally well received, though it
was not without admirers nor entirely without influence. And the
considerable place that Norris occupies in the gossip of Dunton's
Life and Errors shows that he was no unknown figure in the literary
world of his time. [31]

As he got older, Norris left the ardent polemics of his youth
behind. He became more careful of the exact truth of what he asserted, and more humble in the claims that he made for his own
views. In later life he was a notably fair opponent in controversy,
and was generally recognised as such. But it is essentially from
his writings that Norris can be known. In this book we shall attempt
to trace the development of his thought, and to present his developed
teaching on the main subjects that he treated. In the final chapter
his thought will be considered as a whole and its sources will be
examined, and an attempt will be made to assess his posthumous
reputation and influence.

Addendum to Chapter I: Norris's views on secular and ecclesiastical politics.

During his time at Oxford Norris was, in common with the great majority of the university, a strong Tory.[32] But, as many of the poems in his Miscellanies testify, he early determined to take no active part in political controversy, and he adhered to this decision throughout his life. His only later intervention in questions of secular politics was of a purely private nature. In 1693 a young lawyer named William Melmoth wrote to ask his advice on the morality of taking the oath of allegiance to William and Mary. The remains of the ensuing correspondence were published in 1796 by Melmoth's son, then an old man, in the Memoirs of a late Eminent Advocate which he wrote about his father. Norris's reply to Melmoth was in essence that obedience was always due to the de facto government, and that therefore it was permissible to confirm this obedience by oath. This was an essentially non-political view, non-resistance divorced from the divine right of kings. It agreed with the view expressed by William Sherlock in his Case of Allegiance (1691), and was common amongst Tories who accepted the Revolution; but it did not really amount to a developed political philosophy.[33]

If Norris took no further part in secular politics, however, he remained throughout his life a High Churchman in ecclesiastical matters. In the course of a sermon on the text "Blessed are the Peacemakers" in his Discourses upon the Beatitudes (1690), he affirmed that the Dissenters were guilty of the sin of schism in separating themselves from the Church of England. This charge was particularly resented on account of the recent passing of the Toleration Act of 1689, and Norris replied to their objections in The Charge of Schism Continued (1691). Although this work was first published anonymously, Norris made no serious attempt to disguise his authorship, and he later republished it in 1701 after including it in his Treatises upon Several Subjects (1697). In this work Norris argued that all that the Toleration Act of 1689 had done was to remove the penalties for infringing the acts which enjoined conformity to the Church of England, without removing the obligation which those acts imposed. For in his view, though sanctions might be necessary for the practical enforcement of a law, they were not necessary for its obligation, which depended only (apart from the intrinsic reasonableness of what was commanded) on its being enjoined by an authority having a right to be obeyed.[34] Moreover, he continued, even without any positive civil law on the subject, to separate without sufficient reason from the National Church would always be sinful, since the New Testament itself enjoined peace and unity amongst Christians. Only a sincere conviction that communion with the National Church was illicit would justify separation, and Norris was convinced that the practice of "occasional conformity" showed that most Nonconformists did not regard this communion as strictly illicit.

In the course of The Charge of Schism Continued Norris declared on the one hand his opposition to the Toleration Act, but also affirmed that, if the Dissenters were sincerely convinced that it would be illicit for them to communicate with the Church of England, they must follow their consciences: they should in that case now enjoy in peace the benefits which the Toleration Act had brought them, just as previously they should have accepted the penalties which the law imposed. Norris's attitude to toleration was therefore ambivalent: the State had the duty of preserving the religious unity of the people, but the individual must nevertheless follow his own conscience. This view was in fact an application of the doctrine of non-resistance to the case of the laws enjoining conformity to the Established Church. It was not widely different from the attitude taken by some States in modern times towards conscientious objectors to military service.

The Charge of Schism Continued elicited two replies from Nonconformists. In his anonymous Defence of Mr. M. H.'s Brief Enquiry into the Nature of Schism and the Vindication of it (1693), which was primarily written in defence of a work by Matthew Henry, William Tong devoted five pages to Norris's book. He argued that Norris had not sufficiently examined the terms of the Toleration Act, which did not confine itself to exempting Dissenters from the penalties attaching to non-attendance at Anglican services, but which explicitly allowed them to open their own places of worship. Norris, he declared, gave too strong a sense to the word "establishment" when referred to the "Established Church"; in reality this meant only that the Church of England possessed certain legal privileges, - a fact which noone denied. But Tong's remarks on Norris's book were written only in passing. A much fuller reply was that of Simon Browne, a dissenting minister at Portsmouth, who published The Charge of Schism Discharged in 1710, at a time when the subject had again become topical due to the controversy about the proposed Occasional Conformity Bill. Throughout his book Browne treated Norris with respect as one whose works had greatly served the cause of Christianity, and his argument was all the stronger for being based on principles with which Norris himself agreed.

On the legal side of the question, Browne's argument was similar to that of Tong: Norris understood in too strong a sense the "establishment" of the Church of England. But, unlike Tong, Browne also replied to Norris's argument from the New Testament on the

unity of the Church. He pointed out that the New Testament nowhere enjoined that all the Christians of a particular country should
worship in the same way; it called only for a unity in the basic essentials of faith and worship. No Church could command the obedience of Christians unless it had a divine authority to interpret
the Bible; short of that, Christians would be wrong to let themselves be determined by other people's judgements. "In short",
he wrote, "either an infallible judge must be set up, or men must
be left to the conduct of their own private judgement."[34] The views
which Browne expressed on the necessity of private judgement in
religious matters were in fact identical with those of Norris himself, and Browne was clearly convinced that, if Norris could set
aside all political prejudice, he would agree with him on the rightness of a generous toleration. He asked Norris to reply to his book,
and concluded in a most friendly style: "I am persuaded Mr. Norris
is doing service to God and the Church, 'tis my hearty prayer he may
do much more, and I can see no reason from our different sentiments on earth, why we may not meet in the same heaven hereafter,
or why we should not love like brethren and members of the same
Body here."[35] The Charge of Schism Discharged appeared, however,
in the same year as Norris's last book; and Norris, who died eigh-
teen months later after a long illness, never replied to it.

Norris's devotion to the Church of England was expressed in
many places. In an anonymous pamphlet of 1705 entitled The Distinction of High Church and Low Church he wrote that a High Churchman was "one that is truly and sincerely for the Church of England,
... that allows and consents to her doctrine, that reverences her
order and discipline, that heartily likes and approves her worship,
that beauty of holiness, that reasonable service that appears in
all her offices and ministrations; and in one word, that wishes well

18

to and has a zealous concern for her whole constitution, which indeed is truly Christian and primitive",[36] while a Low Churchman was "one that is but coldly and indifferently affected towards the Church, and not much affected by what becomes of her."[37] And in his last work, A Treatise concerning Christian Prudence, he wrote of how one ought to choose one's religion. As compared with Judaism and other religions, he held, Christianity was seen to be true both by the excellence of its teaching and by the miracles that confirmed it. But what particular Church was one to join? Most people took over their Church allegiance without question from their families, but, he declared, "our prudent Christian will not act after this manner in any thing, much less in so weighty a concern as that of religion; but laying aside all sorts of prejudice, and considering nothing but the pure merits of the cause, what is in itself true, just, and right, and having prayed to God for his blessing and direction, he consults and makes use of his reason in the best manner that he can, which he directs by Scripture, the great rule of it in all matters of faith."[38] Like his friend Mary Astell, Norris was convinced that an impartial and objective examination of this sort would lead one to the Church of England as being uniquely apostolic and primitive both in doctrine and in form of government.[39] But Browne seems to have been right in thinking that such an approach, where each person's judgement was to be the final arbiter of his ecclesiastical allegiance, naturally supposed a complete toleration on the part of the State. Norris's Toryism, and the attitude on toleration which went with it, were in fact purely traditional. His love of the Church of England was real and deep, and he could not help thinking that anyone who looked at it dispassionately would see its unique merits. But his philosophy, with its insistence on the personal search for truth in religion as in all else, naturally pointed to complete toleration; and this was in fact the attitude of those of his admirers, such as Henry Needler, who did not share his traditional High Church outlook.

CHAPTER II   EARLIEST WRITINGS, 1682-1684

Many of Norris's earliest publications were translations of
Latin or Greek works, and it would be wrong to suppose that they
necessarily represent his own thought. But they all throw light on
his interests during his early years at All Souls, and one of them,
the translation of Hierocles upon the Golden Verses of the Pythagoreans, has a considerable importance in the development of his
own philosophy.

In 1682 Norris published Effigies Amoris in English: or the
Picture of Love Unveiled. This was a translation of Effigies Amoris
by Robert Waring (1613-58), a Latin essay on love and friendship
first published in 1649 which had become highly popular. Waring
seems to have intended his book in a somewhat light-hearted vein,
and it may be that Norris took it more seriously than its author
intended. Waring did indeed adopt a high and "platonic" view of
love, but the specific characteristics of Norris's later theory of
love and friendship are entirely missing, and on many points Norris's view is directly opposed to that of Waring. It seems probable
that Norris simply wished to exercise his talent as a translator
on a book which was fashionably popular, and whose subject interested him. Later, in his Reflections upon the Conduct of Human
Life (1690), Norris expressed regret that his energies at Oxford
had sometimes been devoted more to frivolous subjects and to the
increase of his reputation than to his own moral or intellectual
satisfaction, and it seems that this translation was probably one
of the works that he had in mind. It has been suggested that the
second edition of Effigies Amoris in English, published in 1701,
may have been printed without Norris's authorisation by the pub-

lisher, James Good, who wanted to take advantage of the author's reputation which had been increased that year by the publication of the First Part of his Theory of the Ideal World, and this suggestion may well be correct. [1]

Also in 1682 Norris published A Meditation of Life and Death. Translated with some Alterations out of the Works of the Learned and Ingenious Eusebius Nierembergius, an abridged translation of the last chapter of the De Arte Voluntatis of the Spanish Jesuit E. Nieremberg, one of the most popular spiritual writers of his time. This same passage, on the miseries of the present life and the joys of death, had already been translated into English by Henry Vaughan the Silurist; but Norris's version was notably shorter than Vaughan's without sacrificing the sense of the original work, and was also written in a considerably more elegant English style. This meditation has many parallels among the later works of Norris, for the consideration of death remained one of his favourite subjects, and he will doubtless not have felt the same scruples about this translation as he did about Effigies Amoris. But Nieremberg's teaching did not differ from that which was common to the Christian ascetical tradition, and there is no reason to think that he had a special influence on Norris.

If these two translations do little more than give some indication of subjects in which the young Norris was interested, the case of Hierocles upon the Golden Verses of the Pythagoreans, translated by Norris directly from the Greek and published the same year, is very different. For this work is a fine example of the sort of Platonism which formed the starting point of Norris's own thought, and which represents the principal philosophical influence that he underwent before he encountered the writings of Malebranche. Hierocles, who lived at Alexandria in the middle

22

of the fifth century, was a Neoplatonist philosopher who was considerably influenced by Christianity, and his commentary on the
Golden Verses of the Pythagoreans contains ideas which were to
be fundamental to Norris's thought throughout his life. According
to Hierocles, there is only one Creator God; the other "immortal
gods" were created by him, and if they are immutable this is only
because they "always and in equal manner contemplate the great
God their Maker, and are constantly intent upon his goodness; so
that they are secure from either change or separation, being as
it were the images of the all-productive Cause, neither disturb'd
with passion, nor tainted with evil."[2] Their constant attention to
God is in fact the root of their changeless goodness, while man's
distracted and wandering attention is the root of his changeableness. "Neither is the title of Immortal Gods intended to distinguish
them from humane souls, but only to show that they incessantly
enjoy the divine felicity, and never forget either their own nature
or their Father's goodness. Whereas, the souls of men are subject to passions, whence it comes to pass that they sometimes attend to God and their own excellency, and sometimes are diverted
from both."[3]

For Hierocles, moral virtue and intellectual knowledge are
interdependent; the spiritual soul cannot give itself to the contemplation of the truth until it has overcome the bodily passions, but
it is by attention to the truth which it already knows that it can overcome its tendencies to sin. "For when better things are unknown,
there is a necessity of being enslaved to worse. From which there
is no other way to be redeem'd than by recollection to return to
oneself and God."[4] Truth is identical with God himself, and God
is intimately present to the soul of every man, so that the way to
truth and virtue is the attentive contemplation of the truth within

23

one. But though God is present and manifests his truth uniformly and constantly to all men, "he does not actually <u>show</u> it to all, because at the time when he holds it forth, the eye of contemplation in most men is shut, or fix'd downward upon worser objects."[5] It is clear that the views of Hierocles in this matter have much in common with St. Augustine's theory of illumination.

These teachings of Hierocles correspond with two of Norris's most fundamental convictions. Throughout his life Norris will insist that truth is eternal and unchangeable, identical with the nature of God himself, and is immediately present to every soul, though it cannot be known except at the price of close attention and thought. Whether Norris's conviction on this matter was in some degree derived from Hierocles, or whether he chose to translate the latter's Commentary on <u>The Golden Verses of the Pythagoreans</u> because he already agreed with the basic view which it expressed, cannot now be known. In addition, Norris himself points out that these passages of Hierocles foreshadow certain aspects of his own theory of freedom as dependent on the power to direct one's attention, a theory which he first developed in his sermon on <u>The Root of Liberty</u> (1685) and which he maintained throughout his life. Both these doctrines have much in common with the theories of Malebranche; the teaching of Hierocles goes far to explain how Norris was able to arrive independently at many of the same conclusions as Malebranche, and why he was to greet with such enthusiasm the latter's more systematic exposition and development of their common ideas.

Apart from this central theme of the presence of unchanging truth to the human mind, there are other aspects too of the teaching of Hierocles which reappear in Norris's later writings. Thus for instance Hierocles and Norris both hold that God created the world

24

purely out of his own superabundant goodness, since he himself can receive nothing from his creatures. They both hold, too, that it is the soul or spirit that is the real person; provided one remembers this, one can say that one is never required to do anything that is unprofitable to oneself, for only knowledge and virtue are profitable to the soul. Other theories held by Hierocles met with a less complete acceptance from Norris. Thus Hierocles held that the soul not only will not die with the body, but also was not created with it, and that its present position, exiled in some degree from God and subject to bodily passions, is the penalty for sins committed before its "fall" into this world. This theory was a not uncommon one in the Platonic tradition, and was held in the seventeenth century by such Cambridge Platonists as Henry More, Joseph Glanvil, and George Rust, but Norris never accepted it as certain, though in some of his writings he suggested it as a possible explanation of the human condition. Again, Hierocles, in common with many Platonists as well as theosophists of all sorts, held that the soul, apart from the terrestrial body which is dissolved at death, has also an immortal, "lucid" body, "the subtle vehicle of the soul."[6] Unlike More, Norris never accepted this theory as certain, though he did at times envisage the existence of such a "vehicle" as possible or even probable. However, this strange speculation, which is not easily reconcilable with the Cartesian theory of the soul that Norris adopted, plays no part in his systematic thought, and appears in his later writings as an echo of the Platonic studies of his youth rather than as a true part of his own system.

Norris's translation of Hierocles shows him in contact with a philosophy which contains in germ many ideas which were later to be characteristic of his own thought. It was introduced by a preface in which for the first time Norris expressed opinions of his own on questions of philosophy and theology. The preface is essentially a defence of Hierocles against those Calvinists who act "as if they thought it the characteristics note of a true Christian, zealously to run down the morality of the heathen, as they do of a true Protestant, to rail stoutly against popery."[7] Against all such narrow views, Norris insists that the Mosaic Law is a transcription of the Natural Law, which can be discovered, though not without difficulty, by the light of reason, and that the Natural Law in turn is but a transcript of the essential holiness of God. Norris does not at this time seek to define the precise relationship between the Natural Law and the nature of God, but he is already convinced that the moral law is founded on the divine nature, and that it can be known by man even without revelation. In taking this view Norris was of course in agreement both with the Scholastic tradition and with the Cambridge Platonists.

The following year, 1683, saw the publication of three original works by Norris. One of these was of little importance for his subsequent development, if indeed it was by him. A Murnival of Knaves, or, Whiggism plainly Display'd and (if not grown shameless) Burlesqu't out of Countenance is a burlesque poem attacking the Whigs in general and Titus Oates and the Earl of Shaftesbury in particular. Its coarse style is in marked contrast to the urbanity of Norris's later writings, and he never included this anonymous poem (published under the pseudonym of "Philanax") in any list of his works, but there seems no sufficient reason to doubt the accuracy of its contemporary attribution to him. 1683 marked the culmination of five years of plots and crises, and Norris, like the great majority of the University, was ardently royalist and Anglican. Norris always remained a Tory and High Churchman, but though he later wrote several

26

short pieces on ecclesiastical politics, this poem remained his only public intervention in current political controversy, a sphere, in fact, from which he deliberately turned away.

It was in this same year that Norris published his Latin treatise on the Galvinist doctrine of predestination, Tractatus adversus Reprobationis Absolutae Decretum. It was to this work that Anthony Wood referred when he wrote: "Upon the first coming out of the said book, the author (a conceited youngster) was look'd upon as over pert, bold and pragmatically daring to engage in so profound a controversy by publishing his little and raw judgement concerning the said decree" (of reprobation),[9] but it is not now possible to tell whether his adverse judgement was widely shared. The tone of this book is indeed often sharp and the arguments are sometimes carried to extremes, and it is apparent that it is the work of a young man; but the arguments advanced are serious and important both in themselves and for the light that they throw on the development of Norris's thought.

In his preface, Norris traces the development of his own religious beliefs. He tells us that he was brought up as a Calvinist from his earliest childhood, and had no doubt of the truth of that doctrine until he met "a most learned man" who pointed out to him its terrible consequences. But he did not then immediately abandon Calvinism, he tell us; he hesitated for a long time between Calvinism and Arminianism, until he finally undertook a systematic reading of the authors on both sides, which eventually led him, after much reflection, to reject Calvinism. This account recalls the parallel movement of most of the Cambridge Platonists from Calvinism to what may be described as Arminianism, though they, unlike Norris, seem not to have known the works of the Dutch Arminians at the time when their opinions were being formed. We do

not know the identity of the vir   pereruditus who first showed
Norris the difficulties of Calvinism, nor even whether this change
of view took place while he was at Winchester or at Oxford. But
Norris does tell us the names of many of the authors whom he
read: on the Calvinist side, Piscator (Johann Fischer), Zanchius
(Girolamo Zanchi), Pierre du Moulin, and Calvin himself; on the
Arminian side, Episcopius (Simon Bischop), Curcellaeus (Etienne
de Courcelles), and Henry More.

The Tractatus adversus Reprobationis Absolutae Decretum
is divided into two parts. In the first, Norris aims to show the falsity of the Calvinist doctrine of absolute reprobation (predestination
to eternal punishment antecedent to any consideration of human sin)
from the way in which it conflicts with the divine attributes and from
its opposition to scripture; in the second part, he examines the evil
consequences that flow from this doctrine, or that would flow from
it if people were to conduct their lives according to its principles.
From the point of view of the development of Norris's thought, it
is the first part, concerning the attributes of God, that is the most
important. For Norris insists that God's attributes are identical
with God himself, so that it is impossible for him to act against
them. This is, of course, traditional Augustinian and Scholastic
doctrine. Moreover, goodness, holiness, justice, and truthfulness
have the same meaning when applied to God as they have when
applied to men, though the divine attributes are infinitely superior
in degree to these virtues as found in human beings. If this were
not so, the frequent command to imitate God would be senseless.

Now these four attributes of God, Norris declares, are all
contradicted by the Calvinist doctrine of absolute reprobation. The
creation of beings precisely in order to damn them cannot be recon-

28

ciled with God's goodness, here understood in the sense of his propensity to do good to his creatures. It is contrary to God's holiness to be the author of sin, yet Piscator, Zanchius, and Calvin himself declare that God directly wills and decrees in as a means to the damnation of the sinner, a doctrine, declares Norris, which makes him much more truly the author of sin than is either the devil or the sinner himself. It would be contrary to God's justice to punish anyone for faults that he had no power to avoid. Finally, the doctrine of reprobation makes a hypocrite of God: Piscator asserts that God offers his grace by promise to many to whom he has no intention of actually giving it, and that, though God commands the reprobate to believe in the gospel, he does not will that they should do so. Such hypocrisy, Norris declares, cannot be reconciled with the truthfulness of God. The idea of God that is left when goodness, holiness, justice, and truthfulness have been removed, is made up of power and will only, and is more like the devil than the true God.

Norris then goes on to give a series of biblical texts which explicitly contradict Calvinism, and to argue forcefully that the predestinarian doctrine undermines the whole scope of the biblical revelation. In the second part of his Tractatus he argues that the doctrine of predestination and reprobation destroys the foundations of religion and morality. If God is neither good nor holy nor just, man can neither love nor trust him. If man is not free but simply acts for good or ill as God decrees, then virtue and vice are meaningless and rewards and punishments will be as ineffective as they are unjust. If one still wishes to speak of the "virtues" of the Elect, these can only be "infused virtues", direct effects of the divine action produced without any cooperation on man's part.[10] The Calvinist doctrine breeds despair, for it leaves man as a mere

29

plaything in the hands of a God who is a stranger to morality and whose rule approximates to that of a blind and inexorable fate. Norris ends his essay with an impassioned attack on the Calvinist teaching, which he compares unfavourably with that of heretics such as the Socinians. The latter, he declares, have an inadequate view of God, since they deny the trinity of persons, but the Calvinist teaching is not merely inadequate, but depraved, since it entirely destroys the moral nature of God.

Despite its polemical vehemence which was far from the serene tone of his later writings, the Tractatus adversus Reprobationis Absolutae Decretum shows two preoccupations which were always to be fundamental to Norris's thought. In particular, he always continued to insist on the absolute nature of moral values as attributes of God, and on the realism of our knowledge of them. This insistence, which reflects the Platonic tradition of which Hierocles was a preeminent exponent, explains why Norris, like the Cambridge Platonists and Malebranche, always rejected, not only Calvinism, but also the Cartesian theory of the created nature of truth. Closely related to this insistence on the moral character of God is Norris's defence of human freedom as the essential precondition for moral action. This is also the subject of a Latin address which Norris delivered before the University not long before he received the degree of Master of Arts, and which was printed as an appendix to the Tractatus adversus Reprobationis Absolutae Decretum.[11]

With the third work published by Norris in 1683, we reach a real turning point in the history of his writings. The works that have been considered up to now were published anonymously, and Norris seldom referred to them later; but An Idea of Happiness, in a Letter to a Friend, Enquiring wherein the Greatest Happiness

attainable by Man in this Life does consist was published under his
own name. It was reprinted the following year as part of Poems
and Discourses occasionally written and, with the whole of Poems
and Discourses except for two Latin poems, was incorporated in
the Miscellanies which, first published in 1687, and revised for
the fourth edition in 1706, became and remained one of his most
popular works.

Norris had been asked by his friend, whose identity is unknown, what was the greatest happiness that was attainable by man
in this life; but in order to answer this question he first examined
the nature of happiness in general and that of the summum bonum,
the supreme happiness. By happiness in the general sense, Norris
understands the enjoyment of any good. He insists that the good
that is enjoyed may be either real or merely apparent, and that
this difference in the object enjoyed makes no difference to the
reality of one's happiness. "I think it impossible for a man to
think himself happy, and (during that persuasion) not really to be
so."[12] There is no such thing as merely imaginary happiness.

Going on to the question of the summum bonum, Norris declares that this must be conceived as a state in which no evil is
feared, no good desired and not possessed. But, he asks, is such
a state possible, when, in our experience, fruition never fully
satisfies? In Norris's view, this disappointment is always due
either to the imperfection of the objects that we enjoy, or to the
imperfection of our enjoyment of them. Perfect happiness, therefore, can consist only in the perfect fruition of an infinite object.
It follows that it can never be enjoyed in this life, since our fruition
of God, the only infinite object, is imperfect here below. Combining the views of the Thomists and the Scotists, Norris affirms
that this fruition involves both knowledge and love, and that both

31

are equally essential. Perfect happiness consists in the loving contemplation of God, "of whom all nature is the image, of whom all the harmony both of the visible and invisible world is but the echo."[13]

After these preliminaries, Norris returned to the question that had originally been put to him. Perfect happiness is not attainable in this life, but what is the greatest happiness that is attainable? After examining the opinions of various ancient authors, Norris concludes with the Pythagoreans and Platonists that the greatest happiness that can be attained in this life consists in the contemplation of God and the unitive way of religion.[14] It consists, in fact, in the highest participation that can be had on earth of that supreme happiness that can be fully enjoyed only in heaven. Such a contemplative union with God, he holds, presupposes the perfection of the moral life, the happiness of which it retains while adding its own. To describe the nature of this contemplative life, Norris appeals to "the masters of mystic theology", Plato and the Platonists, Augustine and Thomas Aquinas, Robert Bellarmine and Jeremy Taylor, but he does not enter into the details of their teaching. For his own part, he defines intellectual contemplation as "an habitual, attentive, steady application or conversion of the spirit to God and his divine perfections",[15] and declares that this must be joined with a love of God which can be both intellectual and passionate. By intellectual love, the soul joins itself by will to God who is perceived as its good, but this intellectual love can overflow into man's sensitive nature and thus become a passion. If one's contemplation of God is intense, one's love will be so too, and may attain the level of what Norris calls "seraphic love" by which a man consecrates himself wholly to God, finds his whole delight in praising and serving him, and desires only to see him face to face in heaven. Such a state, Norris concludes, represents the greatest happiness that man can attain in this life.

Concluding his letter, Norris declares that its teaching was derived primarily from his own experience and reflection. The experience of which he writes seems to be that of an ardent affective religion rather than of mysticism properly so called. This affective religion is seen in largely Platonic terms, which no doubt accounts for the absence of any reference to the need of grace in order to attain to it. Although, as has been seen, Norris continued to republish An Idea of Happiness throughout his life without substantial alteration, his views on this subject later underwent some development. As time went on, he became less and less satisfied with the knowledge of God that could be had in this life, and so came to insist that the one thing that mattered was to reach heaven where God would be seen face to face. In his Discourse concerning the Origin and Relief of all Trouble and Uneasiness of Mind, which formed part of the third volume of his Practical Discourses (1693), he declared that the consolations of the Holy Spirit depended entirely on God's good pleasure and that, apart from these joys which were not subject to man's control, the most solid happiness of the present life was derived from a good conscience in the practice of one's moral and religious duties and from reflection on the goodness of God and on the joys that he had prepared for those who loved him. The knowledge and love of God always continued to have the central place in Norris's thought, but this emphasis gradually became more specifically Christian and less Platonist.

A year after An Idea of Happiness there appeared a collection of Norris's writings entitled Poems and Discourses occasionally written. This volume consisted of fifteen poems and six essays, one of which was An Idea of Happiness, and the whole of it, apart

33

from two Latin poems, was afterwards included in the Miscellanies
of 1687. Norris's poems will be considered later. [16] Of the five
new essays, only one was of central importance in the development
of Norris's thought. The other four need hardly detain us.
A Letter of Resolution concerning some Passages in the foregoing
Treatise, to the same Person, followed on directly from An Idea
of Happiness and replied to some difficulties which it seemed to
raise for the doctrine of heaven. A Discourse concerning Heroic
Piety argued that the counsels of Christian perfection were distinguished from the commandments and provided man's only op-
portunity of showing his gratitude towards God. The Discourse
concerning Heroic Piety already showed the direction in which
Norris's mind was moving regarding the love of God. God alone,
he argued, can satisfy the natural dynamism of man's love: "We
must needs therefore be miserable in our love, unless God be the
object of it. But neither is our happiness sufficiently secured by
making God the object of our love, unless we concenter our whole
affections upon him, and (in the strictest sense of the phrase)
love him with all our heart and with all our soul. For otherwise,
whatever portion of our love does not run in this channel must
necessarily fix upon disporoportionate and unsatisfying objects,
and consequently be an object of discontent to us."[17] Norris had
to develop further his analysis of love before he could affirm that
the concentration of all one's desire on God was both possible
and obligatory. At this time he still held that "such an absolute
and entire dedication of our love to God as this is not always practicable in this life."[18] But he was already convinced that such a
dedication was both uniquely reasonable and desirable for man's
own sake. Of the Care and Improvement of Time emphasises the
brevity of life and man's responsibility to God for the use that he

34

makes of it. Of Solitude affirms that while society is a blessing
to man, the society that one actually meets in the world is often
more a hindrance than a help. A relative solitude is essential for
anyone who wishes to make progress in the contemplative life,
but even for intellectual progress a considerable measure of solitude is desirable. This little essay does not give the more fundamental reasons for the need of solitude which Norris later advanced
in Of the Advantages of Thinking, in his Miscellanies (1687), but it
already shows his conviction that the search for truth is an essentially individual quest.

But much the most important essay in Poems and Discourses occasionally written is Norris's reply to two further questions
from the correspondent whose query had led him to write An Idea
of Happiness. This is entitled Another Letter to the same Person,
concerning the true Notion of Plato's Ideas, and of Platonic Love.
Norris frequently refers to the first part of this letter in his later
writings, generally calling it simply his Letter of Ideas, and although it professes to be a straightforward exposition of Plato's
teaching it is also in reality the first expression of Norris's own
theory of the divine Ideas. Norris begins by recalling the account
given by Aristotle of Plato's Ideas as universal abstract essences
eternally subsisting by themselves, separate both from the mind
of God and from the singular beings that are modelled on them.
"Sir", he comments, "I suppose you can hardly forbear smiling
at the oddness of the conceit, but as ridiculous as you may think
it, 'tis said to be maintained by no less a man than Plato, and has
been thought of that moment too, that multitudes of great men have
set themselves very seriously to confute it as a dangerous heresy,
and have opposed it with as much zeal as ever St. Austin did the
Manichees or the Pelagians".[19] Aristotle himself, Norris declares,

35

cannot sincerely have thought that his account represented Plato's true opinion; rather did he father this theory on Plato with a view to attacking it and expounding his own view on the subject. Norris bases his own interpretation of Plato's theory of Ideas mainly on the Timaeus: Plato, he declares, regarded the world as made by an intelligent agent, who must have had in advance an idea of the work that he was going to produce, since this would otherwise have been a fortuitous rather than an intended effect of his action. Hence Plato had to suppose eternal forms, models, or patterns existing in the mind of God, according to which he formed the world. And these eternal forms he called Ideas, ta prota noeta, the first Intelligibles, the measures of the things that are.

Norris always continued to maintain the validity of this interpretation of Plato, but the rest of the Letter of Ideas is concerned with the theory of Ideas considered in itself rather than as an expression of Plato's thought. Norris envisages two difficulties that can be raised. To the objection that the multiplicity of Ideas is hard to reconcile with the simplicity of God and with the Scholastic doctrine that there is nothing in God which is not God himself, he replies that the Platonic Ideas are not to be understood as essences distinct from the divine essence, but that they are identical with the divine essence itself, considered as imitable by possible creatures. This is of course the traditional Scholastic reply. But the second objection that Norris envisages is one that gave him occasion to reply with a distinction which was to be of importance in all his thought on the divine Ideas.

According to Plato, as has been seen, the divine Ideas are not only the exemplary causes of things, but also the measure of their truth: does not this, it might be asked, imply that truth is dependent on the speculative understanding of God, and that hence

God does not understand something because it is so in its own nature, but rather things are of such a nature because God chooses
to understand them in that way? Such a theory, Norris delcares,
is

"... full of mischief and absurdity, as you may see compendiously
and yet evidently demonstrated in Dr. Rust's little Discourse of
Truth. Now for the clearing this difficulty, 'tis to be observed that
the Essence of God, according to Plato, is distinguished into nous
neoros and nous noetos, the counterpart whereof in English is conceptive and exhibitive. By the Mind of God Exhibitive is meant the
Essence of God as thus or thus imitable or participable by any
creature, and this is the same with an Idea. By the Mind of God
Conceptive is meant a reflex act of God's Understanding upon his
own Essence as exhibitive, or as thus and thus imitable. Now if
you consider the Divine Understanding as Conceptive or Speculative, it does not make its object but suppose it, (as all speculative
understanding does), neither is the truth of the object to be measu-
red from its conformity with that, but the truth of that from its conformity with its object. But if you consider the Divine Understanding
as Exhibitive, then its truth does not depend upon its conformity
with the nature of things, but on the contrary, the truth of the nature of things depends upon its conformity with it. For the Divine
Essence is not thus or thus imitable because such and such things
are in being, but such and such things are in being because the Divine Essence is thus and thus imitable; for had not the Divine Essence been thus imitable, such and such beings would not have been
possible. And thus is Plato to be understood when he founds the
truth of things upon their conformity with the Divine Ideas, ..."[20]
This distinction between the mind of God as exhibitive and conceptive (the distinction, in other words, between God's essence

and his reflex knowledge of that essence) makes it clear that the
truth of things is ultimately based on the divine essence itself.
The mind of God is the measure of all truth, but truth is as necessary as the essence of God, with which indeed it is identical. Norris always continued to make use of this distinction, but in the
First Part of his Theory of the Ideal World (1701) he replaced
the term "exhibitive" by "intelligible", and "conceptive" by "intelligent", words which undoubtedly express his meaning better
than those which he employed in the Letter of Ideas. In Reason
and Religion (1689), Norris suggests that it was Descartes' ignorance of this distinction that made him "blunder so horribly" in
making truth depend on God's decision to understand things in the
way he does. It is clear, then, that Norris attached great importance to this distinction, and it is worth examining where he derived it from.

The Discourse of Truth of Dr. George Rust, Bishop of
Dromore, was published in 1682, twelve years after the death of
its author. With Joseph Glanvil's Lux Orientalis, first published
in 1662 and aimed to prove the pre-existence of the soul, it formed
part of Two Choice and Useful Treatises, edited anonymously by
Henry More the Platonist with long annotations of his own. In his
short Discourse of Truth, Rust argues that all natural and moral
truths would be undermined if truth depended on the will of God.
No conclusion, whether in geometry or in ordinary reasoning, would
follow with certainty from its premisses, and there would be no
ground for saying that fidelity, justice, and mercy were more perfect than their opposites or were characteristic of God himself.
Truth, then, must be grounded in the nature of God if it is to have
a firm foundation. Rust's objection to the Cartesian theory of the
creation of truth has much in common with Norris's objection to

38

the Calvinist doctrine of predestination, for both are concerned
to establish the realism of man's knowledge of moral absolutes.

As has been seen, Norris in his Letter of Ideas attributes
the distinction between nous noeros and nous noetos to Plato himself. In the revised edition of 1706, however, which shows a much
greater concern for historical accuracy, he attributes it simply
to "a distinguished Platonist". This distinguished Platonist was in
fact the anonymous Henry More, author of the annotations to
Rust's Discourse of Truth. Norris must have read Rust in this
edition, the only one published at the time, and he would certainly
have read the annotations at the same time. More makes precisely
this distinction on pages 178-9 of his annotations, and again on
page 246, where he writes:
"I think it may plainly appear from what has been said ... that
the truth of the Divine Intellect quatenus conceptive, speculative,
or observative, which a Platonist would be apt to call nous noeros,
as the Divine Intellect exhibitive nous noetos, ... does consist in
its conformity with the Divine Intellect exhibitive, with the immutable Ideas, respects, and references of things there."
It is clear that this is the source from which Norris drew his distinction, though he surpassed More by the clarity of his explanation
of the source of the plurality of Ideas, and later by his use of the
terms "intelligible" and "intelligent" to describe the two aspects
of the divine mind.

In the second part of this same letter, Norris treats of the
true notion of "Platonic love". After recalling various false conceptions of its nature, he declares that Platonic love is concerned
with the ascent of the soul to God through the steps of created
beauty. Platonic love rises from the love of bodies to that of souls,
from the love of souls to that of virtue, from the beauty of virtue

to that ocean of beauty which is the Idea of Beauty itself and which is identical with God. The divine beauty, like the midday sun, is too bright and too sublime to be at once the object of our love: the soul must begin by loving the reflected beauty of creatures, till it grows strong enough to raise its eyes to their source. So Platonic love is "the love of beauty abstracted from all sensual applications and desire of corporal contact, as it leads us on to the love of the first original Beauty, God"[21] It was later objected to Norris that this teaching did not agree with the doctrine that he finally adopted, according to which God was the only proper object of the love of desire, and this objection was justified. Norris accordingly amended this passage in the fourth edition of his Miscellanies (1706), reducing the role of created beauties to that of simple signs recalling to us the divine beauty. But in 1684 Norris was not yet in possession of his final theory of love.

The early works that have been examined in this chapter show us Norris's thought in the making. In particular, his translation of Hierocles upon the Golden Verses of the Pythagoreans contains the seeds of his central theory of the identity of truth with God and of its immediate presence to the soul. This view is seen at work in Norris's rejection of Calvinism, and is developed in the Letter of Ideas with the aid of More's distinction between nous noeros and nous noetos. The early writings also show the beginnings of Norris's thought on the love of God, and the root, in Hierocles, of his conception of freedom as based on the power to direct one's attention. Norris in these early days was a Platonist and an Arminian in the style of the Cambridge Platonists; but the roots of his own particular line of thought can already be detected.

40

CHAPTER III   THE ROOT OF LIBERTY (1685) AND NORRIS'S
CORRESPONDENCE WITH HENRY MORE.

The year 1685 saw the publication by Norris of his late
father's Discourse concerning the Pretended Religious Assembling in Private Conventicles,[1] and the publication of a translation of Xenophon's Life of Cyrus, the last four books of which
were translated by Norris. But of much greater importance was
the correspondence with Henry More which Norris initiated in
January 1685 and which continued until early in the following year.

As has been seen, Norris agreed with More in his rejection
of Calvinism, and was indebted to him for his distinction between
nous noeros and nous noetos. Indeed he seems to have conceived
a great admiration for More, and his first letter, in which he asked
More the sense in which he understood certain concepts in his En-
chiridium Metaphysicum, seems to have been written largely with
a view to introducing himself to the Cambridge scholar. The details
of Norris's questions, which concerned More's conceptions of space
and of spiritual beings as extended, need not concern us, since Norris never accepted More's views on these subjects and never referred to them again. From his point of view they had fulfilled their
function by serving as an introduction to Henry More.[2]

The correspondence continued on other subjects. In his next
letter Norris asked More for his views on the nature of the "moral
turpitude" of sensuality. Was the indulgence of sensuality (understood as sexual pleasure) wrong in itself, or should it be condemned
only when accompanied by "civil incommodities", as in the case of
adultery and fornication? "The more modern masters of morality",
such as Grotius, Cumberland, and Puffendorf, favoured the latter

view, as did the lawfulness of marriage, whereas many ancient writers, with some passages of Scripture, seemed to favour the former opinion. This theme was continued through several letters, by the end of which Norris had reached full agreement with More in holding that no moral blame attached to the perception of sexual pleasure as such, but that the evil of sensuality, in those cases where it was forbidden, did not arise only from its bad effects on society. Sexual pleasure was naturally ordered towards the propagation of the race, so that to seek it in abstraction from this end would be sinful, just as it would be sinful to seek the pleasures of taste if one had no need to be sustained by food. Moreover excessive indulgence in any bodily pleasure would be wrong, because of its tendence to captivate the soul and prevent its concentration on higher goods; and this was particularly true of sexual pleasure, whose spell was so powerful. On these questions More's letters seem to have helped Norris to clarify his views.

But by the time Norris had reached full agreement with More on this subject, it had ceased to be the main topic of their letters to each other. On Mid-Lent Sunday 1685, Norris, who had been ordained priest the previous year, preached before the University of Oxford in the church of St. Peter's in the East, on the text of Romans 12, 3. In the course of this sermon he advanced a hypothesis on The Root of Liberty which represented one of the most important philosophical statements of his early years. The sermon was printed, and Norris dedicated it to Henry More, to whom he sent a copy. It now became the principal subject of their letters to each other, with More criticising Norris's hypothesis and Norris defending it. The sermon on The Root of Liberty was reprinted in 1687 as part of the Miscellanies, and in 1688 Norris published his correspondence with More (who had died in 1 Sept. 1687) as a supplement to his "Moral Essay" on The Theory and Regulation of Love. In the "Advertisement to the Reader" with which he introduced the published version of their correspondence, Norris declared that he had decided to publish their letters not only as a tribute to his dead friend, but also because More had urged every objection that could be made to his hypothesis on The Root of Liberty. His conviction of the truth of his theory had been confirmed by its ability to withstand the arguments of "so severe a speculatist".[3] For the benefit of those who did not have a copy of his sermon, Norris appended a summary of its argument to the published correspondence, the rest of which can indeed be understood only in the light of his theory on the nature of freedom.

In the text on which Norris's sermon was based, St. Paul enjoined his reader "... not to think of himself more highly than he ought to think; but to think soberly, according as God hath dealt to every man the measure of faith." Norris's sermon had three main divisions: "First, I observe that we are not at our own liberty to entertain what opinions we please concerning ourselves, but that we ought to regulate them by some standard ... Secondly, I observe that the standard whereby we are to regulate our opinions concerning ourselves are those excellencies and perfections which we are really endowed with ... And in the third place I shall consider the absurdities and ill consequences of transgressing this standard, ..."[4] On the second point, Norris emphasised that man was not obliged to a false humility. The "severe masters of spiritual mortification" were wrong when they declared that one ought to despise oneself and to be unconscious of any excellence that one might possess, for one could never be obliged to form a false judgement, and Christianity itself called on man to have "a good conscience towards God" (I Peter 3, 21), which implied that he must be permitted to judge

43

well of himself. Moreover, most sins sprang from forgetfulness of the true dignity of man. The more common danger, however, Norris agreed, was that of pride, overestimating one's own excellences, and in the third and last section of his sermon he examined the evil consequences of such immoderate self-esteem. But it was the first point of Norris's sermon which obliged him to propose his hypothesis on The Root of Liberty.

In order to prove that man was obliged to conform his judgement of his own merits to the standard of truth, Norris had first to show that he was subject to obligation in respect of his intellectual judgements, and it was this which led him to examine the whole relationship of reason with free choice. Not only was the understanding subject to obligation, Norris affirmed, but it was the primary and immediate subject of it, since it was also the primary and immediate subject of freedom. Norris's argument may be given in the form in which he summarised it at the end of the published version of his correspondence with Henry More.

"1) That a creature void of liberty cannot be capable of law or obligation, virtue or vice, reward or punishment, is certain.

2) That man is capable of all these, is certain.

3) That man therefore is endowed with liberty, is certain.

4) That liberty is a rational perfection, or a perfection belonging to an intellectual nature, is certain.

5) That therefore this liberty must be subjected either in the understanding or will, or (to speak more properly) in the soul as intelligent or in the soul as volent, is certain.

6) That it cannot be subjected in that part which acts necessarily, is certain.

7) That the will necessarily follows the dictate of the understanding, or that the soul necessarily wills according as she under-

44

stands, is certain.

8) That therefore this liberty cannot be immediately subjected in the will, or in the soul as volent, is certain.

9) That therefore it must be subjected in the soul as intelligent, is certain.

10) That even the soul as intelligent, so far as it acts necessarily, cannot be the immediate subject of liberty, is also certain.

11) That the soul as intelligent necessarily judges according as the object appears to her, is certain.

12) That therefore the soul as judging or forming a judgement can no more be the immediate subject of liberty than the soul as volent, is certain.

13) That, since the soul necessarily wills as she judges, and necessarily judges as things appear, we have thus far no glimpse of liberty, is certain.

14) That therefore our liberty must be founded upon the no necessity of some certain things appearing thus or thus, or that we have no liberty at all, is as certain.

15) That things appearing thus or thus (unless in self-evident propositions) depends upon the various degrees of advertency or attention, and nothing else, is certain.

16) That therefore we have an immediate power of attending or not attending, or of attending more or less, is certain.

17) That therefore this indifferency of the soul as to attending or not attending or attending more or less is the prime root and immediate subject of human liberty, is no less certain, which was the point to be demonstrated."[5]

In the fuller version of Norris's argument contained in the original sermon, more emphasis was placed on the real identity of the understanding and will with each other and with the substance

45

of the soul, "because in the contrary hypothesis either judgement must be ascribed to the will, and then the will immediately commences understanding, or the assent of the will must be blind, brutish, and unaccountable, both of which are as great absurdities as they are true consequences"[6], but the general line of reasoning was identical with that quoted here. Norris's theory of freedom is a clear one. The will necessarily follows the final judgement or "dictate" of the understanding; one cannot but choose the course of action which seems better at the time, since the object of the will is apparent good; the understanding (or rather, the soul as intelligent) necessarily conforms its judgement to the way the object appears to it; but the way the object appears to one depends on one's attention, and one's attention depends on oneself. The power to direct one's attention, then, is the root of man's freedom of choice.

Norris's theory of The Root of Liberty bears a striking resemblance to Malebranche's teaching on this subject. For Malebranche as for Norris, it is the power to direct one's attention that is the root of freedom and moral responsibility.[7] Moreover, in his later years at all events, Malebranche too declined to distinguish the intellect and will as faculties really distinct from the soul.[8] Despite the close general likeness between their theories, however, there are differences. At this period Norris unhesitatingly attributed the act of judgement to the intellect, saying that it would be "a great absurdity" to attribute it to the will, while Malebranche followed Descartes in restricting the rôle of the intellect to the passive perception of ideas and their relationship and assigning the act of judgement to the will. Later, in a series of texts in which he based himself explicitly on Malebranche, Norris adopted the Cartesian view on this point, though it does not seem that

46

he ever attached much importance to this question, as indeed he scarcely could in view of his denial of any real distinction between the intellect and the will.[9] Meanwhile, despite this difference of conceptual framework, Norris's theory of freedom had from the start the same mental and psychological structure as that of Malebranche.

In view of this it is interesting to observe that Norris was not dependent for his theory on Malebranche. He never attempted to hide his debts to other thinkers, and when he read Malebranche he did so with an enthusiasm that one cannot fail to notice. Indeed it was his reading of Malebranche that later led him to modify his theory of judgement. But Norris made no secret of the sources which did provide the starting point for his hypothesis on freedom. It was from the Thomists that he adopted the view according to which the will necessarily follows the dictate of the understanding, and in his sermon he explicitly referred to St. Thomas in this connection. But he was not satisfied with the rest of the Thomist explanation, and the idea of seeking the solution of the problem in the power to direct one's attention was derived from his Platonic studies, and particularly from the work of Hierocles that he had translated. In his sermon on The Root of Liberty, after proposing his hypothesis, he adds: "Neither is this accound wholly unlicensed by authority, for I find some hints and intimations of it in the school of Plato, where the reason why those middle sort of beings called Heroes are not so uniformly pure as the Athánatoi Theoí or Nóes is assigned to be because they do not so equally attend to the beauty of the Supreme God." A marginal note to the word school adds: "See Hierocles upon the Golden Verses of Pythagoras."[10] But if Norris's theory had its roots in Thomism and in the Platonism of Hierocles, it was nevertheless an independent construction of his own. His theory was a consistent and unified one, and he continued to uphold it throughout his life.

As has been seen, Norris sent Henry More a copy of his sermon on The Root of Liberty soon after it was printed. More's first criticisms of Norris's theory were contained in his third letter to Norris, dated 16 January 1686, and, apart from some hesitation regarding the tone of his criticism of the "severe masters of spiritual mortification", his objections concerned two main points. Though agreeing with Norris that the will and intellect were not two faculties really distinct from each other or from the soul, More did not agree that one's choice necessarily followed one's judgement. "Methinks you run yourself into an unnecessary noose of fatality, by granting the soul necessarily wills as she understands; you know that of the poet: Video meliora proboque, deteriora sequor". [11] Furthermore, in More's view, attention to moral or intelligible objects would not be sufficient of itself to give the soul the power to choose them. Only a soul that had been purified from moral corruptions and regenerated by divine grace was in a position to choose the truly good, for only in such a soul could the attraction of heavenly things outweigh the natural attraction to the things of earth.

In his reply to this letter, Norris assured More that nothing but the desire for truth could lead him to dispute his judgement. Having said this, he firmly maintained his own position. If, he declared, the soul cannot will evil as evil, it cannot choose what seems the lesser of two goods; hence it is determined by its judgement of what seems to it the greater good. Moreover the judgement is necessarily determined by the appearance of the object, but this appearance varies according to the greater or less attention that one pays to it. Coming to More's detailed objections, Norris agrees that the Video meliora proboque, deteriora sequor of Ovid

48

is the experience of every man, but affirms that it is explained
by the distinction between speculative or habitual knowledge on
the one hand and practical knowledge on the other. One may know
in a speculative or habitual way that a certain action is a sin and
therefore to be avoided, but yet when the occasion arises one may
fail to attend to this knowledge and judge that, in the present circumstances, that action is to be preferred to the discomfort of
avoiding it. To More's second objection, that attention is not sufficient to enable one to choose what one sees to be best, Norris
replies that "I confess I can easily conceive how a man may be defective <u>in his attention</u>, but not how attention itself, if duly applied,
can be defective towards <u>true illumination</u>, though in the midst of
<u>moral corruptions</u>. All that can be said is, that these moral cor-
ruptions may divert the soul from sufficiently attending to the
beauty of holiness, and this I take to be the true and ultimate ground
of all sin, and here 'tis I fix the necessity of <u>grace and divine</u>
<u>assistance</u>."[12] This in fact always remained Norris's view. In
his later writings he placed more emphasis on the need for grace
and moral purity, both in order to make good moral choices and
also in the search for truth; but the rôle of grace always remained
that of leading the soul to attend to true values. In Norris's view
such attention, once given, could never fail of its effect.

The final exchange of letters (More's fourth and last letter,
dated 22 February 1686, and Norris's final reply) served to clear
up a number of outstanding points. More's letter showed that he
had not understood what Norris meant by attention, and had hence
failed to grasp one of the most essential points of his theory. For
More asked Norris whether, in speaking of a power of attending or
not attending, or of attending more or less, he meant anything more
than the simple power, which every man had, of undertaking a

49

sincere search for truth and goodness. However sincere such a search may be, he declares, it will not be sufficient, so long as it remains merely speculative, to ensure that one chooses in accordance with the dictates of one's understanding. But a search of this kind, implying an effort of all the faculties with a view to discovering a truth or a good as yet unknown, was not at all what Norris meant by attention. In his final letter he explained his position. "Whereas therefore the operations and powers of the soul as intelligent are usually divided into these three, apprehension, judgement, and discourse, I find it necessary to add a fourth, that of attention, which I look upon as really distinct from the other three, they being conversant with their objects as true and false, but this only as intelligible; and is only in short a general power of converting the acies of the understanding towards any intelligible object, whether simple or complex, and answers exactly to the application of the eye to a sensible object, and accordingly is as distinct from either apprehension, judgement, or discourse as this application of the eye is from the very act of vision."[13] This definition of attention would not have satisfied Norris later in life, insomuch as he came to reject the scholastic triple division of the acts of the understanding; but insofar as it defines attention itself this definition exactly describes not only what Norris himself always understood by it, but also the sense in which Hierocles, St. Augustine, and Malebranche used that term. Indeed it is surprising that More, with his wealth of Platonic learning, had not himself seen from Norris's sermon and letters that this was the sense in which he used the term "attention".

From these final letters it also transpired that Norris and More did not use the term "practical judgement" in the same sense. According to More, Norris's distinction between speculative and practical knowledge was invalid. All judgements were basically speculative; a "practical" judgement was merely a speculative judgement on which the agent acted, and the fact that one judgement rather than another became practical depended only on the agent's choice. This however was not what Norris meant by a practical judgement. In his view the practical judgement was the choice itself, the judgement by which the agent actually decided to act in a certain way. On this point Norris followed the Thomist analysis, while More's position approximated to that of Suarez and the majority of non-Thomist scholastics.

To Norris's argument that the soul must choose what, at the moment of choice, seemed better to it, More replied by distinguishing two orders of goods: moral good and natural good. An unregenerate soul, he declared, can always choose the merely natural good, bonum jucundum or utile, in preference to the moral good, even while knowing in the abstract that the moral good ought always to be preferred. In his final letter, however, Norris denied the applicability of this distinction to the case in point. If someone chooses the merely natural in preference to the moral good, this implies that he judges that the natural good is in the present circumstance the greater good for him; "Which conclusion", he tells More, "you yourself seem unawares to slip into, by using the word (prefer), for what is to prefer but to think or pronounce upon the whole matter to be better or more eligible?"[14] In its final, practical, judgement, the soul chooses, not in accordance with the type of good, but according to which good seems in all the present circumstances to be the greater. More however could not conceive how one could forget one's habitual knowledge that the moral good was always to be preferred at the very moment when it became relevant to action. When one chose the natural in preference to the moral good, the understanding (or the soul as intelligent) continued to judge that the moral good ought to be preferred; but in such a case reason, despite its protestations, was overcome by the passions, and it was the soul as sensual or animal which chose sin.

In his reply, Norris once again repeated that the person who chose to commit a sin certainly chose it as preferable. "Now this must come to pass", he continued, "in one of these two ways, either by his not attending to it as sin, or not as a greater evil. The first of which I can easily conceive as possible, and the latter in all cases I think certain. And this methinks you yourself run into by saying ... that the animal appetite bears the soul in hand, that such a sin with pleasure and profit is better than an act of virtue with pain and worldly loss. For what is this but in other words to say that the concupiscible may be so strong and rampant that the soul may judge pro hic et nunc the uneasiness of abstaining to be a greater evil than an unlawful indulgence, so as upon that judgement to choose the latter?"[15]

In this whole matter, it seems, one can hardly deny the superiority of Norris's analysis. Experience shows that it is certainly possible to forget one's principles under the pressure of the passions, while More's view that it is "the soul as animal" which chooses sin seems to cast doubt on the unity of the person as a conscious and morally responsible agent. Nevertheless More's objection is not entirely without foundation, for when one chooses the merely natural in preference to the moral good it is not reason, considered as attentive to truth, which makes the decision. On the contrary, as Norris himself emphasises, attention to truth is what is lacking, while the soul attends only to lower attractions and fears. All in all it seems preferable to say that it is the soul, the

person himself, who makes the choice, whether the good chosen
be a moral or a merely natural one. From this point of view,
while admitting the real unity of will and intellect, there is much
to be said for the Cartesian view which attributes judgement to
the will as marking the adherence of the person to truth or to what,
for lack of sufficient attention, has a false appearance of truth.
This view was also that of Malebranche and, as has been seen, was
later adopted by Norris under his influence. In this matter as in
others, Malebranche's writings were to help Norris to formulate
his own views more satisfactorily than he had been able to do on
his own. But even at this early period Norris was able to give a
better explanation of sin and of free choice than was More.

The letters of More and Norris are marked by great courtesy
on both sides, though their tone differs considerably, as one would
expect in view of the very different ages of their authors. Norris
shows the greater penetration in logical argument: his aim in these
later letters was to develop and test out his hypothesis on attention
as the root of freedom. More on the other hand was moved by a less
philosophical and more directly religious interest, and seems at
times to suspect his young correspondent of a lack of religious
seriousness and of a superficial rationalism. In the course of their
correspondence Norris learned from More new elements of his
moral theory, especially in the matter of sexual ethics, and also,
no doubt, a new appreciation of the importance of grace. But it
is clear that, on the central question under discussion, Norris's
theory that the power to direct one's attention was the root of
human freedom had indeed shown itself well "able to withstand
the shock" of More's objections. This correspondence showed that
Norris, at the age of twenty-nine, was, in penetration of mind,
more than equal to the most respected English philosopher of the

time. His theory on The Root of Liberty was one of the chief philosophical achievements of Norris's early years, and was always to remain an essential part of his thought.

CHAPTER IV   THE MISCELLANIES OF 1687

The publication in 1687 of A Collection of Miscellanies,
consisting of Poems, Essays, Discourses, and Letters, occasionally written, marks the culmination of the first period of
Norris's literary activity. Though some of his later, more spe-
cialised writings were reprinted more often, the Miscellanies
were the most popular of all Norris's works with the cultivated
public in general. In the middle of the eighteenth century Richardson, in his novel Clarissa, gives a picture of young ladies ex-
changing money by folding notes between the pages of their copy
of the Miscellanies, a book which was then no doubt to be found in
many a family bookcase; and even in the nineteenth century we
read in 1813 that "his Miscellanies are still read and applauded"[1],
and in 1824 that "this is the most popular of all his works, and
affords the picture of a truly amiable mind"[2]. The Miscellanies
are in fact a collection of the most diverse pieces, in which everyone would find something to interest him; but taken as a whole they
form a résumé of Norris's thought in this first period of his life,
and include all those of his early writings which he thought worthy
of being preserved.

Both the Poems and Discourses of 1684 and the sermon on
The Root of Liberty were incorporated in the Miscellanies, which
also included sixty new poems in addition to thirteen of the fifteen
first published in 1684. These poems will be examined in the second section of this chapter. The Miscellanies also contained the
following essays which now appeared for the first time: Of the Advantages of Thinking; A Metaphysical Essay towards the Demonstration of a God, from the Steady and Immutable Nature of Truth;

A Letter concerning Love and Music; A Letter concerning Friendship; Contemplation and Love: or, The Methodical Ascent of the
Soul to God, by Steps of Meditation; Considerations upon the Nature of Sin; The Christian Law asserted and vindicated: or, A General Apology for the Christian Religion, both as to the Obligativeness and Reasonableness of the Institution; A Discourse concerning Perseverance in Holiness; Of the Slightness of all Secular,
and the Importance of minding our Eternal, Interest; The Copy of
a Letter written to my Friend F. B. concerning the Death of my
dear Niece M. C.; Of Seriousness; Of Courage.

In the fourth edition of the Miscellanies, in 1706, Norris
made considerable changes in some of these essays. Some of these
changes consisted in the omission of personal details that had been
included in the original letters, while others were due to Norris's
greater carefulness, later in life, in the interpretation of other
philosophers; but some of them reflected changes and developments
in his thinking. Where these changes are of some importance they
will be noticed in this survey.

1. **Prose Essays**

The little essay Of the Advantages of Thinking was placed
by Norris at the head of the prose section of his Miscellanies. It
takes up the theme of the essay Of Solitude in Poems and Discourses, but gives the more fundamental reason for Norris's recommendation of solitude for the attainment of true knowledge. In intellectual matters reading is useful but thinking is necessary; reading
which is unaccompanied by critical reflection may help to make a
commonplace book but does not contribute to the growth of knowledge. Independent, attentive, and careful thought is the only means
by which the obstacles that hinder the progress of knowledge can
be overcome, obstacles which include the prejudices one may have
imbibed in infancy, exaggerated respect for tradition and "authori-

56

ties", and the ambiguity of the terms that are generally employed.[3]
It is only by thinking freely and carefully that one can obtain clear
and distinct ideas of things. Other obstacles to the search for
truth, such as passion, temporal interests, jealousy, and fear,
are evidently unreasonable, and the best way to overcome them
is to think about their unreasonableness and convince oneself of it.
Finally, the practice of reasoned thought is as much an aid to moral improvement as it is to intellectual progress. To do one's
duty, one must first know it and the reasons which urge one to
accomplish it, and then one must attend to this habitual knowledge
when the time comes to act. A thinking and reflective man will be
accustomed to this necessary mental attention.

The theme of this short essay is clearly Cartesian. Norris
refers explicitly to "the excellent Descartes", and several passages are direct echos of the Discours de la Méthode. But although
Norris had begun his philosophical career by the translation of a
Platonic work and his early writings were full of a traditional
Platonism, it would be wrong to think that this Cartesian emphasis
on the need for personal reflection marked a radically new departure in his thought. For what Norris had above all drawn from the
Platonists was the conviction of the immediate presence of truth
to the soul. Truth therefore must be sought within one's own mind,
by attentive thought. This conviction is common to Platonists and
Cartesians, and a Platonism which depended on tradition would be
contrary both to the fundamental intuitions of Plato and to the necessary implications of his theory of knowledge. Norris has sometimes been thought of as a traditionalist, no doubt on account of
his sometimes exaggerated liking for quotations, but he certainly
did not feel himself obliged to submit to any intellectual authority.
On the contrary, his ideal of a philosopher is clearly expressed in

Of the Advantages of Thinking: "He addicts himself to no author, sect, or party, but freely picks up truth wherever he can find it; puts to sea upon his own bottom; holds the stern himself; ..."[4]

A Metaphysical Essay towards the Demonstration of a God, from the Steady and Immutable Nature of Truth is a short essay fourteen pages in length, but despite its brevity it constitutes, with the sermon on The Root of Liberty, one of the most important of Norris's early writings. Its teaching, foreshadowed to some extent by the Letter of Ideas, reappears frequently in his later works, and expresses what seems to have been his most fundamental metaphysical insight.

Norris begins his Metaphysical Essay by remarking on the difficulty of finding an argument for the existence of God that has not already been proposed by someone else. Even the arguments of Descartes were not entirely original, and Norris was not prepared to say that his own line of reasoning was completely new. It was, however, based on his own reflections. His argument begins with a traditional analysis of the meanings of the word "truth"; he is concerned, not with "subjective" truth (the conformity of the mind with its object), but with "objective" truth, and in particular with the "complex truth of the object", the relations or "habitudes", whether positive or negative, of things to each other. That such objective relations or habitudes do indeed exist, Norris shows by pointing to some of them, such as the relations between a faculty and its object or between an end and the means of attaining it. Furthermore, he argues, that there are such relations is as certain as that any proposition is true, for logical or subjective truth consists in asserting such relations. But some of these relationships are steady and immutable: there are not only truths, but eternal truths. That truth exists is a proposition that cannot be denied without contradiction and that is thus eternally true; but Norris gives a whole series of other examples, taken from logic, physics (that all local movement is successive), metaphysics, and mathematics (the truths of geometry). "These and such like", he declares, "are standing and irrepealable truths, such as have no precarious existence or arbitrarious dependence upon any will or understanding whatsoever; and such as all intellectual operations do not make, but suppose."[5]

But if these relations are eternal, Norris argues, it is evident that their terms must be so too, for the relations subsisting between things or essences could not be eternal if the essences themselves were not. These simple essences, however, do not subsist eternally in the world of nature, for no created things are eternal; they must, therefore, have another, ideal, subsistence which is eternal. Put in another way, essences can exist either in a mind or outside it; the simple essences of things exist eternally, but they do not exist eternally in the world of nature, outside the mind; hence they must exist eternally in a mind, in an intelligence which itself must therefore be eternal. There are thus two sorts of essences: on the one hand the created essences of existing things, and on the other hand the eternal essences of which these created ones are copies. The eternal essences must exist in an eternal mind which, since it contains all the essences or Ideas, will also know all their relationships; it will therefore know all necessary and eternal truths. This mind will be as unchangeable as the essences and truths that it contains, especially if these essences and truths are really identical with aspects of itself.[6] "Lastly", he concludes, "'twill follow that this Mind is not only eternal, immutable, and omniscient, but that in a word 'tis endowed with all possible perfection. For to have, and itself to be all the essences and habit-

59

udes of things is to <u>have</u> and to <u>be</u> all that can <u>possibly</u> be, to be
the <u>rule and measure</u> of all perfection, to be supreme in the <u>scale</u>
of being, and to be the <u>root</u> and spring of all <u>entity</u>, which is the
same as to be <u>God</u>. This mind therefore so accomplished is no
other than <u>God</u>, and consequently <u>there is a God</u>, which was the
thing I undertook to demonstrate."[7]

The argument which Norris advances in his <u>Metaphysical</u>
<u>Essay</u> to prove the existence of God is of course a variant of the
argument from the eternity of truth which is found not infrequently
in thinkers of the Augustinian tradition. The essential point of this
argument consists in the recognition that our minds are in direct
contact with the eternal. We have immediate experience of truths,
such as those of geometry, which impose themselves upon our
minds, and which are strictly necessary and eternally true; and
the eternity of these truths implies that of the essences whose relationships they express. But this is also the point which would ex-
cite the objections of all those who would deny the real eternity of
truths and essences and claim that their necessity was hypothetical
only, not dependent on actual existence. Such in particular would
be the objection of the Scholastics to Norris's proof. Norris later
replied at length to this objection in the First Part of his <u>Theory</u>
<u>of the Ideal or Intelligible World</u>, where he also developed the
whole argument of the <u>Metaphysical Essay</u> more fully. But the core
of his reply to this objection was already contained in the Post-
script that he appended even to the first edition of this essay.

In this Postscript Norris tells his readers that he had written
the <u>Metaphysical Essay</u> a considerable time before publishing it
in the <u>Miscellanies</u>. During this time he had put the essay aside,
and had afterwards "reviewed it with all the <u>coldness and indiffer-</u>
<u>cy</u> of a <u>stranger</u>, and with more <u>severity</u> perhaps than I am likely

to meet with from the most prejudiced reader."[8] He had remained
fully satisfied with his original reasoning, but had foreseen two
possible objections to which he now replied. The first of these was
that of the Scholastics: the relations expressed in the "eternal
truths" are not attributed to the simple essences as actually existing,
but are only hypothetical, in the sense that whenever the essences
may exist they will have such relations. To this anticipated objection
Norris made a double reply. First, he denied its validity: "For
when I say, for instance, that every part of a circle is equally
distant from the centre, this proposition does not hang in suspense,
then to be verified when the things shall exist in nature, but is at
present actually true, as true as it ever will or can be."[9] But
secondly, he added, even if one admitted the objection, "thus much
at least is attributed to the simple essences at present, that when
they shall exist such and such habitudes will attend them ... But
now, how can anything be said of that which is not? There is therefore another way of existing besides that in rerum natura, namely
in the mundus archetypus or the Ideal World, where all the rationes
rerum or simple essences of things whereof there are standing and
immutable affirmations and negations have an eternal and immutable
existence, before they ever enter upon the stage of nature."[10]

    To reinforce this point, Norris continued: "Nor ought this
ideal way of subsisting to seem strange, when even while things
have a natural subsistence, the propositions concerning them are
not verified according to their natural, but according to their ideal
subsistences. Thus we demonstrate several propositions concerning
a right line, a circle, etc., and yet 'tis most certain that none of
these are to be found in nature according to that exactness supposed
in the demonstration. Such and such attributes therefore belong to
them, not as they are in nature, but as they are in their ideas. This

is a notion very frequently glanced at by Saint <u>Austin</u>; and 'tis the conclusion of <u>Aquinas</u> that the soul <u>Omnia vera cognoscit in rationi-</u> <u>bus eternis</u> (Part I, qu. 84, art. 5). And of late years this notion has been much improved by the ingenious philosopher Du Hamel in his book <u>De Mente Humana</u>. And if this be true in propositions whose subjects are in <u>nature,</u> much more is it in <u>eternal</u> proposi- tions, whose simple essences have not always a <u>natural</u> existence. These can no otherwise be verified, but by the <u>coeternal</u> existence of <u>simple essences</u> in the <u>Ideal World</u>."[11]

The reasoning of this passage, which takes as its basis the fact that the pure mathematical essences are imitated only imper- fectly in the natural or empirical world, became one of the main pillars of Norris's metaphysics, serving to establish both the dis- tinction between the natural and intelligible worlds and the parallel distinction between intellectual knowledge and sensible perception. But the passage is also of interest as showing that Norris had al- ready read the <u>De Mente Humana</u> of the French philosopher Jean- Baptiste Du Hamel (1624-1706), an Oratorian priest who became the first secretary of the <u>Académie Royale des Sciences</u> and who strove in his philosophical writings to reconcile the new Cartesian philosophy with Scholasticism on largely Augustinian lines. Du Hamel strongly emphasised the distinction between intelligible geometrical essences and their imperfect manifestations in the empirical world, and it seems probable that Norris may have derived from him the idea of including this supplementary argu- ment in the Postscript of his <u>Metaphysical Essay</u>.[12]

In the final paragraph of his Postscript, Norris replied to a second possible objection. Was he not guilty of inconsequence in asserting on the one hand that truth was presupposed to all in- tellectual operations and did not depend on any mind, and finally making it depend nevertheless on the mind of God? To this objection Norris replied that the contradiction was only apparent. He referred his readers back to the distinction that he had made in his Letter of Ideas (which was of course reprinted in this same volume of Miscellanies), and declared that truth did not depend on any mind qua "conceptive" or speculative, but that it depended on the divine mind as "exhibitive" or intelligible. If per impossibile there were no God, there would be no essences and no truth.

There is no reason to doubt the truth of Norris's statement that the argument of the Metaphysical Essay was the fruit of his own reflections, though it is evident that it was dependent in a broad sense on his whole Platonic background. Norris's line of thought is very similar in logical structure to that of St. Augustine, who had based his reasoning on necessary truths which could be explained neither by sense experience nor by the experience of the changing human self, but only by the presence to the mind of an unchanging rule or standard of truth which in the end was identical with God himself, though Norris's presentation seems drily logical when compared with the psychological finesse of Augustine's style. But Norris seems at this period to have known Augustine's theory of knowledge only second hand, through Du Hamel, who did not make use of this theory to form the basis for a proof of the existence of God. Norris's argument also bears some resemblance to one of those advanced by Ralph Cudworth in his True Intellectual System of the Universe (1678). Cudworth had argued, in a passage that was certainly later known to Norris, that man's knowledge of eternal truths and eternally true ideas was possible only because his mind was a created participation in the mind of God, a created reflection of its contents. Cudworth's argument, however, which was not developed at length, differed from Norris's in presupposing

63

the theory of innate ideas.

A much closer approach to Norris's argument is to be found in some of Malebranche's writings. In La Recherche de la Vérité Malebranche had used an indirect argument to establish his theory that man is in direct contact with the divine Ideas, proceeding by the elimination of other hypotheses, but he later advanced a positive argument to prove the same thesis; and this positive argument, which first appeared in the IOth Eclaircissement to La Recherche, was developed in Méditations Chrétiennes, and reached its final form in the Entretiens sur la Métaphysique, was very similar to the argument of Norris's Metaphysical Essay. "If our ideas are eternal, immutable, necessary, you can see that they can exist only in an immutable nature", says Theodore, Malebranche's spokesman in the Entretiens.[13] But Norris did not at this time know Malebranche's works. As we shall see, all the evidence points to his having begun to read them during the two years which followed the publication of the Miscellanies.

The reasoning of the Metaphysical Essay recurs repeatedly in Norris's later writings, particularly in Reason and Religion (1689) and in the Theory of the Ideal or Intelligible World. The First Part of the Theory (1701) is in essence a fuller statement of the teaching of this little essay and a defence of this teaching against possible objections, while the Second Part (1704) owes much to Malebranche. But even there Norris reproduced the reasoning of the Metaphysical Essay in addition to Malebranche's very similar argument. He thus duplicated much of the reasoning without bringing any really fresh argument, but his doing so shows that he regarded Malebranche's argument as distinct from his own, and thus gives further evidence of their separate origin.

Malebranche's argument was of course primarily intended

64

to establish a theory of knowledge, whereas Norris's was intended to demonstrate the existence of God. But Norris's argument implied a theory of knowledge similar to that of Malebranche, at least so far as concerns those ideas which form the bases of necessary and eternally valid truths. For if the truths that we know and the ideas whose relationships they express are strictly eternal and necessary, then they can exist only in God's mind and can be known only where they are. Norris had not yet developed any special theory regarding man's knowledge of contingent events and changeable objects, and, as other essays in the Miscellanies show, he had not yet clearly excluded the possibility that man might have certain innate ideas. In these respects his theory of knowledge was as yet far from complete, and needed to be supplemented with the help of ideas drawn from Malebranche. But Norris always remained more deeply convinced of the truth of the fundamental proposition advanced in this essay - that man has a direct knowledge of eternal and necessary truth, and that this truth is an aspect of the nature of God himself - than of that of any of the detailed theories which he later added to it. In this sense the Metaphysical Essay is fundamental to any study of Norris's metaphysics, for it expresses the insight or conviction which was central to all his thought.

A Letter concerning Love and Music and A Letter concerning Friendship were originally replies to the questions of a correspondent who had asked Norris how love, particularly in the case of love between man and woman, was distinguished from lust, whether the pleasure that came from listening to music was sensual or intellectual, and whether true friendship could subsist between a husband and his wife or whether man and woman were too unequal for this to be possible. The main importance of these letters is that they show Norris for the first time making that radical distinction between the loves of desire and benevolence which was to be fundamental to his later theory of love. The love of desire or concupiscence is a simple desire for or tendency towards the good, he declares in accordance with traditional teaching, while benevolence or charity is the wishing of good to someone. The love of desire can be either intellectual or sensual, according to whether the object desired is an intellectual or a sensible good. Lust is of course a sensual desire for a woman, and when a man is said to be "in love" with a woman, Norris declares, this is the sort of love that is meant. But the word "lust" is usually reserved for the desire of sensual pleasure in forbidden instances, which is sinful, whereas in itself sensual desire for a woman is not.

The one-sided picture of love between man and woman that Norris gives in this letter is balanced by what he says in his <u>Letter concerning Friendship</u>. Friendship, he declares, is a special form of the love of benevolence, a benevolence that is specially intense, mutual, and mutually known. It does not require an absolute equality between the parties, but only that the superior should not take advantage of his privileges. There is thus no reason why true friendship should not exist between husband and wife, and in his <u>Theory and Regulation of Love</u> (1688) Norris calls marriage "the strictest of friendships".[14] According to Norris, then, husband and wife should be linked by two distinct forms of love: by the sensual desire which makes them in love with each other and which is essentially egoist, and by an especially close friendship, a benevolence by which each desires the good of the other. The distinction between the two loves was traditional, and Norris may well have derived his formulation of it from Aquinas,[15] though he later developed it in a way very different from that of the Thomists.

The subject of love continued to occupy Norris's thoughts during the year following the publication of the Miscellanies, when he expanded and developed the teaching of these two letters in The Theory and Regulation of Love.

As has been seen, Norris was also asked whether listening to music was a pleasure of the senses or of the intellect. His reply to this question opens with an analysis of what it means to describe a pleasure as sensual or intellectual. This analysis underwent a significant change in the revised (fourth) edition of the Miscellanies in 1706. In 1687 Norris wrote that a sensual pleasure was one that primarily and directly affected the body, and affected the mind only by way of secondary participation, whereas in the case of intellectual pleasure the position was reversed. If the distinction was understood in this way, there could be no doubt that the pleasure derived from music was an intellectual one, since music consisted of the harmony and proportions between notes, which could be perceived only by the mind. Individual notes might please the ear, but a tune could be appreciated only by the understanding. Later in life, however, Norris adopted from Malebranche the Cartesian theory according to which all consciousness, including that of the senses, was proper to the spiritual soul, so that it could not be said that any pleasure primarily and directly affected the body. For this reason he specifically retracted his passage from the Letter concerning Love and Music in the Second Part of his Theory of the Ideal or Intelligible World (1704), and completely rewrote it in the new edition of 1706. "Sensual pleasure", he now wrote, "is that which the soul receives by the mediation of the body, upon the occasion of some motion or impression made upon it; whereas intellectual pleasure is that which the soul perceives immediately by itself, and from her own thoughts, without any such occasion from the body."[16] One might expect that, as a result of this new definition, Norris would relegate music to the rank of sense pleasures, as Malebranche did in his Méditations Chrétiennes;[17] but Norris, who shows himself in his poems and elsewhere to have been a great lover of music, did not agree. He continued to regard music as an intellectual pleasure, for essentially the same reason as had moved him in 1687. Sound in itself was a sensation, a sentiment in the soul resulting from a movement in the body, and the pleasure of hearing it would be a bodily pleasure; but "the harmony and proportion of sounds (which is that wherein music formally consists) is an abstract and intelligible thing, and the pleasure of it arises not from any bodily movement (as the other does), but from the soul itself contemplating the beauty and agreement of it."[18]

In Contemplation and Love, a series of philosophical meditations, Norris aimed to establish the religious attitude which was natural and reasonable for every created spirit. Love, he declares with St. Augustine, is the "weight" of the soul, which tends towards its good in the same way as bodies, in the Aristotelian system, tend towards their "centre" or natural place; and man's only adequate good is God. In a passage which throws a pleasant light on his own personality, Norris admits that he himself finds such pleasure in some of the things of earth that he is almost tempted to think that they could fully satisfy him. The pleasures in question are "... conversation with select friends, or men of harmonical and tunable dispositions; reading of close and fine-wrought discourses; solitary walks and gardens; the magnificence of the heavens; the beauty of the spring; and above all, majestic and well-composed music."[23] But a closer examination of experience shows, he concludes, that although the created world is truly good, it can never altogether satisfy man. Only God, who is infinite Truth, Goodness, and Beauty,

68

can fulfil all man's desires. One ought, therefore, never finally
to set one's heart on anything short of God. Whatever else one
chooses should be referred to him either actually or habitually.
In these meditations Norris comes very close to what was to be
his definitive teaching on the love of God alone. Norris was a true
child of his time in his concern for natural religion, but it is clear
that his understanding of it was very different from the somewhat
pedestrian outlook of many of his contemporaries.

Considerations upon the Nature of Sin is an essay which marks
the first expression of Norris's views on the general principles of
ethics. Sin, he begins, is a voluntary, and thus morally imputable,
transgression of law. But of what law is it the transgression? The
final answer cannot be the divine positive law (the Mosaic Law and
the Law of the Gospel), since some actions would be sinful even if
there were no revealed law. Nor does the final answer lie in the
law of reason, of that reason which Norris, in a phrase reminis-
cent of the Cambridge Platonists, describes as "that Candle of the
Lord that lights every man that comes into the world in his passage
through it".[25] The ultimate foundation of the law is that "there are
certain antecedent aptnesses or qualities in things, with respect to
which they are fit to be commanded or forbidden by the wise Governor of the world ..."[26] After emphasising that sin, in the strict
and formal sense, supposes that the agent knew (or could and ought
to have known) that the action was forbidden, and that he did it freely,
Norris then examines the question of whether sin is to be regarded
as positive or negative in character. The essay concludes with reflections on why sin ought to be avoided. The course of the argument has shown that sin can be committed only when one is not attentive to its true nature. Such inattention is culpable, but Norris,
in precise accordance with the teaching of his sermon on The Root

69

of Liberty, insists that the habitual knowledge that sin is the worst of evils remains the starting point for repentance. And without repentance there can be no forgiveness.

Norris however soon became dissatisfied with the detailed positions taken up in this essay, and no part of the Miscellanies underwent so many changes as did this in the revised (fourth) edition of 1706. The principle changes concerned two points: the nature of the law of reason, and the positive or negative nature of sin. In the first edition of Considerations upon the Nature of Sin Norris supposed a certain innate knowledge of moral principles. "By the Law of Reason", he then wrote, "may be understood that original stock of rational tendencies or practical sentiments which prevent all discourse and reasonings about what is to be done, and answer to speculative principles. For as the animal and sensitive nature is not only furnished with sense and perception, but also with certain connatural instincts and impressions whereby animals are directed and inclined to sensitive good, so ... God has furnished the rational nature not only with the faculty of reasoning, but with certain common principles and notions, whereby 'tis inclined to the good of the reasonable life."[27] Norris never regarded these innate first principles of ethics as constituting the fundamental basis of morality, for the law of reason in this sense was part of the positive or revealed law. But in the fourth edition he decisively rejected the existence of any such innate moral knowledge, speaking of "the unphilosophicalness and indeed unintelligibility of the supposition of any such original impressions".[28] Norris had shared his early acceptance of innate moral principles with such Cambridge Platonists as Henry More, but he soon abandoned this early view, realising that his own conception of the immediate presence of truth to the mind made such innate knowledge unnecessary. In his Cursory

Reflections upon a Book call'd, An Essay concerning Human Understanding (1690), Norris made clear his own rejection of innate ideas even while criticising Locke's argument against them, and emphasised the distinction between such a view and his own theory.

The second important change in the fourth edition of Considerations upon the Nature of Sin concerned the positive or negative nature of sin. Almost all Christian thinkers have regarded evil as a privation, an absence of good, rather than as something positive in its own nature, but Norris in 1687 took the contrary view. A sin was an action which not merely did not promote the common good, but which actively opposed it, just as pain was not merely an absence of pleasure, but its contrary; and contraries were equally positive. This applied to sins of omission too: "Their irregularity does not lie in the not doing or the not willing to do what ought to be done, but in the willing not to do it."[29] All sin therefore was of a positively evil nature. But Norris soon changed his mind on this matter, and did not wait for the revised (fourth) edition of the Miscellanies to say so. Already in 1690 he added a post-script to his Cursory Reflections on Locke's Essay, in which he wrote: "Whereas in a certain discourse of mine entitled "Considerations upon the Nature of Sin" I made sin to be of a positive nature, upon better consideration I find intolerable consequences to follow upon that supposition, and do therefore freely own myself to have been in a mistake, and do here retract it under my hand."[30] In the fourth edition of the Miscellanies the whole passage was of course changed, and Norris adopted the traditional view which he had rejected in 1687. What seems to have happened is that Norris changed the perspective in which he saw sin. When he wrote the original version of Considerations upon the Nature of Sin, he had been thinking of sin as an action opposed to the common good, since the natural tendency of an action

71

to promote or oppose the common good was the very quality which made it "fit to be commanded or forbidden by the wise Governor of the world"; and in this context it was natural to think of sin as positive. But Norris soon came to see that such a view did not fit in with his psychological and metaphysical doctrine, according to which no choice could be made except in virtue of the desire for God as universal good. In this context sin could only be seen as the stopping short of this movement towards God on an inadequate object, and hence as a privation rather than as something positive.

The Christian Law asserted and vindicated is described by Norris as A General Apology for the Christian Religion, both as to the Obligativeness and Reasonableness of the Institution. In this essay Norris expresses for the first time his view of the relations between Christianity and natural religion. Against all whe assert either that Christianity contains no moral obligations or that it contains obligations which are contrary to reason, he aims to prove that it is "a state of service" and "a reasonable service."[31]

On the first point, Norris declares that Christianity has been utterly deformed by those who deny the necessity of good works. The antinomians claim that Christ freed his followers from the obligations of the moral law, while others hold that Christianity is purely a matter of orthodox belief, with no special reference to conduct; and the "solifidians" assert that all that is required for the justification of the Christian is trust in the merits of Christ. Against all such views (which he tends to over-simplify and thus to caricature), Norris declares that Christ in no way absolved us from obedience to the moral law. Indeed Christ was himself a legislator, perfecting and completing the law of which Moses had given a first draft, and thus increasing its exigencies. On the other hand, Norris declares, Christianity is not only a law but also a

covenant of grace, and as such it brings the possibility of forgiveness. The perfect fulfilment of the law is no longer the absolute
condition of salvation, but faith and repentance can bring to the
sinner a pardon which would have been beyond his grasp but for
the sacrifice of Christ. Christ's sacrifice does not save a man
despite himself, but it opens the way to pardon if he repents. In
offering forgiveness, but only in return for repentance and the
serious effort to fulfil one's duties, Christianity exemplifies both
the goodness and the wisdom and justice of God.

 Having shown that Christianity is a state of service in that
it makes moral demands, Norris next proceeds to show that the
service it demands is in accordance with reason. Natural religion,
he declares, is obviously reasonable, but so too is Christianity
both in what it requires one to believe and in its moral teaching.
As has been seen, the general design of Christianity is eminently
reasonable, since it reconciles the truth, wisdom, and justice of
God with his mercy and goodness; and furthermore noone who reflects on the arguments that attest the divine origin of the Christian
religion (the Old Testament prophecies and prefigurations fulfilled
in Christ, his miracles and the sublimity of his teaching, his death
and resurrection, etc.) can doubt that it comes in fact from God.
The mysteries of Christianity, it is true, such as the doctrines
of the Trinity and the Incarnation, are above reason and cannot be
fully understood, but reason can find no contradiction in them,
while the resurrection of Christ does not seem in any way impossible to God's power. As to the moral teaching of Christianity,
"the Christian Law is nothing else but the Law of Nature retrieved,
explained, and set in a clearer light."[32] Christ completed the
Mosaic Law by adding to it refinements of which the Jews of Moses'
time were incapable, but he added nothing to the Natural Law, which

73

always remains the final criterion of morality. And neither the Christian nor the Natural Law commands anything that does not have "a natural connection with the well or ill-being of man, either as to his private or political capacity."[33]

Norris then briefly examines some of the Christian commandments. Understood even in its most literal sense, the command to love God with one's whole heart and soul is strictly in accordance with the nature of the will, while the command to love one's neighbour as oneself clearly tends to the good both of the individual and of society. Even such difficult commandments as those which forbid the returning of evil for evil, command one to love one's enemies, or forbid divorce save for adultery, can be seen to be for the ultimate good of mankind. Christian morality, therefore, contributes to the interest of mankind, but it is also obligatory by virtue of God's rightful authority over all his creatures, and it is a sign of his goodness that he has commanded us nothing but what is in our own interest. It is true that some of the commandments are difficult for fallen man to observe, since, although they are reasonable, man cannot always easily follow reason; but man has then the assistance of grace, and forgiveness is offered to repentance.

At the end of The Christian Law asserted and vindicated, Norris draws certain conclusions from his argument. It follows from the reasonableness of Christianity that no doctrine which is evidently contrary to reason can be part of the Christian religion. It follows too that noone ought to be persecuted for his religion unless he disturbs the public peace, "for since God has required nothing of us but what is agreeable to our reason, why should man?"[3] And finally it follows that sin, being unreasonable, is the height of folly. In this essay Norris advanced for the first time his view of

74

the relation of Christianity and reason. The adversaries whom he had in mind were chiefly those who denied that reason had any rightful part to play in religious matters. But Norris's conception of reason was very different from that of the Deists and Socinians, and even from that of Locke. Norris had no hesitation in accepting the mysterious side of Christianity, and he interpreted the Natural Law in such a way that it included even the most exigent Christian commandments. In An Account of Reason and Faith (1697), one of his most successful works, he returned to this subject, to defend Christianity against those who, agreeing with him on the rationality of religion, drew from it very different conclusions from his own.

A Discourse concerning Perseverance in Holiness appears probably to have been preached in the first instance as a sermon. In it Norris aimed to prove two points: that man has sufficient power to persevere, if he wishes, till death in a life of holiness, but that it is also possible for him to fall from such a life. The holy life of which Norris speaks does not involve a complete absence of sin, but it excludes any habit of serious sin and any sin committed with entire deliberation, and it involves a sincere effort to overcome those faults and weaknesses which can never be entirely excluded in this life. Such a life of holiness is called by Norris the state of sincerity, and to die in this state is regarded by him as the condition of salvation in the Christian dispensation. It is not necessary for salvation always to have been in such a state; one may have fallen into serious sin and risen out of it by repentance. Salvation comes from the merits of Christ, bringing forgiveness of sins; but if one is to receive this forgiveness one must be in the state of sincerity. If, however, to be saved, one must die in such a state, it must in principle be possible always to remain in it, since man does not control the moment of his death.

But though it is possible to persevere till death in a life of holiness, it is also possible to fall from it. One might think that the moral and religious life was so eminently reasonable that noone could abandon it, but experience proves the contrary, for man does not easily let himself be guided by reason. The habits of a holy life can be broken, and though God has promised us sufficient grace to be saved and will not allow us to be tempted beyond our strength, there is no reason to expect him to intervene with irresistible graces to save us from ourselves.

In the original edition of the Miscellanies Norris refers at this point to the theory of pre-existence which was held both by Hierocles and by such Platonists as Henry More. According to some Platonists, he recalls, most souls are sent into this world as a punishment for faults committed in a previous existence, but some few come either out of generosity or sent by God's providence to be examples of virtue to others; and these souls, they think, are assured by God's favour of perseverance in virtue and an eventual return to their native heaven. Norris does not comment on the presuppositions of this theory, but contents himself with conceding that God may reward those who have served him particularly faithfully with such a measure of his grace that they are sure to persevere. But such cases, he considers, are rare, and even these favoured individuals have spent most of their lives subject to the possibility of falling away. It is clear that Norris's teaching on this point takes no account of the reason the Platonists advanced for the indefectibility of these souls, so it is not surprising that all reference to these Platonic speculations was omitted from the revised edition of 1706.

Of the Slightness of all Secular, and the Importance of Minding our Eternal, Interest is an essay which seems originally to have been a sermon, devoted to the proof of two propositions, "Ist, that no interest relating purely to this present world is of any great moment or concern to man; 2ly, that to be very careful of our final interest, and to make sure to ourselves a happy eternity, is indeed a thing of vast moment and importance."[35] Norris does not mean that what one does on earth is unimportant, but that one ought to live and act in this life with eternity in view. Those who subordinate religion to earthly objectives reverse the order of things and display their own stupidity. Like all Norris's writings on practical religion, this essay is of a highly lucid reasonableness which foreshadows Eighteenth Century ways of thought. His teaching does no more than to take entirely seriously doctrines which every Christian would claim to believe and most of which Norris would claim to be capable of rational proof. It was in this direction of a Christianity all of whose implications were taken entirely seriously that Norris's writings were to have their most lasting influence on English life and thought.

The Copy of a Letter written to my Friend F.B. concerning the Death of my Dear Niece M.C. is, in its original form, a most moving document. Norris was profoundly upset by the tragically premature death of his niece, who seems from her initials to have been the daughter of his sister Mary, who was married to a certain Richard Cooper, of Newbury, Berkshire, and seven of his poems, in addition to this letter, are dedicated to her memory. Her death, he tells his friend, is the worst sorrow that he has ever felt, not for her sake, for her happiness with God is assured, but for his own, for "My pretty little dear Niece and Scholar, she whom I loved, admired, and delighted in, she for whose sake I once thought life, as now I think death, a blessing, ... is dead."[36] But after giving free rein to his grief, Norris pulls himself up.

Grief and regret, he declares, is the most foolish of passions, for it can change nothing. If we believe that the world is governed by an omnipotent being of infinite goodness and wisdom, we must believe, at least implicitly, that all things happen for the best. At present we cannot see all the connections of things, but we must trust God who only permits evil in order to draw greater good from it. LEIBNIZ

The revised edition of 1706 suppressed most of the personal references in the letters which formed part of the Miscellanies, but nowhere did this suppression have a more far-reaching effect than in this letter, which became simply The Extract of a Letter written upon the Death of a Friend. All the paragraphs in which Norris spoke of his sorrow, of his love for his niece, and of her charming personality, disappear, leaving only the moral and philosophical teaching on the absurdity of grief and the rational duty of accepting whatever God allows as best. As a result this teaching now gives an appearance of Stoic insensibility, whereas in its original form the letter showed Norris's extreme sensibility and the struggle that he had had to make reason prevail.

The two short essays which alone remain to be examined in the prose section of the Miscellanies need not detain us long. In Of Seriousness, Norris declares that true seriousness, an essential concomitant of virtue, does not consist in gravity of appearance or slowness of gait; the truly serious man is "one that duly and impartially weighs the moments of things, so as neither to value trifles nor despise things really excellent."[37] The truly serious man, in fact, is the rational man. Of Courage affirms that courage is essential in order both to begin a life of virtue and to persevere in it. True courage is not foolhardiness, but the definitions suggested by Aristotle and the Stoics are not helpful. In Norris's view, the

78

virtue of courage is "a firm and constant <u>schesis</u> or disposition
of mind, whereby a man is fixed and determined never to dread
any evil so far as to decline it when the choosing it is the only
remedy against a greater."[38] Norris illustrates this definition
with the example of martyrdom: the martyr chooses to accept pain
and death in order to avoid the greater evil of sin. Like every virtue,
courage for Norris is an expression of reason.

2. Norris's Poetry

To consider Norris from a literary point of view as a poet
is outside the scope of this book, but it is interesting to note that
historians of literature have often rendered more justice to Norris
than have historians of philosophy.[39] Our aim is the more restricted one of considering those aspects and passages of Norris's
poetry which throw light on his philosophical thought or on his
character. The great majority of Norris's poems date from his
youth. <u>Poems and Discourses</u> (1684) contains fifteen poems, all
of which, with the exception of two in Latin, were republished in
the <u>Miscellanies</u> of 1687, together with sixty new ones which appeared there for the first time. In the last poem of the <u>Miscellanies</u>
Norris took leave of his muse, and though these same seventy-
three poems were reprinted in each new edition of the <u>Miscellanies</u>,
he never added to them. Only twice did Norris in later life break
into poetry. Once in each Part of his <u>Theory of the Ideal or Intel-</u>
<u>ligible World</u> (1701-4), moved by the grandeur of the doctrine that
he was expounding, he expressed himself in a poem of great beauty
and solemnity.[40]

Though his ambitious "pindaric odes" cannot be considered
very successful, many of Norris's simpler poems possess a real
beauty. As one would expect, many of his poems reflect the same

philosophical and religious views which are expressed in his prose writings of the same period. Amongst the themes of his poems are to be found the soaring flight of Platonic love towards God, the divine Ideas as sources of order in the universe, the inability of earthly goods to satisfy man, and the desire for eternity. The poem Seraphic Love speaks of beauty as consisting in harmony and proportion, while The Grant echoes An Idea of Happiness by affirming that

>"Even a dream of happiness
>
>With real joy the soul does bless."

Some of the poems are provided with "annotations" to explain their meaning. Thus in a note to the poem The Elevation, Norris refers his readers to the works of More, Glanvil, and Rust for an explanation of the hypothesis of the pre-existence of souls, a hypothesis which is presupposed by this poem but on whose truth he himself does not pronounce. In another poem Norris sings the praise of Henry More; in another he evokes friendship and music as the highest and most lasting of earthly joys. In seven of his most touching poems he mourns his niece who had died so prematurely. [41] From our point of view, however, the greatest interest attaches to those poems which reveal aspects of Norris's thought or character which are not apparent from his prose writings.

In several of his poems Norris seems to turn against the ideal of rational knowledge which he normally prized so highly. Thus in the poem Against Knowledge he complains that knowledge, by showing the vanity of earthly goods and pleasures, destroys man's happiness in this world, while The Curiosity represents the search for knowledge as an unending labour which brings but little reward. But if these two poems do no more than echo the Book of Ecclesiastes, the poem The Discouragement is more radical. Perhaps what we think of as knowledge is no more than a false appearance of truth; perhaps the blessed in heaven reason according to quite other rules than ours; perhaps our "truth" is regarded there as an absurdity.

> "We truth by a refracted ray
> View, like the sun at ebb of day.
> Whom the gross treacherous atmosphere
> Makes where it is not, to appear."

It is clear that this verse expresses a doubt of the most fundamental kind about the validity of human knowledge. It would doubtless be wrong to insist too strongly on this poem, which according to its title betrays a moment of discouragement in its author. But one may wonder whether Norris would have underlined so strongly, against Descartes and the scholastics, that the ideas and truths which we see are the very ones that God knows in his own essence, if he had never found himself in danger of falling into total scepticism. At all events, as appears particularly from his Theory of the Ideal or Intelligible World, Norris was convinced that the theory according to which man is in immediate contact with the divine ideas was the only one which made it possible to avoid scepticism and to give a firm foundation to human knowledge; and the scepticism to which this theory replies is the very sort of scepticism which is expressed in this poem.

The verses that we have been considering do not, however, mark the end of the poem. They reflect, so to speak, the blackest moment of discouragement, expressing a radical doubt which Norris was never to formulate again. The last verse expresses a less radical point of view, a merely relative disavowal of human knowledge. Even if true knowledge is to be found here below, it is difficult to acquire and does not extend far; at death, on entering heaven, we shall acquire all knowledge instantaneously, without

81

any effort on our part. Accordingly it is unnecessary to seek all knowledge during this life; the only knowledge that is really necessary, apart from what is needed for practical purposes, is that which aids man to reach heaven, where alone his desire to know all truth can be fulfilled. This attitude is frequently expressed in Norris's later writings, particularly in his Reflections upon the Conduct of Human Life. As time went on, Norris became less and less satisfied with human knowledge, less and less easily convinced. His respect for truth grew ceaselessly, so that in later life he tended to advance many of his theories as no more than hypotheses. In this, no doubt, he was partly following Malebranche's recommendation to use one's freedom as much as possible and never to consent to a proposition unless one was forced to do so by evidence that could not be gainsaid, but he was also giving expression to that sceptical side of himself which had been expressed in these poems. Norris was often regarded by his adversaries as an "enthusiast", but in fact he had a highly developed critical sense; and though he never seems to have practised a systematic doubt in the Cartesian sense, his poems show that he well knew the temptation of total scepticism. No doubt this was why he attached such great importance to the immediate presence of divine truth to the soul.

Several poems in the Miscellanies, together with the dedication of the whole work to Leopold-William Finch, James II's nominee as Warden of All Souls, show Norris's Tory sympathies, but these few political references are less significant than the series of poems in which he expresses his renunciation of all involvement in politics. The honours of this world are vanity, ambition is a snare, and most political disputes are senseless. One is happier and more free if one leaves the state to its feverish life of plots

and intrigues, and lives a quiet life of peaceful study. This desire
for a peaceful life was shared by Norris with the Cambridge Platonists. In Norris's case it was linked with a love for the country
and the longing for a rural retreat. These poems, it is true, form
part of a literary genre which was then popular, reflecting the
Beatus ille of Horace, [42] but they also seem to represent his true
feelings, since he often expresses elsewhere his love for the beauties of nature and his whole philosophy presupposes the desirability
of solitude for reflective thought. The poem Sitting in an Arbour
contains a description of a garden running down to a river, a garden in which the author could give himself to thought with no other
distraction than that of the "winged choir" of birds. This poem
seems an almost perfect anticipated description of the garden of
Bemerton Rectory, which, however, did not become Norris's
home until 1692. Norris in fact left Oxford and retired to the
country in 1689, but he did not find his idyllic picture of rural
life altogether realised; his parochial duties did not leave him the
leisure for which he had hoped for his literary work. [43] Nevertheless he seems always to have retained his love for the country and
his esteem for solitude as the necessary condition for thought.

In her study The Happy Man: Studies in the Metamorphoses
of a Classical Ideal, Maren-Sophie Røstvig has traced the changes
in interpretation which the Horation ideal of a rural retreat underwent in the course of the seventeenth and eighteenth centuries. In
this development, she finds that Norris's poems represent a turning point. On the one hand she emphasises the Epicurean tone of
Norris's verses on this subject, which she finds typical of his time.
There is no doubt that this element is present in Norris's poetry,
but it should not be exaggerated in view both of his conviction that
a rural retreat was the best setting for intellectual activity, and

of the seriousness and devotion with which he gave himself to the work of a philosophical and religious writer. On the other hand, and more importantly, she brings out clearly the contrast that exists between Norris's conception of nature and the quasi-mystical views of his predecessors. Despite his respect for the Platonists of the mid-seventeenth century, Norris shows no interest in their belief in the penetration of the material world by the spiritual. Norris's poetical forerunners - Henry More, Vaughan, Thomas Traherne - had a Hermetist conception of Nature as alive and quasi-divine, but Norris saw in the material world the reign of order and harmony, and its beauty led him above nature and direct to God. In this, Røstvig declares, Norris is a precursor of the eighteenth century and the age of Pope.[44] These poems reflect the views that Norris also expressed in his prose writings. By his rejection of occult powers in nature and by his insistence on the reign of physical law, Norris belonged to what Henri Gouhier has called the Cartesian "anti-renaissance",[45] but Røstvig has seen the essential modernity of Norris in comparison with the Cambridge Platonists more clearly than have those who have written expressly on his philosophy.[46]

3. Conclusion

The Miscellanies of 1687 was the first of Norris's writings to achieve a wide popularity; it was also the last work that he wrote before he began to read Malebranche. Not that one can exclude the possibility that Norris had some indirect knowledge of Malebranche's thought before this date, but it seems certain that he had not yet begun to read his works. The first signs of Malebranche's influence on Norris are to be found in the books that he wrote in the years immediately following the publication of the Miscellanies.[47]

Accordingly it will be worth while at this point to see how far Norris's speculations had taken him by this time.

On two fundamental matters, Norris had already reached his definitive position before 1687. The proof of the existence of God which he advanced in his Metaphysical Essay, together with the view that he had already proposed in his Letter of Ideas (1684) on the two aspects of the divine mind and on the relation to it of the Ideas, was to be the foundation of the whole of his thought on the "intelligible world". Again, the theory which identified the power to direct one's attention as the root of liberty, and which Norris first proposed in his sermon of 29 March 1685 and defended in his correspondence with Henry More, was always to remain essential to his system. Both these theories have their roots in the Platonism of Hierocles, for they both presuppose that immediate presence of absolute truth to the human mind which was the essential of Hierocles's teaching. But both theories had been eleborated with considerable originality by Norris himself.

Apart from these subjects on which Norris had already attained his permanent position, the Miscellanies give evidence of the direction that his thoughts were taking on several other issues. Thus the distinction between the loves of benevolence and desire is already expressed, though the consequences that this distinction was to have in his later works are not yet apparent. Again, the concentration of all one's desire on God, the centre towards which the soul gravitates, is already recommended, though this demand has not yet attained the rigour and clarity which it later received after Norris had adopted Malebranche's theory on this subject. More generally, the theocentric spirit that was to characterise all Norris's later writings, the strong sense of the reality and central importance of God, is already apparent in the Miscellanies.

There were several subjects, on the other hand, on which Norris in 1687 had not yet clarified his ideas. Thus the theory of innate knowledge which was presupposed by Considerations upon the Nature of Sin was rendered superfluous by the teaching of Norris's other essays on the immediate presence of divine truth to the mind, while the theory of the positive nature of sin was hardly compatible with the view that every choice was made in virtue of the desire of absolute good. In particular, Norris's moral theories had not yet been systematised. Often he speaks of the universal good as the only criterion of morality, but at other times he regards individual perfection as a parallel standard; the relations between these two criteria and Norris's theory of love have not yet been specified. But on one fundamental point Norris's position was already fixed: the moral law is reasonable and naturally advantageous to man, but its obligation as law derives from the fact that it is enjoined by God.

On the nature of sensation and the related question of the soul of animals, Norris at this period had not yet formed any special opinion. No doubt he accepted, without having specially thought about it, the scholastic view on these questions, which he was later to answer in terms borrowed from Malebranche. Again, he had not given much thought to matters of physics at this time. But in truth these were subjects in which he never had more than a secondary interest. Norris's real interest was always to be reserved almost exclusively for metaphysics, morality, and religion.

If we leave aside these questions to which he had not yet given much attention, we cannot fail to observe a remarkable convergence between the views which Norris had worked out for himself as a young man, and those which he was to find, more fully developed, in Malebranche's writings. This is especially true of

Norris's theory of freedom, despite the difference of analysis that resulted from the fact that he at this time attributed the act of judgementto the intellect whereas Malebranche attributed it to the will. As has been seen, the same convergence is also found in their theories of knowledge. For Norris as for Malebranche, the eternal truths that we know and the ideas on which they are founded are in God. Norris had reached this conviction by a different path from that of Malebranche, and his theory was at this time confined to purely intellectual ideas and the necessary truths which flow from them. Norris was, and always remained, more of a Platonist, less of a Cartesian, than Malebranche; but even at this time one cannot deny the similarity of their views on intellectual knowledge.

For the completion of many aspects of his philosophy, and especially for the full development of his theory on the love of God and for his theory of sensation, Norris was to owe much to his reading of Malebranche in the years following the first publication of the Miscellanies. But already one can see why Norris was so disposed to welcome the teachings of his French contemporary and even in many cases to adopt his precise formulation of them. The philosophy of Malebranche forms in fact the natural complement of Norris's own independent reflections. In some of his later works Norris's enthusiasm for Malebranche went so far that it is easy to forget that the ideas expressed were as much his own as they were Malebranche's. In Malebranche Norris found his own ideas, often better expressed than he had managed to formulate them himself; and he also found further doctrines which enabled him to fill the gaps in his own thought. But in many cases, as we shall see, Norris remained less fully convinced of these parts of Malebranche's philosophy which went beyond his own original position. Honest and not easy to convince, he was inclined to accept these theories only as probably hypotheses, while his own doctrine of the intelligible world was always to remain the heart of his metaphysical system.

CHAPTER V THE IDEAL WORLD: GOD AND HUMAN THOUGHT

Norris's theory of the "Ideal or Intelligible World", which
was at once a theory of knowledge and a natural theology, was the
centre of all his thought. As has already been seen, the roots of
his developed system are to be found in his earliest writings. Thus
in the work which Norris translated, Hierocles identified truth with
the God who was immediately present to every soul: truth therefore
was to be found within oneself, though only at the price of assiduous
attention. Again, Norris's essential objection to Calvinism was
that the doctrine of reprobation was irreconcilable with the goodness, holiness, justice, and truthfulness of God, values which
were valid for God in the same sense as they were for man, though
God exemplified them to an infinitely higher degree. The Letter of
Ideas of 1684 insisted that the divine Ideas were to be identified
with the essence of God, considered as intelligible and imitable in
various ways by possible creatures, so that truth was an aspect
of the divine nature. These various indications of Norris's theories
of truth and knowledge were drawn together by his Metaphysical
Essay towards the Demonstration of a God, from the Steady and
Immutable Nature of Truth, published in the Miscellanies of 1687.
In this essay, it will be remembered, he affirmed that certain
propositions known to man were strictly necessary and eternally
true. The eternal truth of these propositions, he argued, implied
the eternal reality of the essences whose relationships they expressed. Since these essences did not subsist eternally in the world
of nature, they must have another, "ideal", existence, in an eternal mind, a timeless system of essences and truths. This mind
must be eternal, immutable, and omniscient, and was therefore

identical with God.

From his earliest writings, therefore, Norris held that the divine Ideas were immediately present to the human mind. The existence of such Ideas in the mind of God was of course the common doctrine of the Scholastics, who derived it from St. Augustine, but Norris went beyond them by his insistence that the truths which man knows are themselves strictly eternal. In his view, truth is directly experienced as necessary and eternal, and it imposes itself inescapably on the mind of anyone who sufficiently attends to it. Norris had not yet explicitly elaborated a theory of knowledge, but his teaching on truth presupposed that we know necessary truth "in God", since it is seen as an aspect of his nature. This truth, Norris held, was present, in God, to every soul, but it could be attained, in the face of the prevalence of false opinions and prejudices, only by attentive, careful, and independent thought.

In his early years, then, Norris had already formulated a definite theory of truth or of "the Ideal World"; his later writings on this subject served mainly to explain this teaching and to defend it against possible objections. This view of truth implied a certain theory of knowledge, but at the time of writing the Miscellanies Norris had not yet attempted to formulate this theory in any detail. When he did come to formulate a theory of human knowledge, Norris did so in terms that were largely borrowed from Malebranche. This made his views on this subject appear more dependent on Malebranche than they really were. Norris's first references to Malebranche are found in his Theory and Regulation of Love (1688), but the first work in which Malebranche's teaching affects his theory of knowledge is Reason and Religion, which was published in the following year. Norris's theory of truth in itself and his theory of man's knowledge of this truth run like two separate strands through his later writings, the former essentially the result of his own reflections, the latter owing more to his reading of Malebranche. It will perhaps be more helpful to consider the development of Norris's thought on these two aspects of his theory separately.

1. Truth and God: the Ideal World in itself

After the Miscellanies, the first work in which Norris returned to the subject of the nature of truth and its relation to God was Reason and Religion, first published in 1689 shortly before his departure from Oxford. Reason and Religion was a series of philosophical meditations on the nature of God and the nature of man; it belonged to the same class of literature as Contemplation and Love, in the Miscellanies, but was written in a condensed and concentrated style which at times prevented Norris from explaining his meaning with adequate clarity. But though it was thus not an entirely satisfactory work, it remained the only systematic exposition of his metaphysical ideas until the publication of the Essay towards the Theory of the Ideal or Intelligible World, and it was from Reason and Religion that Locke, for instance, derived his knowledge of Norris's system.

Norris's teaching on God and truth is contained in the first part of Reason and Religion, concerned with the nature of God, in which he first considers the general idea that we have of God, our fundamental conception of his essence. He declares that he had formerly followed Descartes and Henry More in holding that the most fundamental idea that we could form of God was that of an absolutely perfect being; but he had now come to the conclusion that God's perfection could be proved a priori from his identity with Being itself, and that this latter was therefore our most funda-

91

mental conception of the divine essence.

Like many Christian thinkers, Norris attached great significance to God's revelation of his name to Moses (Exod. 3:14). God
is there represented as calling himself "I AM", which, Norris declares, must signify "Being itself, or Universal Being, or Being
in general, Being in the abstract, without any restriction or limitation. As if God had said, "You enquire who I am, and by what
name I would be distinguished. Know then that I am he that am, I
am Being itself"."[1] But although Norris thought that the identification of God with Being was rooted in the Bible, he also considered
that it was rationally demonstrable. In the Metaphysical Essay he
had already shown that essences had an existence that was independent of and prior to their realisations in the empirical world; there
must therefore be an essence or Idea of Being, existing independently
of and prior to particular beings. In his Letter of Ideas he had
shown that the divine essence contained all other essences, which
were merely aspects of its intelligibility, considered as imitable
by possible creatures. But if the divine essence contained in this
sense the essences of all possible beings, then it must itself be the
plenitude of Being.

From this conception of God as identified with Being itself,
Norris next proceded to demonstrate his absolute perfection, thus
showing in passing that the former rather than the latter was the
more fundamental idea of God. "Being itself", he argues, "contains in it all the degrees of being, and consequently all possible
perfection."[2] Every perfection is a degree or aspect of being, and
Being itself contains all the degrees of being, since it is indeterminate and hence unlimited and infinite. Furthermore, he adds,
imperfection is a lack of being, so that what is utterly removed
from non-being must be utterly perfect. From this same consid-

eration of God's identity with Being it also follows that he contains within himself the perfections of all his creatures. But these perfections are in God in a more excellent way than they are in creatures. The world is full of beauty, for all created things have some likeness to God; but creatures are beautiful only in a derivative, particular, and limited way, whereas God is Beauty itself. And the same applies to all other perfections.

It is important to notice that, when Norris speaks of God as "Indeterminate Being", he uses the term "indeterminate" in the sense of unlimited or infinite. It has been suggested that the teaching of Reason and Religion, according to which God is indeterminate Being, does not accord with his later view, expressed in the Theory of the Ideal .. World, that God contains the essential perfections of created things in such a way that, when one knows these perfections, one knows something which is part of the divine essence. [3] But this objection rests on a misunderstanding. For Norris, unlike Aristotle or Hegel, indetermination does not at all imply poverty of content. On the contrary, in Reason and Religion Norris proves that God contains all perfections precisely from the fact of his indeterminateness: "Whatever is indeterminate in being has all the degrees of being." [4] Already in Reason and Religion Norris affirmed that God contains the perfections of created beings; and he implied at least that, in knowing these perfections, one knows something of God. His teaching on this point became more explicit in the Theory of the Ideal .. World, but it did not change. For Norris, as for Malebranche and indeed for Aquinas, indetermination, like illimitation, is a perfection.

It is clear that, when Norris sought to define our essential idea of God, he was not thinking of an idea like other ideas. For God is not one being amongst others: he is Being itself. Norris later declared explicitly, with Malebranche, that God is known immediately, by his own essence which is present to the mind and obscurely seen by it, and not by any representative idea. What he meant here by our idea of God was simply our fundamental conception of his essence. And he considered that the most fundamental idea that we could have of God was that of Being itself; but reflection was needed in order to see that this Being was indeed God. Norris's teaching on Being as the essence of God contains echos of several other philosophers. Aquinas had made Being the essence and, so to speak, the definition of God, and Norris's argument from the indeterminateness of God to his unlimited and infinite perfection was Thomist in its inspiration. But in addition it was the view of Descartes that, when one conceived being in itself, it was infinite being that one conceived, while Malebranche constantly identified indeterminate being with the infinite being of God, and regarded this as the most proper characterization of the divine essence.

It is clear that, in his identification of the divine essence with Being, Norris was not consciously following Descartes, whom he regarded on this point rather as an adversary. He was no doubt influenced both by Aquinas and by Malebranche, though his view of being differed from that of the Thomists in that, where Aquinas regarded existence as primary, Norris approached being from the side of essence, and regarded mere existence as the lowest and emptiest of concepts. Norris's teaching was closer to that of Malebranche, but remained more Platonist in its conception: essences exist prior to and independently of the beings which exemplify them, and in this Platonic sense God is the Idea of Being, the essence which gathers, includes, and unifies all essences. Norris's teaching on the divine essence in Reason and Religion was of course fully in accord with the theory of the Intelligible World that he had already formulated in his earlier writings.

In a later section of the first part of Reason and Religion, Norris treats of God's omniscience. In his Metaphysical Essay he had already proved the omniscience at the same time as the existence of God, and he now repeated, in a slightly condensed form, the arguments which he had advanced in that work, together with considerations taken from the Letter of Ideas. He insisted that the divine Ideas were identical with the divine essence considered as imitable in different ways, and that truth therefore depended on the divine mind considered as "exhibitive" (or intelligible), but did not depend on it considered as "conceptive" (or intelligent). Norris attached great importance to this distinction which, as has been seen, he derived from Henry More, because it enabled him to affirm the strict necessity of truth while agreeing that truth depended on God.

"'Twas for want of the help of this notion", he added, "that that keen wit Descartes blundered so horribly in stating the dependence of propositions of eternal truth upon the intellect of God. He saw 'twas necessary (as indeed it is) to make God the cause of truth, and that truth must some way or other depend upon him. But then he makes it to depend upon the mind of God as conceptive, and that things are so only because God is pleased so to conceive them. And this he carries so high as to say that even in a triangle three angles would not have been equal to two right ones, had not God been pleased so to conceive and make it. Now I am for the dependence of truth upon the divine intellect as well as he, but not so as to make it arbitrary and contingent, and consequently not upon the divine intellect as conceptive, but only as exhibitive. That is, that things are therefore true inasmuch as they are conformable to those standing and immutable Ideas which are in the mind of God as exhibitive and representative of all the whole possibility of being."[5]

For Norris, truth depended on God only in the sense that it was an aspect of his nature. The experience of the eternal necessity of truth was the starting point of his metaphysical reflection, and for this reason he found the Cartesian theory of the creation of truth not only unacceptable but also incomprehensible.

In the formulation of Norris's theory of knowledge, Reason and Religion marked a decisive step forward under the influence of Malebranche, but it did not add much to the theory of truth in its relation to God that was contained in his earlier works. These same ideas lay at the base of the First Part of the Essay towards the Theory of the Ideal or Intelligible World (1701), which was to be the definitive statement of Norris's position. Norris had already spoken in 1690 of a book that he intended to write on this subject. In Reflections upon the Conduct of Human Life he referred Lady Masham (to whom that work was dedicated) to his Theoria Mundi Idealis, sive Metaphysica Platonica which was soon to be published, while in his Cursory Reflections on Locke's Essay he spoke of the Theory of the Ideal World that he was writing. In both places he declared that the new book would fill in the gaps left by Reason and Religion, and would present for the first time the whole of his teaching on the Intelligible World. But in the Preface to the First Part of the Theory he tells us what had become of that project:

"'Tis true indeed that some years ago, when I had the honour to be one of the Fellows of All Souls College in Oxford (which God for ever bless and prosper), I began a treatise upon this subject in Latin, whereof I there finished two chapters with a

96

good part of a thirt. But, whether discouraged by the difficulty
of the undertaking or diverted from it by other avocations, so
it was that I went no further, but laid it, and almost the thoughts
of it, quite aside, without meddling with it for many years. And
when very lately I resumed this work into my hands, I found I
could like neither the form nor the matter of my former performance, so that I was forced to begin the edifice upon a new
foundation and to build as it were from the very ground, employ-
ing only here or there a stroke of the old materials."[6]

We cannot know what Norris now found unsatisfactory about his
earlier unfinsihed work, of which no trace remains. He had, no
doubt, been distracted from it largely by the controversies in which
he had in the interval became involved. But Norris had determined
to return to the subject for two reasons. His other writings contained many references to the Intelligible World, but since he had
never completely expounded his theory these references were apt
to be dismissed by some as mere "Platonic gibberish". And on the
other hand the subject was too important and central both for metaphysics and morals to be left in the dark. It seemed unlikely, furthermore, that anyone else would undertake this work, when even
Malebranche, the philosopher whe had done most to investigate
the nature of the world of Ideas and who "would perhaps have been
the fittest person of the age to have given a just and complete theory
of its systems", [7] had stopped short half way in his description of
it. Norris considered that Malebranche had very well described
the manner of man's knowledge of the Ideas, which was why he so
largely followed him in the Second Part of his own Theory; but
Malebranche had not treated in any detail of the world of Ideas in
itself. This accordingly was the task that Norris now set himself,
building on the foundation of his earlier works on the subject. It is

97

not proposed here to follow the detailed order of his exposition, but rather to examine the central affirmations of his theory in this its fully developed state.

Norris begins his argument with a preliminary description of what he understands by the "natural" and "ideal" states of things. A thing exists in the natural state when it has been created by the free choice of God. It then has a de facto, contingent existence, in time, and the collection of all such contingently existing beings is the natural world. In the intelligible or ideal state, on the other hand, things exist necessarily, permanently, and immutably. Their existence in Idea is not merely prior to their created existence, but is also the exemplar and intelligible measure of it. The Ideal or Intelligible World is the necessary, eternal system of these essences, the measure both of what exists and of whatever can exist. The aim of Norris's book is both to prove the reality and to analyse the nature of this Ideal World.

Norris considered that the existence of eternal, immutable essences was implied by many expressions that were in daily use. People often spoke of justice itself, beauty itself, truth itself, or of the idea of a line, a circle, or a square. But though in such ways they implied the existence of the Ideal World, they frequently denied it when it was posed as an explicit thesis. To prove its reality he proposed a total of six arguments. Norris's first argument was based on the fact that the natural world seems not always to have existed, in which case it must have been created by a being of infinite power, whom we call God. Now either this world was created in accordance with a plan, or else it was made without thought, fortuitously. That it was not made thoughtlessly, however, is evident both from the nature of God and also from the clear marks of design that can be observed in the world. But if the world was made in accordance with a plan, then God knew in advance what he was going to create, and the essence of things could be known before the creation of the natural world. Essences have therefore an intelligible existence prior to and apart from the natural or created world.

Norris's second argument was taken from the uniformities that can be observed in nature. The determinate size and configuration of parts that are to be found in all the members of any given species of plants or animals can be accounted for, he argues, only on the supposition that they are all made in accordance with the same Idea or all exemplify the same essence. The occasional irregularities that occur, as in the birth of "monsters", serve only to highlight the normal uniformity of nature, and are to be explained along the lines of Malebranche's principle that God acts according to general laws of great simplicity. Furthermore, he adds, insofar as we have any insight into the inner natures of things, the specific essence of each kind appears to be reproduced exactly in all the members of a species, without that element of latitude that attends their precise size and shape. Essences therefore are prior to the individual existing things which exemplify them.

In the third place Norris reproduced a consideration which he had first proposed in the post-script of his Metaphysical Essay. The intelligible essences with which geometry is concerned are never perfectly reproduced in the empirical world, yet they are certainly known since it is their perfection which enables one to judge that their empirical representations are imperfect. The proofs of geometry concern pure intelligible essences, and their truth is independent of the existence of any empirical figures whatever. The consideration that the truths of geometry were concerned with purely intelligible essences led Norris on to his fourth argument, which reproduced the reasoning of the main body of his Metaphysical Essay, which he had already repeated, in another context, in Reason and Religion. Eternal essences were implied by the eternity of truth, and truth imposed itself necessarily on us since it was implicitly affirmed even in the act of denying it. Norris now expanded this argument very considerably, since he undertook to reply in detail to the objections of the Scholastics and to show that their own principles ought to lead them to accept the reality of a world of Ideas or eternal essences. To the Scholastic objection that eternal truths were hypothetical and did not imply actual existence, he gave essentially the same reply as in the post-script to his Metaphysical Essay. Suarez may say that "Man is an animal" can be resolved into "If man is, he is an animal", but, Norris argues, even this hypothetical statement involves an absolute affirmation: the connection affirmed between "man" and "if he exists is an animal" is an absolute one. In other words, Norris argues that one could not affirm that man, once he existed, would be an animal, if the ideas of "man" and "animal" did not have an eternally valid meaning. These eternal essences, however, were not to be found in the natural world, where everything was contingent, changeable, and temporary, so the existence of an Intelligible World of essences must be admitted.

Norris's fifth argument was in the nature of an argumentum ad hominem to the Scholastics, who followed Aristotle in holding that all science concerned what was necessary and immutable. Recognising that individual existants were changeable and contingent, they held that science was of the universal, while affirming that these universal ideas were mental abstractions, inadequate conceptions of natural objects. Against this conception Norris argued that, on such a view, the universals themselves must be

100

in the natural objects, changeable and contingent with them, or
else they must be mere constructions of contingent human minds.
Science, he argues, cannot truly be a knowledge of what is necessary and immutable unless it attains essences, laws, or ideas that
are themselves strictly necessary.

In Norris's view these five arguments established beyond
all doubt the reality of the Ideal or Intelligible World of unchanging essences; but they did not immediately decide the question of
its nature. Is the world of Ideas and truths in God, identified in
some way with his essence, or does it have an independent existence as a world of Ideas existing on its own? Prior to the Theory
of the Ideal .. World Norris had never seriously considered the
second alternative, but now he set out to prove explicitly that the
Ideal World was to be found in God. His principal argument to this
effect was a repetition of the reasoning that he had used in Reason
and Religion to prove that Being was the essence of God, and it also constituted a sixth proof of the real existence of the Intelligible
World. If God was universal, infinite Being, ipsum esse subsistens
as Aquinas said, then he contained all the perfections of being and
was hence, in Ficinus's phrase, "omniform". Norris further argued
that, while God must know all things, one could not suppose that he
was illuminated by his own creatures, as he would be if he derived
his knowledge from them. On this point Malebranche and the Scholastics were agreed, and Norris brought quotations from Aquinas,
the Portuguese Dominican Magallaneus, and the Lutheran Scholastic Christoph Scheibler to show that they all agreed that God
knew creatures in the act of knowing his own essence as imitable.
Norris was right in thinking that this was the common teaching of
the Scholastics, who derived it from Augustine, though he somewhat overloaded his text with quotations in order to show that it

was. The Scholastics accepted the reality of the divine Ideas, and hence of the Ideal World, as fully as Norris did, but, unlike him, they denied that these Ideas had any relevance to human knowledge. The first part of Norris's argument for the identification of the Ideal World with God was considerably more cogent than the second. For if God were not Being itself or infinite Being, then one could not affirm that whatever existed either was God or was created by him; and in this case one could not exclude the possibility of the existence of eternal essences and truths which were neither created by God nor identified with him. But if God includes in his essence all the perfections of being, then there is no possibility of essences or truths existing independently of him, and the "Intelligible World" must be identified with him, in a way that remains to be elucidated.

At this point in his analysis, Norris was so moved by the thought of what he had proved that he gave expression to his sense of the grandeur and beauty of God in an ardent prayer of praise, culminating in the first poem that he had written since the publication of the Miscellanies in 1687. [8] Before going on to examine in more detail the nature of the Ideas and truths and their precise relationship to the divine essence, Norris then considered the question of whether the existence of the Intelligible World, which he had now established, was more or less certain than that of the natural or empirical world. His answer to this question, however, depended on his views on the nature of sense knowledge, and will be examined later.

Returning to the Ideas, Norris declares that ideas in general are representations in the mind by which things are known. But whereas our ideas are generally supposed to be derived from the objects which they represent, created things are copies of the divine Ideas and not vice-versa. Created things differ among themselves as being different degrees of or participations in being, and the divine Ideas too are different degrees of being or perfection in the divine nature, so far as these are imitable by possible creatures. It is on these changeless divine Ideas that created things are modelled. It is clear, then, that the Ideas are independent of the created things whose patterns they are, but there is a sense in which they are also independent of God himself. At this point Norris repeats the distinction which he had first advanced in his Letter of Ideas of 1684 and which he had repeated in Reason and Religion: the Ideas do not depend on the mind of God considered as conceptive or, as he now calls it, intelligent, for the divine mind, like every other mind, presupposes its object and does not construct it. The object of the divine mind in all its knowing is God's own essence considered as intelligible or, as Norris had formerly expressed it, exhibitive of whatever can exist. The Ideas, therefore, are not arbitrary, and God himself could not know them otherwise than they necessarily are.

Norris next suggests that this "emanation" of the Ideas can be identified with the eternal procession of the Word, the Second Person of the Holy Trinity, who is "the Wisdom of God, and the brightness of his glory, and the express image of his Person", [9] an image which expresses both the divine nature itself and also every possible creature. In the divine nature there are, Norris holds, some degrees of perfection which cannot be reproduced in creatures, while others represent possible creatures. All these perfections are represented in the Word, but only the latter ones are, strictly speaking, what we call Ideas, so that the Word, the intelligible image of God, remains beyond our full understanding. This identification of the world of Ideas with the Word, God the Son, was of course traditional among Christian Platonists; it is found in Malebranche, and is particularly characteristic of St. Augustine. But it does not form an essential part of Norris's theory.

Since God is infinite, Norris continues, he contains all the degrees of being, some of which are imitable by possible creatures. The divine essence, insofar as it is imitable, is the Idea of a creature in general; considered as imitable in a certain way or to a certain degree, it is the Idea of a particular type of creature. Accordingly God has Ideas even of the most imperfect of beings, and Norris points out that St. Augustine, St. Thomas, and Malebranche all agree that God knows even pure matter, the idea of which is called "intelligible extension" by Malebranche. Norris's whole discussion of the nature of the Ideas shows that he considered that the views of the Platonists, the Scholastics, and Malebranche on this subject were fundamentally the same. And in this he was, at bottom, correct. Nevertheless his own views on this matter were closer in detail to those of the Platonists and the Scholastics than to those of Malebranche. Norris spoke unreservedly of Ideas of different species and kinds of creatures, and he equated Malebranche's "intelligible extension" with what the Scholastics would have meant by the idea of matter. It was not until he came to write the Second Part of his Theory that he came up against the other aspects of what Malebranche meant by intelligible extension.

If God knows the essences of possible creatures through knowing his own essence, he knows their existence through knowing his own decrees or decisions to create them. Norris's teaching on this point was entirely traditional, and he did not go into the subject any further by asking, for instance, how in that case God could know the free actions of human beings. Instead he went on to consider the part played by the Ideas in the creation and govern-

104

ment of the world. The Ideas were, in Scholastic terms, exemplary causes: the models in accordance with which God created things. The Ideas, on which the diversity of creatures depended, were also the source of the beauty and harmony of nature. The Cambridge Platonists had spoken of "plastic principles" in nature; the Scholastics spoke of "substantial forms", while other Platonists spoke of a soul of the world; but in Norris's view the only true source of the activity, harmony, and regularity of nature, which these authors sought to explain by means of these imaginary principles, was the activity of God in accordance with the Ideas. The regularity of nature resulted, he held, from the laws of movement, which represented the firm will of God; but these laws were derived, in the final analysis, from the essences which existed eternally in the divine mind, the Intelligible World.

Following Malebranche, Norris held that God directed the activity of bodies in accordance with comparatively few general laws, the beauty of whose simplicity more than compensated for the occasional imperfections the resulted from it.[10] In an interesting way, Norris pointed out the similarity between Malebranche's explanation of the origin of "monsters" or imperfections in nature and that proposed by the Scholastics as represented by Suarez. Suarez holds that God always desires, in a general way, that natural causes should produce perfect effects, but adds that this desire on God's part is not absolute: "God will have a perfect effect to follow, as far as it shall be able to follow according to the order of natural causes."[11] God does not normally interfere with the activity of the natural causes that he has established, and it is for this reason, in Suarez's view, that, through the interaction of natural causes, "monsters" sometimes occur. If the Scholastic "natural causes" are replaced by God's direct causality, regulated by the Ideas, then

Suarez's explanation of the imperfections of nature is the precise
equivalent of Malebranche's theory, which Norris himself held,
according to which "monsters" are to be explained in terms of the
generality and simplicity of the laws by which God administers the
world. Sometimes Norris seems not to have been aware of the
divergences between the views of the various authors whom he
quotes, but in this matter of the parallel between the Scholastic
"natures" and Malebranche's "general laws" he seems to have had
a better appreciation of the basic identity of the two conceptions than
did either Malebranche himself or his Scholastic contemporaries.

Norris concluded his examination of the Ideas by considering
their relationship to the infinity of God. The finite cannot represent
the infinite, but the infinite necessarily represents whatever can
exist. But are the Ideas themselves to be regarded as finite or infinite, Norris asks? On the one hand it seems that they are finite,
since they represent the finite essences of creatures; but on the
other hand they are identified with the infinite essence of God. Norris
solved this difficulty with the aid of a distinction which he borrowed
from Suarez. Every Idea is infinite in its esse reale, since it is
identified with the divine essence; but every Idea which represents
a creature is finite in its esse formale or repraesentativum, since
the perfection that it presents is finite. The multiplicity of the Ideas
does not conflict with the simplicity of the divine nature, moreover,
since in their esse reale they are all one with it.Only a real diversity
of component parts would be contrary to the unity and simplicity of
the Godhead.

After dealing with the nature of the Ideas, Norris's next aim
was to examine the status of the eternal truths. If his teaching on
the Ideas was essentially a development of the views he had already
expressed in his Letter of Ideas of 1684, what he said on the truths

106

was to a large extent a restatement of the teaching of his Metaphysical Essay of 1687 and a defence of this teaching against his opponents. Many of Norris's reflections on the eternal truths did little
more, however, than repeat what he had said on the Ideas, and
need not be repeated here. As he pointed out, in his theory the Ideas
and truths are strictly correlative, each implying the other.

In order to establish the precise relationship that obtains
between the truths and the Ideas, Norris found himself obliged to
examine the relationship of relations in general to their terms. On
this matter he followed the analysis of Suarez, according to whom
a relation is a reality, in the sense that it is not a creation of the
human mind, but a reality which is not really, but only formally,
distinct from the terms whose relationship it expresses. The relation of similarity, for example, which subsists between two white
objects, is found, not created, by the mind of man; but it is not
really distinct from the two whitenesses which give rise to it,
though it is formally distinct from them in that it refers one on
them to the other. In the case in point, "Likeness in the thing is
not anything else than the very whiteness itself as respecting another
whiteness as of the same or like nature."[12] In accordance with
this analysis, Norris was able to affirm that the eternal truths
really existed, but were not really distinct from the Ideas whose
relations they were. They were, however, formally distinct from
them, in that they added, to the formality of each Idea, a reference
to one or more other Ideas. In Norrs's view, therefore, the truths
bear the same relationship to the Ideas as the Ideas themselves bear
to the divine essence, since the Ideas, as has been seen, are not
really distinct from the divine essence, though they are formally
distinct from it in that they represent possible creatures. The
eternal truths, therefore, like the Ideas or eternal essences, are

really identical with the divine essence, though they are of course formally distinct from it.

Truth, therefore, Norris affirms, is part of God's nature. When God conforms himself to it, as he necessarily does in all his activity, he is not subordinating himself to any rule outside himself; he is merely acting in accordance with his own nature. At this point Norris repeats his usual strictures on the Cartesian theory of truth as created and therefore not strictly necessary, and adds that all who recognise truth as necessary, immutable, and eternal ought to agree in admitting its identity with God. This argument from the eternal necessity of truth to the existence of God was, of course, the theme of the Metaphysical Essay of 1687, but Norris now envisaged the possibility that he might be accused of arguing in a circle: was he not at the same time basing truth on God and basing God on truth? However he had little difficulty in showing that his reasoning was only apparently circular. In his view, truth depends on God, or rather is really identified with him, so that if there were no God there could be no truth; but God depends on truth only in the sense that man's knowledge of him depends on it. Man can know particular truths before he knows that there is a God, for truth, though really identified with God's intelligible essence, is formally distinct from it. In Norris's view, it is by analysing the nature and characteristics of the truths that he knows that man finds that he is in contact with the eternal, necessary, and omniscient being whom he calls God; for truth is experienced as eternal, and imposes itself on the mind.

The last subject of importance with which Norris dealt in the First Part of his Theory of the Ideal or Intelligible World was that of "the notion and distinction of Essence and Existence".[13] "There is hardly anything", he writes, "... upon which metaphysical and

Scholastic pens have bestowed more exquisite subtilty, and yet after all have left more intricate and confused, than the notion of essence and existence, and the distinction that is between them."[14] The dispute between Thomists, partisans of a real distinction between essence and existence, and Suaresians who denied it was already a classical one in Norris's time, and has continued amongst Scholastic philosophers until the present time without reaching any agreed conclusion.[15] But Norris was convinced that the whole Scholastic discussion rested on a misunderstanding which could be removed by his own theory of the intelligible world.

The essence of a created thing is that which makes it intelligible, or makes it what it is, while its existence is that by which, ceasing to be merely possible, it becomes real and actual. The essence or nature of a thing answers the question of what it is, quid sit, while existence answers the question of whether it exists, an sit. The Scholastics agree in taking essence and existence for metaphysical degrees or elements intrinsic to every created being, and they tend to regard essence as the element of potentiality in a thing which existence realises. Now created things are contingent: they have not always existed and they can cease to exist. It is for this reason that Thomists affirm that the essences of creatures do not contain existence but are really distinct from it. Suaresians, on the other hand, argue that one cannot conceive either a non-existent essence or an existence that is not the existence of something, and accordingly they deny the real distinction of the two principles. In Norris's view both schools are largely right in what they affirm, but neither has seen that what is mistaken is their common presupposition. For in Norris's view there are two sorts of essences. The intelligible essences are necessary and eternal, and are really identified with the divine essence; consequently they are really and

109

and entirely distinct from creatures. But there are also created essences, constitutive of creatures, and these are not to be distinguished from their own existence. The true distinction, for Norris, is not, in short, between essence and existence, but between intelligible essences and those created essences which are constitutive of creatures. Accordingly the Thomists are right to affirm the real distinction between intelligible essence and created existence, while the Suaresians are right in insisting on the real unity of created essence and existence. But these two affirmations do not contradict each other, and it is for lack of an adequate theory of the intelligible world that the Scholastics have continued to argue so interminably about them.

Norris's discussion of essence and existence shows him at his best. His reasoning is clear, and throws real light on the question in dispute. Since his distinction between intelligible and constitutive essence, which he had already made in the course of his examination of the Ideas, [16] was an integral part of his whole theory of the Ideal World, he naturally felt that his teaching as a whole received a confirmation from the light that it threw on this Scholastic imbroglio. It is interesting to note that Norris's conception of essence as "what a thing is", a conception which is common to both the Scholastic and Cartesian traditions, differs very considerably from Locke's conception of substance as the unknown substratum beneath or behind appearances. This divergence of conception had repercussions on the positions taken up by the two philosophers on various disputed questions, including in particular the question of whether matter could think. [17]

Norris's views on the Ideal World in itself are clearly Platonic and Augustinian in their general inspiration. These views attained their fullest expression in the First Part of his Theory of the Ideal

... World, but they were in essence remarkably constant since his earliest writings on the subject. Since then, however, Norris had come to realise the considerable measure of agreement that existed between his own theory of the intelligible world and traditional Scholastic teaching, which accepted both the presence of Ideas in the mind of God and the fact that these Ideas were not dependent on God's will. It is clear that, before writing his Theory, Norris had re-read several Scholastic works, and in particular the Disputationes Metaphysicae of Suarez, and that these studies had not only given him a greater respect for the Scholastic philosophers but had also enabled him to express the relationship of the Ideas and truths to the divine essence with greater exactness than he had previously done or than Malebranche was able to do. But Norris's new esteem for the Scholastics did not alter his essential opposition to their theory of knowledge. In the Scholastic view, man's knowledge begins with sense experience; although God possesses Ideas and there are in consequence eternal truths, man's ideas are obtained by abstraction from sense data, and the truths that he knows are hypothetical and do not imply any real existence. For Norris on the other hand, the truths that man knows are strictly necessary and eternal, and are immediately apprehended as such. Since these truths are really aspects of the divine nature, Norris's theory implies that man has a certain direct knowledge of God: necessary truths can be derived neither from the changeable world of nature nor from man's own changeable mind, except insofar as the eternal Truth itself is present to it.

Although Norris frequently expressed his respect for Descartes, by whom he was in fact much influenced in other matters, no theory is so contrary to his views on the Ideal World as the Cartesian theory of the created nature of truth. And Norris was well aware of

111

this fact. Taken as a whole, his theory of the Intelligible World in itself is closer to Malebranche than to any other thinker amongst his contemporaries. It fits in very naturally with Malebranche's theory of knowledge. Nevertheless Norris was not indebted to Malebranche for the essentials of his theory, which was primarily the fruit of his own reflection, beginning in 1682 with his translation of Hierocles upon the Golden Verses of the Pythagoreans. As will be seen, Norris was greatly influenced by Malebranche in his explanation of man's knowledge of the intelligible and natural worlds; but his assurance of the reality of the Ideal or Intelligible World was more fundamental in his mind than any detailed theory of how it was known.

2. Man's Knowledge of Truth: the Ideal World in relation to Human Understanding

From the time of his earliest writings, Norris had taken the view that truth was to be found within oneself. Truth was an aspect of the nature of God, who was immediately present to every soul, and accordingly it could only be known in some sense "in God". In this sense Norris was fully justified in claiming, in Reason and Religion, that the idea that "we see and know all things in God" was "a notion which I very early lighted upon, by the natural parturiency of my own mind, before I had consulted with any authors that might imbue me with it", [18] though his view was of course dependent on the whole Platonic background of his thought.

The fact that truth was immediately present, in God, to every soul did not mean, for Norris, that it was easy to know it. On the contrary, much of what passed for truth was mere prejudice or erroneous opinion, derived from one's early impressions, from uncritical acceptance of the opinions or assertions of other people, and

112

from lack of sufficient attention in one's own thinking. To distinguish truth from error and mere opinion, there was need of careful, critical, and independent thought. Above all, one must reason
only on clear and distinct ideas, and never give one's assent to a
proposition which one saw to be open to doubt. The presence of God,
and with him truth, to every soul meant that the search for truth
must be an essentially individual quest. The thoughts, experiences,
and writings of others might provide, so to speak, the raw material
of knowledge; they might raise problems or suggest solutions, but
each man must judge of their validity in terms of the light of truth
which was present to himself. Norris's insistence on careful and
systematic attention and on independence in one's thinking was one
of the strongest aspects of his thought, and his detailed rules for
critical thinking will be examined in a subsequent chapter.[19] At
this point it suffices to say that, although many of his prescriptions
for thinking would be valid irrespective of the truth or falsehood of
the rest of his philosophy, in Norris's own mind they derived from
the identity of truth with God and his presence to every soul.

Though truth was in this sense present to everyone, Norris
held that most people failed to discern it for lack of sufficiently
careful attention. Instead they gave their assent too hastily, judging
on first uncritical impressions and giving their assent to what merely had the appearance of truth. In Norris's view it is in the act of
judging that one gives one's assent to the truth or to what, for lack
of sufficiently careful and critical attention, falsely appears to be
true. At the time of writing his sermon on The Root of Liberty and
of his subsequent correspondence with Henry More, Norris held
the traditional view that judgement was an act of the intellect, but,
as has already been seen,[20] this view did not fit entirely satisfactorily with the rest of his theory since, in a false judgement, due

intellectual attention was precisely what was lacking. Norris held
that the intellect and will were not faculties really distinct either
from each other or from the soul; rather they were the soul as intelligent and the soul as volent. In this case, if judgement is seen,
as Norris saw it, as the adhesion of the person to what is seen to
be true or to what for lack of attention falsely appears to be true,
it seems preferable to attribute it to the will. By the time of writing Reason and Religion (1689), Norris had come round to this view,
which he had found expressed in Malebranche's Recherche de la
Vérité, [21] and which Malebranche in his turn had adopted from Descartes. Referring to the Scholastic triple division of intellectual
operations into apprehension, judgement, and discourse, Norris
now writes: "I am rather of Monsieur Malebranche his mind, that
there is no other operation of the intellect but only perception, and
that judgement and discourse more properly belong to the will, as
being an embracing of and an adhesion to the truth." [22] There is no
doubt that Norris adopted the attribution of judgement to the will
from Malebranche, whom he began to read during the years 1688-9,
but this view fitted in better with his whole theory of knowledge and
of freedom than did the traditional one. Neither Norris nor Malebranche, however, at least in his later years, seem to have attributed a great importance to this question, in view of their denial of
a real distinction between the intellect and the will.

Norris, then, from his early years, considered that truth was
known "in God", since it was a relationship of essences which existed
necessarily and eternally as aspects of the divine intelligibility. But
this conception of "knowing in God" refered, of course, to necessary truths only. Norris recognised that knowledge of the natural,
empirical world depended on experience. As he was later to write
in the Second Part of his Theory of the Ideal or Intelligible World,

it is only necessary truths that can be known simply be the application of the mind: "In all other truths our senses are concerned,
and we must be beholden to our eyes, and to our ears, and to our
hands, for the knowledge we have of them; and a man would be ridiculous that should go to prove by mere reason that such a one
won the plate at a horse-race."[23] In his Reflections upon the Conduct of Human Life (1690), Norris gave two criteria of what is
worth knowing: only the knowledge of necessary truth perfects the
mind, he declared, because that alone is a knowledge of God (that
is, of aspects of his intelligibility); but it can be important also
to know matters of contingent fact, so far as these are relevant to
our interests. Norris, then, recognised two radically different sorts
of knowledge. What account did he give of empirical knowledge?

Norris does not seem originally to have had any particular
theory as to the cause or nature of sense experience. In Reflections
upon the Conduct of Human Life he refers in passing to the external,
material world as the occasional cause of our sensations,[24] but it
was not until 1693, in the course of A Discourse concerning the
Measure of Divine Love, that he explicitly proposed the occasionalist
explanation of sensation which he had learned from Malebranche. In
this Discourse, which will be examined later,[25] Norris was arguing
against those who claimed that, since the bodies around us were the
causes of our pleasure, they were proper objects of our desires.
Norris attacked the basis of this argument by denying that bodies
had, strictly speaking, the power to cause pleasure or any sensation in us. The common philosophy, he agreed, held that bodies were
the causes of our sensations, and that they had in themselves the
qualities which they implanted in us; fire, for instance, was itself
hot, and made us hot. "The modern reformers of philosophy",[26]
by whom Norris doubtless meant in particular Descartes and Locke,

115

had indeed rejected the formal presence of such qualities in bodies, but they continued to hold that bodies had in themselves the power to produce sensations in us. Only one philosopher, Norris declared, had thought otherwise and further than this: and that was Malebranche. All other philosophers had fallen victim to the prejudice which concludes that, since a certain sensation invariably follows a certain bodily impression, therefore it is caused by it. In Norris's view, however, regular concomitance was no proof of causal dependence, and in this case there were clear arguments to show that bodily objects could not be the causes of sensations in human beings.

When a needle pricks the hand, one feels pain. When one approaches a fire, one feels warmth. But there is no more reason to suppose that the fire is hot than that the needle is in pain, for all that can be conceived as belonging to bodies is extension, figure, and motion. This was the consideration that led the "modern philosophers" to deny the presence in bodies of qualities similar to human sensations; but the same line of thought, Norris argues, ought to have led them further to reject the idea that bodies have the power to produce sensations in us. For it is inconceivable that figure and motion should be able to produce something of such an entirely different, and indeed superior order as a sensation, which belongs to the order of consciousness, of thought in the Cartesian sense.

The foregoing argument cannot be regarded as a strong one, since it does not come to grips with what the adversaries of occasionalism really thought. The Scholastics, for instance, did not think that sensations were produced in man simply by the action of external bodies; they thought rather that they resulted from the interaction of man's faculties with impressions or "species" coming from the objects. But Norris went on to propose a further argument which is interesting as being, it seems, peculiar to himself. The action of

116

bodies, he argues, takes place by movement and shock; it depends on the resistance of one body to another, and thus on their mutual impenetrability. But a spirit is not impenetrable; on the contrary, it can coexist with a body in the same space. "And therefore, since spirits make no resistance against bodies, it is not possible that bodies should have any action or make any impression upon spirits."[27] It is quite conceivable, for instance, that fire should move and agitate the parts of one's body, but not that it should produce the sensations of pleasure or pain that one experiences if one approaches it.

The adversaries of occasionalism would admit, Norris recognises, that fire, like any other body, could not act directly on the soul. But they would claim that it could do so indirectly, by virtue of the union that subsists between the soul and the body. But Norris held that such a reply was ambiguous, and could be understood in three senses: "Either that the fire, by the motion which it imparts to my body, makes it to act upon my soul. Or that there is such a connection or natural sympathy between these two substances soul and body, that what is done to the body will be felt by the soul. Or lastly, that there is such a positive law or order established between them by the author of nature that such impressions, made upon the body, shall be ordinarily followed by such sensations in the soul."[28] Norris considered that the first of these suggestions could be excluded on the grounds that he had already advanced: if matter could not act on spirit, then the human body could no more do so than fire or any other bodily object. The second suggestion, that of natural sympathy, explained nothing, for it was simply false. Norris held that body and soul were two distinct substances, and that no two substances had such a natural sympathy or occult connection that what affected one affected the other too.[29] Only the third possibility remained: that what affected the body affected the soul, not by any physical interaction or natural sympathy, but by virtue of a positive law or order established by the Author of nature, according to which certain impressions made on the body should be followed by particular sensations in the soul. And this was indeed Norris's view, following Malebranche. But in this case, he pointed out, it was not strictly accurate to speak of bodily impressions "causing" sensations in the soul: these impressions were merely the occasions of the law entering into operation. And this law could be nothing other than the expression of the will of God, which ultimately was identical with God himself. God, then, was the real efficient cause of all sensations, and bodies and the impressions derived from them were only occasional causes of them.

It is evident that Norris's occasionalism was inspired by Malebranche, but his presentation of it did not lack originality. Thus Norris's occasionalism was limited to the problem of the action of matter on spirit,[30] while his analysis of the three senses in which one could understand the union of soul and body, and his argument in favour of the third of these alternatives, were peculiar to himself. In A Discourse concerning the Measure of Divine Love, Norris was concerned with occasionalism only with reference to the question of what might be the proper object of man's desires; he did not go on to examine what the occasional causes of sensation might be. But in the Second Part of his Theory of the Ideal ... World he made it clear that he regarded the incidence of light on the eye as the occasional cause of vision.[31]

The occasionalist understanding of sensation of course raises the question of the knowability, and indeed of the real existence, of the external, material world. If what one sees, hears, and touches are merely modifications of one's own soul, could not God produce these equally well if there were no material objects to serve as the occasions of their production? This difficulty occurred already to Mary Astell, whose correspondence with Norris, occasioned by her reading of A Discourse concerning the Measure of Divine Love, was published in 1695 under the title of Letters concerning the Love of God. If there was no natural connection between bodies and sensations, she asked in her last letter, if God could produce sensations equally well without bodies being there at all, was not the material world entirely superfluous? Norris's reply to this objection was strictly malebranchiste. It was not true, on his theory, that bodies were irrelevant to sensation. God had united the soul to that parcel of organised matter which we call our body, and this body was variously affected by other bodies around it. It was for the preservation of the body that God gave us sensation, and pleasure and pain were the natural signs of good or harm to it. Norris's reply does indeed show that, granted the existence of the material world and the fact that the soul is united to a body in it, sensations are not arbitrary and occasional causes by no means superfluous. But one could wish that Mary Astell had pushed her objection further, and questioned Norris as to why he believed in a material world at all. This objection was indeed put by Locke in his Examination of P. Malebranche's Opinion of Seeing all things in God,[32] and it was from similar considerations that Berkeley and Collier partly derived their immaterialism;[33] but Norris himself never doubted the existence of the material world.

In the course of the First Part of his Theory of the Ideal ... World, however, Norris examined the question of the relative certainty with which the existence of the natural or material and the intelligible worlds were known. The reality of the intelligible world, he affirmed, was known with certainty: he himself had advanced six

119

arguments which proved its existence beyond any doubt. But the material world was known in one way only:through sensation. Norris recognised that some people might add that the existence of the material world was also known by faith, as being revealed by God; but he quickly disposed of this objection by saying that our knowledge of revelation itself depended on sensation. "I have no other certainty of the existence of such a revelation than I have of the existence of my _bible_ wherein it is contained. And then again, I have no other certainty of the existence of my _bible_, or of such and such characters in it, than I have of other _bodies_ or of any of those _figures_ whereby they are modified. So that you see all at last resolves into the testimony of sense, which therefore upon an ultimate and final consideration may be said to be the only argument I have for the existence of a natural world."[34]

The material world, then, was known only through sensation. But sense experience, he continued, does not itself furnish us with knowledge. Sensations are only modifications of our own souls, so that strictly speaking we sense neither bodies nor the existence of bodies, but only our own sensations. "I feel a sensation, and thence find myself naturally carried to judge or conclude that there are bodies; but then 'tis not the sensation but my reasoning or judgement upon that sensation that tells me or reports to me that there are such beings."[35] Sensation itself can be clear and evident, Norris agrees: one can know beyond any possible doubt that one is in pain, for instance. But this clarity does not extend to reasoning based on sensation.

"In reasoning upon an intellectual principle I find the conclusion oftentimes so nearly and visibly connected with the principle that I can be as certain of the conclusion as I am of the principle itself. But now 'tis not so when I reason upon a sensation, unless

120

in one instance, and that is when I conclude my own existence from it; and then indeed, I am in pain, therefore I am, or I am in pleasure, therefore I am, is as good an argument as I think, therefore I am. But 'tis otherwise when from sensation I conclude the existence of things without me. There is no such immediate connection then, nor can I with reason pretend to be as certain (however otherwise persuaded or assured I may be) of the existence of those bodies which I prove from sensation, as I am of the sensation itself. For as I do not properly feel bodies, so neither are bodies (or at least it may justly be doubted whether they are or no) the causes of what I feel, as the best philosophers will now acknowledge."[36]

Sensation, therefore, affords no evident proof of the real existence of a material world existing outside ourselves.

If such a proof were to be had, it would in Norris's view have to be along the lines suggested by Descartes, from the consideration of the goodness and veracity of God in conjunction with the regularity of our sensations and our natural tendency to assume the existence of such a world. But Norris held, following Malebranche, that while these considerations were sufficient to establish the reasonableness of believing in the existence of an external world of bodies, they did not amount to a strict proof of the existence of such a world. Since Norris denies himself Malebranche's recourse to revelation to furnish the certainty that reason could not give, he was accordingly compelled to say that no strict proof of the existence of a material world could be given.

Norris's teaching on our knowledge of the external world is, of course, easily assailable. He affirmed on the one hand that it would be extravagant scepticism to doubt the real existence of the natural world, while showing on the other hand that no argument in

121

its favour could be regarded as strictly conclusive. Collier, who was in general an admirer of Norris and whose immaterialist philosophy was largely inspired by him, considered that he had failed to acknowledge the natural consequences of his own reasoning.[37] But Norris's position on this subject was perhaps not as unreasonable as appears. To consider,as he did, that we have very good reason to assume the existence of an external, material world, but that we cannot, strictly speaking, prove it, is, on the contrary, a very reasonable view to take.

Norris held, then, that the external world was known through sensations, which were modifications of one's consciousness occasioned by changes occurring in one's bodily sense organs. His main interest, however, was centred on the knowledge of necessary truths. As has been seen, Norris was convinced from his early days that necessary truths and unchanging essences were known "in God", since they were aspects of the divine intelligibility. But this view had been implied rather than explicitly taught in his earlier writings on this subject, which were concerned with truth in itself rather than with how man knows it. When he came to expound this position specifically, in Reason and Religion (1689), he borrowed a large par of his argument directly from Malebranche's Recherche de la Vérité This proceeding was somewhat misleading, since it suggested that Norris's view was derived from Malebranche, whereas in fact Norris had reached his conviction by an entirely different path from that followed by Malebranche. Malebranche came to his theory of "seeing all things in God" from reflection on the Cartesian dualism of mind and body and by the systematic exclusion of all other explanations of knowledge as inadequate; it was only at the end of his reasoning that he established that the ideas by which one knew were the divine Ideas; whereas Norris was already sure of the divine characte

122

of the Ideas before he asked how they were known. Norris accepted
the Cartesian dualism, and with it he accepted Malebranche's occasionalist explanation of sense experience; Malebranche in his later
writings argued directly from the eternity, immutability, and necessity of our ideas to the fact that they were in God;[38] but though their
views in this sense converged, they had approached them from opposite directions, so that the arguments of La Recherche de la
Vérité do not fit entirely naturally into Norris's exposition.

Norris however saw Malebranche in a Platonic context. Con-
tinguing from a passage that has already been quoted, he wrote, of
knowing all things in God:

> "This is a notion which I very early lighted upon, by the natural
> parturience of my own mind, before I had consulted with any
> authors that might imbue me with it. But afterwards I met with
> some that confirmed me in it. For it is a notion very frequently
> touched upon by Platonists, by Plotinus, by Proclus, by Marsilius
> Ficinus, by St. Austin, by the late French philosopher Du Hamel,
> in his book De Mente Humana, and is sometimes glanced at by
> Aquinas himself; but by none that I know of so copiously, so pur-
> posely, and so dexterously managed, as by the incomparable
> Monsieur Malebranche, who, I think, has established the truth
> of it beyond all cavil or exception, as well as reasonable doubt-
> ing."[39]

Norris was delighted to find in Malebranche what seemed to be a
clear and systematic exposition of the view which he also held, and
accordingly he incorporated Malebranche's arguments directly into his text, despite the fact that they did not correspond with his own
line of reasoning.

In Reason and Religion, accordingly, Norris gave a faithful
but very brief summary of Malebranche's arguments, condensing

into nine pages the contents of six chapters of La Recherche de la Vérité.[40] External objects, Malebranche begins, cannot be seen in themselves, but only by the mediation of ideas. "This proposition", Norris declares, "is most unquestionable, taking ideas in a large signification for images or representations of things. For things that are perceived must be some way or other present to the soul, either by themselves or by their representatives. And since they are not by themselves, they must be by their ideas. And so much is acknowledged on all sides. Here therefore being no controversy, there needs no more proof."[41] Norris then summarises Malebranche's division of the possible sources of our ideas. "It is therefore necessary that these ideas which we have of objects without, should either proceed from these objects: or that our mind has a power of producing those ideas. Or that God should produce them with the mind when he creates it, or that he should produce them as often as we think of any object. Or that our mind should possess in itself all the perfections which it sees in things. Or lastly, that it be united to some absolutely perfect Being, that includes in himself all the perfections of created beings. By one of these ways we must necessarily perceive whatever we perceive."[42]

Norris then gives a brief summary of Malebranche's arguments under each of these heads, agreeing with him in choosing the last alternative. Later, in the Second Part of his Theory of the Ideal ... World, he expanded these arguments very considerably, adding his own considerations to each and identifying the adversaries he had in mind, and we shall examine them in that context. But it can be seen at once that Malebranche's arguments were concerned primarily with our knowledge of the external world. The first hypothesis, in particular, which Malebranche examined and rejected, the theory according to which ideas might come from objects, in the sense that

124

things might be known through the "species" or particles that they emitted, could only refer to ideas or images of material things. But the arguments which Norris added to those which he adopted from Malebranche showed that he himself was still essentially concerned with the knowledge of necessary truths. He began immediately with his most fundamental consideration: "Since knowledge is comprehension of truth, if the truth which I comprehend be in God, and in him only, then I must be said to see and know whatever I see or know in God."[43] The truth which man knows can only be in God, since it is a relationship of necessary and eternal essences which impose themselves on the mind. It is the same for different minds, and for the same mind at different times; it is the same everywhere, and is not made but discovered by the mind. Truth, then, is "one absolute and separate nature, independing upon our understandings, and yet withal intimately and constantly present to them ... Now," he asks, "what can this one, independing, and ever-present nature be, but God? To know truth, therefore, is to know God: and divinity is a larger study than we are aware of."[44] It is not necessary at this point to examine Norris's arguments in detail. They recur, more fully expressed, in the Second Part of his Theory of the Ideal ... World. But it is already clear that his approach to "knowing all things in God" was different from Malebranche's, despite his enthusiastic adoption of the latter's arguments and terminology.

Reason and Religion cannot be regarded as a successful exposition of Norris's theory of knowledge. The chapter devoted to this subject was far too short for him to explain his meaning adequately, or to hope to convince his readers. Nevertheless it remained for sixteen years the only systematic exposition of his theory on this subject, which was, however, referred to in many of his other writings.[45] It was not until 1705, when the Second Part of his Theory of the Ideal or Intelligible World finally appeared, that he was able fully to explain his views on man's knowledge of truth. The Second Part of the Theory was Norris's longest work, but it included a number of discussions which we shall examine in other contexts.[46] We shall be concerned here only with its central theme, man's knowledge of the world of Ideas.

Norris begins his examination of this central subject by analysing the several ways in which things are known. Whatever is known, he declares, must be present to the soul, either immediately by its own reality or by an idea which represents it. Although the soul does not have a clear view of its own essence, it has an immediate consciousness of what takes place within it, of its own thoughts and sentiments. God too, Norris continues, is known by his own immediate presence, without an idea. We have indeed in a loose sense of the term an idea of God, if by "idea" is meant only an objective conception of his essence; but we do not have a representative idea of him, for nothing finite can represent the infinite. In taking this view Norris was following Malebranche, but it was in fact a necessary implication of his own thought, for he had always discerned God in the necessary truth that was immediately present to the mind. And he now added that, with God, the Ideas and truths which were formally but not really distinct from him were also known immediately, for nothing created or contingent could represent eternally necessary truths and essences. In making this assertion at this point, Norris was of course anticipating his principal argument on the source and nature of ideas.

The mind, then, in Norris's view, has an immediate consciousness of its own mental states, and it also knows God by his immediate presence. Bodily objects, on the other hand, are known not by them-

selves, but by ideas which represent them, for the objects themselves cannot be immediately present to the mind. So far as other
spiritual beings were concerned, the essence of one's own soul
and the souls of other men, angels, and so-on, Norris was not
prepared to say whether they were intelligible by themselves or
only by means of ideas; but he was more inclined to the latter view
for two main reasons. To know created spirits in themselves would
not give any knowledge of necessary truth, since they, like all creatures, were contingent; and on the other hand, if the soul were immediately intelligible, one would expect it to have a fuller knowledge
of itself and its nature than it at present possessed. The soul was
conscious of its own activities, but it did not at present have a clear
intuition of its nature, and it seemed that it could have this only if
it saw its Idea, which at present was veiled from its sight.

After this preliminary division of the objects of knowledge,
which explained, as Norris had not done in Reason and Religion,
why the following arguments were concerned specifically with the
knowledge of material things, he repeated the same five-fold division of the possible sources of our ideas that he had already proposed in Reason and Religion. This time, however, Norris expanded
very considerably the arguments which he took from La Recherche
de la Vérité, adding both considerations taken from Malebranche's
Réponse au Livre des vraies et des fausses Idées and also, above
all, modifications and reflections of his own.

The first step of Malebranche's argument consisted of proving
"that material objects do not send out species which resemble them",[47]
but Norris preferred to entitle his chapter "that the ideas whereby
we perceive such objects as are mediately intelligible do not come
from those objects."[48] This, he rightly pointed out, was what was
to be proved: Malebranche's title merely represented an argument

127

in support of this conclusion. Malebranche had assumed that the "species" in question were material effluvia, little bodies continually emitted by all material objects, and had argued against them on the grounds that they would therefore be impenetrable. Since almost an infinity of objects could be seen from any point in the world, it would follow that the whole of space must be filled with these "species" which must converge at every point in order to render the objects visible from there; but it would be impossible for impenetrable, bodily species to do this. Furthermore such "species" could not account for the variations of apparent size and perspective according to the different distance and directions from which objects were viewed, and objects did not apparently diminish in size as one would expect them to do if they continually emitted such effluvia.

To these arguments of Malebranche, Norris added two further considerations which were characteristic of his own approach. We have ideas of perfect geometrical figures, but these ideas cannot come from the material figures which we draw, for instance, on paper, since these are never strictly accurate; and in any case nothing material can be immediately present to the mind. This last argument led Norris on to the second part of his reasoning against the hypothesis which derived ideas from objects. Malebranche had attributed this theory to the "peripateticiens", that is to say the Scholastics, but Norris points out that it was also the view of Bacon, and of the Epicureans and their modern followers the Gassendists. And indeed, Norris rightly insists, the form of the hypothesis which Malebranche described and rejected was that of the Epicureans and Gassendists rather than of the Scholastics. It was the Epicureans who postulated material effluvia as the means by which bodies were known. As for the Scholastics, their "species" were not, "as M.

Malebranche seems to think, and as I once thought myself, substantial emanations, but a sort of corporeal accidents or qualities,
... called impressed species, images, or phantasms."[49] The Scholastics did not regard these "intentional" species as bodies, though
they thought of them as material in the broad sense of being accidents
inhering in bodies. However, in Norris's view the Scholastic theory
was no more satisfactory than that of the Epicureans. The Scholastics regarded their "impressed species" as material in a broad
sense, which was why they postulated an intellectus agens to spiri-
tualise them and render them intelligible. But Norris insisted that
the intellectus agens was a fiction: we were not conscious of having
any such power or faculty, though we experienced all our other
mental activities, such as understanding, willing, sensing, imagining,
and remembering. Furthermore it was contrary to the nature of the
mind to produce its own object, or to convert material beings (even Why?
if they were only accidents) into spiritual ones. And in Norris's
view, finally, no accident could represent a substance. Accordingly
bodies could not be known by any sort of species coming from them.

However, Norris did not consider that his rejection of the
Epicurean and Scholastic theories was sufficient to prove that our
ideas were not in any way derived from objects. For, though "species"
were a figment of the imagination, "if we open our eyes shall we
not find yet something else to come to them from bodies? Yes, there
is light ..."[50] Light does not come from bodies as form its source,
it is true, but they reflect it in various degrees, and thus cause it
to reach our eyes. Might not our ideas of bodies be derived from
the impressions of light which, although it does not itself penetrate
further than the retina, transmits from there an excitation to the
brain, which is the ultimate centre of all sensation from the physical
point of view? Norris agreed without hesitation that the varied in-

cidence of light was the occasional cause of our seeing objects, but he denied that it could be the efficient cause. The "optical men" declared, indeed, that light delineated little pictures on the retina, and though Norris doubted the possibility of this, he did not peremptorily deny it. But he affirmed that several reasons prevented these images, if they existed, from being the immediate objects of our vision. If we saw them directly we should always see double, and we should always see objects upside down.[51] In fact, Norris declares, not even Newton, "the great raiser and improver of the optical science",[52] claimed that these images were the objects of our vision. But Norris's fundamental reason for rejecting images formed by light as the source of our ideas of material things was the same as the reason for which he rejected the "species" of the Epicureans and Scholastics: these images would be material, and therefore incapable of directly affecting the mind.

Before finally leaving this first hypothesis, Norris also examined Locke's teaching, which derived our ideas from sensation, and that of the Scholastics who held that "there is nothing in the understanding but what was first in the sense". At the time of writing his Cursory Reflections upon a Book called, An Essay concerning Human Understanding, Norris had had no doubt that Locke accepted the Aristotelian view of the origin of our ideas, and he had repeated this statement in his reply to Le Clerc's criticism; but now he was no longer so sure. If Locke in fact meant, "as ... I once thought", that ideas came to us from objects, then "it appears by the whole tenor of this discourse that he has derived our ideas from a false original."[53] But if on the other hand Locke, when he derived our ideas of material things from sensation, meant merely that these ideas arose in us on the occasion of sensation, then, Norris considered, one could to a great extent accept his assertion. For Norris agreed with Locke that we had no ideas of material objects which we had not sensed, though he was inclined to make an exception of the idea of extension itself, which he regarded as prior to particular sense experiences. But if one took Locke in this sense, Norris declared, he was telling us nothing about the source of our ideas. Whatever might be the source and nature of our ideas, one could say that they were derived from sensation, in the sense that we perceived them only on the occasion of sensation. In many ways, Locke had rendered great services to philosophy, Norris declared at the end of the Theory: he had deserved well of the public. "But as to the account which he has given us of ideas . . . that, I think, is as lame and defective as anything can well be, since in that sense wherein it would have been to the purpose it appears not to be true, and in that sense wherein it is true it is not much to the purpose."[54] In a subsequent chapter we shall see that, although Locke probably thought that ideas were derived from objects, he was only concerned in his Essay to show that we had no ideas of objects of which we had had no sensations. Unlike Norris, Locke did not seek to establish the source and nature of our ideas as such, but rather the source and extent of human knowledge.

Turning to the Scholastic dictum that there was nothing in the understanding that had not first been in the senses, Norris declared that the same considerations applied as in the case of Locke's view, except that it was less easy to interpret the Scholastic view in a favourable sense, since they spoke of all knowledge while Locke spoke only of "ideas". Furthermore the Scholastics affirmed explicitly that our ideas were derived from bodily objects by the intermediary of "intentional species" which were then spiritualised by the "intellectus agens", and Norris had already examined and rejected this theory.

In La Recherche de la Vérité Malebranche had devoted four pages to refuting the hypothesis that our ideas were derived from bodies; in Reason and Religion Norris had reduced this to two pages. But in the Second Part of his Theory of the Ideal .. World he spent forty-seven pages in considering this theory. Malebranche in fact considered this theory only in its crassest and most easily assailable form, whereas Norris, who in Reason and Religion had simply followed Malebranche, lived in the country of Locke and Newton, and could not dispose of this hypothesis in such a cavalier fashion. Moreover he himself regarded it as "by far the most plausible"[55] of the hypotheses which he rejected. His long discussion of this subject shows a real effort on his part to understand the views of the Scholastics, Locke, and the "optical men". In spite of this, a certain ambiguity remains in his discussion of this matter, as it had in Malebranche's. For the Scholastics did not in fact teach that intellectual ideas were imprinted in man by "species" coming from bodily objects. It was sensation, not understanding, that they explained in this way, and they thought that the mind then had the power to construct abstract ideas on the basis of these sense data. Accordingly it seems that, strictly speaking, the Scholastic theory of "intentional species" had already been eliminated by Malebranche and Norris's critique of sense knowledge, and that the Scholastic theory of the intellectus agens would have been more suitably regarded as one form of the hypothesis according to which the mind had the power to produce its own ideas.

In the next stage of his argument, following Malebranche's division, Norris set out to prove "that the ideas whereby we understand are not the productions of our own souls."[56] Following Malebranche, Norris argues that ideas are real beings, so that the power to produce them would be a strictly creative power, which man does

132

not possess. Even if man did possess such a power, he adds, he could not use it to create ideas, since he would have already to possess an idea of the idea that he was going to create. This was of course the same argument that Norris had already used to prove the eternity of the Ideas in God. But Norris's fundamental argument against this hypothesis was not derived from Malebranche. The ultimate reason why man cannot produce the ideas by which he understands is "because they are not in themselves of a producible nature. For whatever is produced is temporary and contingent and mutable. But the Ideas whereby we understand ... are ... necessary, eternal, and immutable, ... And therefore again we cannot produce them, and that because they are absolutely improducible. Which argument, by the way, will hold as well to show that they cannot be the product of external objects or material beings; nay, it will serve as well to show that they do not fall under the productive power even of God himself, nor have any causal dependence upon his will."[57] This was Norris's essential reason for holding that the ideas by which man understood were "in God", so that there was something artificial about his reproduction of Malebranche's various arguments.

This can be seen again in the next stage of Norris's argument, in which he follows Malebranche in urging that "the ideas whereby we understand are not created in us by God"[58], either when he creates the soul or on the occasion of experience. Norris notes that the latter alternative illicitly extends to our ideas what is, in his view, the true explanation of the source of our sensations; but whereas Malebranche had contented himself with showing the unlikelihood of this hypothesis, the first part of which represented the Cartesian theory of innate ideas, Norris went further and repeated his previous argument: our ideas are not created in us by God, for they are not of a nature that is capable of being created.

133

The last theory which Norris follows Malebranche in rejecting is the view that the ideas by which we understand are the perfections of our own souls. This is God's way of knowing, Norris declares, but it cannot be man's, for man knows many perfections, such as infinity, which are not to be found in his own essence. Norris then goes on to consider another variant of this hypothesis according to which our ideas are modifications of our souls, modalities which are essentially representative of objects. Norris suggests that the Aristotelians may have had "some confuse parturiency"[59] of this theory when they declared that intellectus intelligendo fit omnia, but this is not certain. "But if we cannot find this notion in the ancient Schools, let us go to the Sorbonne; for there we have M. Arnauld in his Book of True and False Ideas (as I learn from the Answer to it, not having the book itself by me) appearing openly and expressly for it."[60] Norris's reply to Arnauld's theory closely follows Malebranche's Réponse au Livre des Vraies et des Fausses Idées. Arnauld, he declares, confuses ideas with sensations, for these latter are indeed modalities of the soul. Our ideas are intelligible essences, whereas our modalities, such as heat, taste, and colour, are felt but not understood; our ideas are universal and can be known by all men, whereas our sensations, being the modalities of particular substances, are particular and peculiar to each person. After these arguments taken from Malebranche's reply to Arnauld, Norris adds his own distinctive consideration: our modalities, being modifications of contingent beings, are themselves contingent and mutable, whereas our ideas are eternal, necessary, and immutable.

After thus repeating and expanding Malebranche's review of the hypotheses which he found unacceptable as accounts of the source and nature of ideas, Norris went on to expound his own view. Malebranche affirmed at this point "that we see all things in God,"[61]

134

but Norris preferred to express this view more accurately, and argued first "that 'tis possible that the ideas whereby we understand may be the divine Ideas",[62] and finally "that the divine Ideas are actually the ideas whereby we understand."[63] Norris preferred his formulation of this theory to that of Malebranche because he thought that the latter might suggest to the unwary that we saw material objects themselves in God, whereas in reality it was their Ideas that we saw, or that we saw, for instance, colours in God, whereas these were only modifications of our own souls. The possibility of this explanation of human knowledge depended, in Norris's view, on two conditions only: that God possessed or contained a world of intelligible Ideas, and that God was immediately present to the soul. These truths had been proved elsewhere. It might, he recognised, be objected that such a direct vision of the Ideas was impossible, not from God's side, but because of the limitation and insufficiency of man's faculties. This was in fact the Scholastic view, but Norris replied that he had already shown that we had a certain direct perception of the divine essence in itself, since no idea could represent God who could be known only by his own immediate presence. If, then, we had some perception, however inadequate, of the essence of God in himself, a direct perception of his essence as relative or imitable (that is, of the Ideas) could not be ruled out as impossible.

Having cleared the ground in this way, Norris proceeded to argue positively that the ideas whereby we understood were the divine Ideas. In Reason and Religion Norris had first repeated Malebranche's arguments and had then added his own, but he now reversed this procedure, beginning with his own arguments and then adding those which Malebranche proposed in La Recherche de la Vérité and in the 10th Eclaircissement to La Recherche, and con-

135

cluding with an "explanatory account" of his system.

Norris began by pointing out that he had already advanced an indirect argument for the theory that we know by means of the divine Ideas, in that he had excluded all the alternative hypotheses.[64] He then proposed his direct arguments. The most fundamental of these was the consideration which had characterised his writings on this subject since his earliest days, and which had served as his principal reason for rejecting all the alternative hypotheses. "The ideas whereby we understand are necessary, eternal, and immutable; but there are no ideas so qualified but the divine; therefore the ideas whereby we understand are the divine Ideas."[65] Norris held that the mind was directly in contact with eternal and necessary ideas and truths which imposed themselves on it, and that nothing was necessary or eternal except the divine essence. The Ideas accordingly must be identified with the divine essence as aspects of its intelligibility, and could be known only where they were: in God. This argument merely drew out the implications of Norris's _Metaphysical Essay_ and of the First Part of his _Theory_. It was undoubtedly the fundamental reason behind his theory of knowledge.

However, Norris added several supplementary considerations at this point. The perception of ideas and truths was the perfection of the mind, but it might be thought that nothing but God could perfect the mind of man.[66] Again, though truth was found within each soul, it was no man's private property. "She dwells indeed in every man, and has an oracle in every breast, but is confined to no man, nor to any place or time, but is always and everywhere intelligible, and to everyone, as being at once a secret and a public light, as St. Austin speaks."[67] Our languages are different, but the truths that they express, and therefore the ideas which form the basis of these truths, are the same everywhere, though found by every man within him-

136

self. In Norris's view this implies that there is one intelligible nature or world of Ideas which communicates itself to every mind that seeks it attentively, and that is monopolised by none. And finally, Norris declares that if the ideas by which we perceive things were not the same Ideas in accordance with which those things were created, we could have no guarantee that they were valid criteria of the things they were supposed to represent.

These three considerations, however, had no more than a secondary importance for Norris, who suggested them only as tentative reflections. The essential thing was the eternal necessity of truths and of the Ideas whose relationships they expressed. "And so far we may be positive, that whatever is eternal, all necessary and immutable natures, with whatever relations that are between them or result from them, must be perceived in God, and that because they are in God, who only is necessary, immutable, and eternal; which, by the way," he adds, echoing his Metaphysical Essay, "plainly demonstrates that there is a God, as also that the divine essence may be, nay actually is, in some degree the immediate object of our intellectual view even in this life."[68] As will become apparent in his "explanatory account", this was in fact the only part of his theory of which he was altogether convinced.

Having in this way advanced his own essential arguments, Norris next brought those which Malebranche had proposed in La Recherche de la Vérité to show that "we see all things in God". He suggested that these arguments of Malebranche could be taken as "a new set of auxiliary considerations that come in for the further confirmation of this hypothesis, that the ideas whereby we understand are the divine Ideas."[69] Malebranche had in fact reached his theory at this time chiefly by the elimination of the alternative hypotheses, and most of the direct arguments that he proposed did

137

no more than show the fittingness of such an explanation of human knowledge. Thus he argued that God always acted in the simplest way possible to achieve his purposes, and that to know by means of the divine Ideas would be the simplest way in which knowledge could be explained. Again, this hypothesis would place man in the greatest possible dependence on God. These and similar arguments can hardly be said to have great weight, but the two more important arguments which Norris quoted from Malebranche were the following. "We find by experience that when we have a mind to think upon any particular thing, we forthwith cast our view upon all beings, and then afterwards apply ourselves to the consideration of the object we propose to think on. But now it is certain that we cannot desire to see any object but that we must see it already, altho' confusely and in general. And therefore since we may desire to see all beings, sometimes one and sometimes another, it is certain that all beings are present to our minds; and it seems that all beings cannot be present to our minds any otherwise than because God is present to them, who in the simplicity of his being contains all beings."[70] And secondly, Malebranche further argued from the idea of the infinite, which man perceives though he cannot comprehend it. This "idea", Norris adds, is nothing else than a certain perception of the divine essence itself; and therefore, if God himself is the immediate object of our minds, it seems reasonable to think that his Ideas may be too.

After these considerations from the body of La Recherche de la Vérité, Norris finally brought, as additional supplementary reasons for accepting his hypothesis, the further arguments which Malebranche adduced in his 10th Eclaircissement to the same work. Malebranche's reasoning in the 10th Eclaircissement, as in all his later works, was much closer to Norris's own thought. He now

138

argued from the universality of reason, which all men can consult, from its infinity, and from the necessity and immutability of truth. Universality, necessity, immutability, and infinity were all divine characteristics; therefore the reason with which we were in contact was the divine reason. As can be seen, these further arguments of Malebranche virtually duplicated Norris's own reasoning, and their inclusion did little to advance his argument, which it weighed down with repetitions. But it seems that Norris wished to adduce every possible witness in favour of his thesis, and the fact that he included these arguments of Malebranche separately from his own is an additional indication, if that were needed, of the independence of his own original reasoning.

After completing his review of the arguments in favour of his hypothesis, Norris finally gave an "explanatory account" of how he understood it.[71] Several parts of his explanation added little to what he had already said, and need only be mentioned here. Thus, while agreeing with Malebranche that the hypothesis of our direct perception of the divine Ideas did not of itself imply that we had a direct vision of the divine essence in itself, he added that we did in fact have such a vision of the essence of God. We could not comprehend God, but we had a certain direct perception of him since otherwise we could have no idea of him at all.[72] Again, he insisted that the divine Ideas were the immediate objects of our thought, and that material things could be said to be seen only in the sense that we saw the Ideas in God which represented them. Furthermore, in all our knowledge of the external world there was sentiment as well as idea, and the sentiments or sensations were modifications of our own souls: only the ideas were seen in God. "The short then is," he wrote, "we see nothing in the Intelligible World but the pure Ideas of things, and all the rest we feel."[73] It was this

distinction between idea and sentiment, together with the realisation that colour was not a quality inherent in bodies but a modification of the human consciousness, which had enabled Malebranche
to affirm that it was not only Ideas and necessary truths, as St.
Augustine had thought, but also changeable and contingent things
that were known in God.

At this crucial point of his explanation of his theory, however,
Norris faltered. He had affirmed that, in our perception of material
things, we saw an Idea in God and had a sensation of colour in our
own souls, but he now found himself unable to say what the Ideas
of material beings that we saw in God were. In particular he was
unable to decide "whether the intelligible world has such a relation
to that which is material and sensible that there are in it particular
and precise Ideas for every thing; as suppose, an intelligible sun,
an intelligible tree, etc., and that we see one of those precise Ideas
whenever we look upon one of those bodies. Or (as Mr. Malebranche
seems rather to think) that we see things in God by the various and
different application which he makes to our minds of intelligible
extension, sometimes after one manner and sometimes after another,
in conjunction with those different sensations which we have with it
upon the impression of bodies, particularly that of colour, which
serve to specify, particularise, and distinguish our ideas, and to
make them represent the several differences of bodies as well as
to inform us of their existence."[74] Norris declared that this doubt
concerned only a "modality"[75] of his hypothesis, which each reader
could be left to envisage in his own way, but in reality it is clear
that, if he could not say whether we saw the Idea of (say) a tree or
part of the Idea of "intelligible extension", he cannot have had any
clear conception of what he meant by the ideas of material beings
at all, in the context of empirical knowledge.

140

In view of this uncertainty as to precisely what Ideas were involved in man's experience of the material world, it is not surprising that Norris felt unable to attribute any very high degree of certainty to this part of his theory. He affirmed that noone could prove that his theory was false, but added that he himself proposed it only as the most likely hypothesis that could be offered to explain human knowledge. But he attributed very different degrees of certainty to the different parts of his theory. He had already affirmed that necessary truths and the ideas whose relationships they expressed must be known in God, and that this part of his theory was certain. He now added: "That the divine Ideas are the ideas whereby we understand seems proved beyond all possibility of reasonable exception. And this part of the theory I am in good measure persuaded of, and can hardly forbear being positive in. That which seems more liable to be questioned, as well as more against the grain of common prejudice, is whether the same divine Ideas are also the ideas whereby we see?"[76] It is clear that the part of his theory of which he was certain was that which was based essentially on his own reflections and which was already implied, for instance, in his Metaphysical Essay of 1687, while the part of which he was less certain was that which was derived from Malebranche and which aimed to explain empirical knowledge. His uncertainty regarding this part of his theory reflected his inability to say what the Ideas of material things that were seen in God were; but this was obviously a very unsatisfactory conclusion to all his reasoning on this subject. It will be worth examining in some detail how Norris came to be so uncertain on this point.

There is considerable evidence in the Second Part of the Theory of the Ideal or Intelligible World to show that Norris's confusion regarding this part of his theory resulted from a very natural misunderstanding on his part of Malebranche's concept of "intelligible extension". In order to appreciate this it is necessary to retrace our steps somewhat, and to consider what he had had to say about imagination and vision earlier in this work. In his earlier writings Norris had identified the pure intellect with "the faculty whereby I apprehend objects, whether material or immaterial, without any material species", while the imagination was the faculty "of apprehending objects as present under a corporeal image or representation."[77] But in the Second Part of his Theory he changed this view, and affirmed: "I would ... assign this for the difference between imagination and intellect strictly and properly so called, that in the former the immediate object of thought is an idea that is representatively material, and that in the latter the immediate object of thought is an idea that is representatively immaterial."[78] It does not seem to have been Norris's intention to undermine the distinction between the intellectual conception of, say, a geometrical figure and its imaginary representation, for he began his discussion by evoking with approval the distinction which Descartes made in the sixth of his Méditations Métaphysiques between the understanding or pure intellect and the imagination in the conception of a triangle or pentagon on the one hand and of a chiliagon on the other; but if his new definition is taken strictly it assigns all thought about material things to the sphere of the imagination and leaves no room to differentiate between the intellectual idea of, say, a triangle and one's imaginary picture of it.[79]

A very similar confusion is present in the account of vision which Norris gave in the Second Part of his Theory. As has already been seen, Norris held that sensations were modifications of the soul produced by God on the occasion of the presence of bodies, and that vision in particular was occasioned by the incidence of light on the

142

retina and the excitation which the optic nerve thence transmitted to the brain. But this was not the whole story, for Norris held that vision or sight was not a simple sensation like smell or touch, a mere modifivation of consciousness, but contained in addition an intellectual element. "Vision has this peculiar in it, ... that it includes idea as well as sentiment, that is, that there is in it an outward perception, or perception of something without us, as well as an inward feeling. Our other senses have only the latter. There is nothing in them but only sensation, some inward feeling or manner of being as to pleasure or pain that we are conscious of to ourselves, and accordingly they may properly be said to be pure senses. Whereas in vision, besides that feeling or sensation which it has in common with the rest, there is also a true ideal perception" (i. e. perception of ideas) "which the others have not, for which reason it is not a pure sense, but has something intellectual as well as sensible in it."[80] Vision, in fact, differed from imagination only in being more vivid and in having a different occasional cause, since vision followed the incidence of light whereas in imagination the nerves were excited by "the course or flux of the animal spirits",[81] that is, by internal factors. Sight like imagination, therefore, attained ideas, and vision was a form of thought.

As an example of what he meant, Norris took the case of a rainbow. "To instance in one of the most beautiful appearances in nature, when I look upon the rainbow I have in the first place an idea which is the immediate object of my vision, that which I truly see and which represents to me that which I am said to see; that is, I have an idea of a certain figure, viz. an arch of a circle, and accordingly I say I see a bow, which indeed I may properly be said to do, though that material one in the clouds should not be the immediate object of my vision, because I see that Idea or intelligible

143

arch which represents it. But then besides that pure Idea which is
the object of my view, I have also at the same instant very lively
and agreeable sensations of certain colours (as they are called),
viz. red, green, etc., which affect me with so very charming a
delight that I thence take a particular occasion to pity the blind."[82]
In this example, Norris speaks as if, in seeing a rainbow, one saw
the intelligible Idea of an arc of a circle, and the only aspect of the
perception that was strictly attributable to sensation was the experience of colour which was attached to that Idea. If this view was
carried to its logical conclusion, Norris would lay himself open to
the criticism which he himself had formulated in the First Part of
his Theory: "If I did see no other figures but those sensible ones
which lie before me, how should I be able to know whether they were
perfect or no?"[83] Norris had always clearly distinguished between
the imperfect, empirical figures that one saw and the perfect, intelligible ones in terms of which one judges the others to be imperfect.
This had been one of his principal arguments for the reality of the
intelligible world. But if the figures that one saw were themselves
the intelligible figures, this distinction would disappear. This was
certainly not Norris's intention, but it is clear that the suggestion
that one literally saw Ideas had landed him in considerable confusion.

This suggestion Norris derived from Malebranche. Malebranche did not indeed make Norris's distinction between sight and
the other senses in this respect: he held that in all sensations extension was attained by the intellect, while colour, pain, warmth,
etc. were sentiments or modifications of the soul.[84] But he did on
occasion speak as if one directly saw the Ideas of geometrical figures, and in a passage of his Conversations Chrétiennes which
Norris quoted he wrote that "When I see the sun, I see the idea of
the circle in God, and I have in myself the sentiment of light which

144

tells me that this idea represents something created and actually existant."[85] This seems to be the passage from which, above all, Norris derived his new conception of seeing Ideas, and his description of what it means to see a rainbow is clearly an echo of it.

But this passage of <u>Conversations Chrétiennes</u> is misleading if it is taken as a full statement of Malebranche's views on this matter. Malebranche in fact meant two things by his idea of "intelligible extension". Strictly speaking, this was for him the purely intelligible idea of extension or matter, an idea which virtually contained the geometrical figures that it rendered possible. And the ideas of these figures were their mathematical definitions, according to which they could be constructed independently of sense experience.[86] An intelligible circle, Malebranche affirms explicitly, has no determinate circumference.[87] But Malebranche also regarded intelligible extension as the undifferentiated backdrop of all sensations, the canvas, so to speak, on which they were painted.[88] In this second sense, intelligible extension had for him the rôle which Kant assigned to the pure a priori perception of space. In this sense, intelligible extension was the <u>a priori</u> condition of all sensation, which is no doubt why Norris suggested that it was presupposed by, and not dependent on, sense experience. Malebranche regarded intelligible extension in this sense as belonging to the intelligible rather than to the sensible order because he regarded it as the principle of the objectification of experience: sensations as such were rigorously individual and subjective, yet we all saw the same world and apprehended it as something distinct from ourselves. But it is clear that this pure perception of space is not an idea in the same strictly intellectual sense as in the purely intelligible idea of extension, and the figures which it may be said virtually to contain are pictures in the imagination rather than strictly intelligible definitions.[89]

145

This dual use of the term "intelligible extension" led Malebranche to miss out several logical elements in some of his descriptions of empirical knowledge. Thus in the passage quoted above from Conversations Chrétiennes, he should strictly speaking have distinguished the intelligible idea of the circle, mathematically defined and without particular dimensions, from the intuitively perceived image or picture of the circle, which has a determinate size and is no doubt, strictly, an imperfect realisation of its definition. It is this latter picture of the circle which is filled with light or colour and thus, in Malebranche's view, determined to represent the sun as actually existant. But in this and some other passages Malebranche omitted some of the steps of his reasoning, and spoke of the imaginary picture as if it was the idea. These were the passages which misled Norris.

In his earlier writings, up to and including the First Part of his Theory of the Ideal ... World, Norris had always taken intelligible extension, to which in fact he had seldom referred, in Malebranche's first, purely intellectual sense; and he had always taken the ideas of geometrical figures as their mathematical definitions. It was only when writing the Second Part of his Theory that he came to realise that Malebranche also used "intelligible extension" in another sense, as the backdrop of sensation. But he did not really understand this aspect of Malebranche's theory, and he was misled by the shortened form in which the latter described vision in Conversations Chrétiennes and elsewhere. It was as a result of taking such passages too literally that Norris came to suggest that imagination and vision should be identified with the perception of representatively material ideas. Norris knew that Malebranche did not share this view of the imagination, but rather agreed with Norris's former definition of it as the faculty of apprehending objects under

146

a corporeal image or representation; but he thought that this was due to inconsistency on Malebranche's part, whereas in reality it was due to Norris himself having misunderstood Malebranche's theory.

It was this misunderstanding on Norris's part which led to his inability to say what Ideas were attained in sense experience, and thus to his relative uncertainty about the truth of this part of his theory. Like Norris, Malebranche too sometimes spoke of our seeing the Ideas of particular material beings and sometimes of our seeing only different parts of intelligible extension. His meaning on this subject was not altogether clear. [90] Malebranche seems to have held that the only strictly intellectual element in our knowledge of the material world was our knowledge of intelligible extension. God indeed had Ideas of particular material things, and these Ideas defined their internal structure, organisation, and configuration; but these Ideas were not normally known to us, and our "ideas" of a horse, a tree, and so-on, were compounded of the general Idea of matter or extension and sensible appearances. The only sense in which material things could be, literally, seen in God was in the sense that Malebranche regarded intelligible extension, the "canvas" or background on which they were seen, as being God's Idea of extension; but all the differences of material beings were known only a posteriori, through sensation. Our intellectual knowledge of material things concerned the laws and properties of matter in general; all the rest of our knowledge of them depended on sense experience. This view was in fact almost identical with that which was implicit in Norris's writings up to and including the First Part of his Theory. In the Second Part of the Theory Norris wad distracted from it by his misunderstanding of Malebranche's theory of intelligible extension, a misunderstanding which seems to have derived largely from his

147

reading at this time of Conversations Chrétiennes and of the Réponse au Livre des Vraies et des Fausses Idées.

Until this time, Norris's theory of knowledge may be summed up as follows. Norris held that there were two radically distinct sources of knowledge: the divine Ideas and sense experience. The Ideas included all necessary and unchanging essences, and all the ideas whose relations were expressed by eternally true proposition. These Ideas were to be found within oneself, though only at the price of careful and attentive thought. External, contingent objects, on the other hand, were known by means of sensation, that is, by impressions implanted in the mind by God on the occasion of the presence of bodily objects. These two sources of knowledge can be clearly seen in the contrast which Norris drew between intelligible or ideal and empirical geometrical figures, where the perfection of the ideal figures is used as the criterion by which the empirical ones are judged imperfect, and it is illustrated particularly clearly by his description, in Reason and Religion, of how a child comes to learn his first language:

"To know a language is to know that such a word is to go as a sign for such a thing. Now of words there are some to which the thing that answers is material and sensible. Others again there are, to which the things that answer are purely intellectual. This premised, I demand how a child comes to understand the first language which he learns? You will say, by frequent hearing the word repeated, when at the same time the thing is pointed to, he begins at length to collect that such a word is to go for such a thing; and so to call a table a table and a stool a stool. True, this serves well enough to explain how we may learn the meaning of such words to which something sensible answers. But this won't at all help us out in accounting for the

understanding words which signify pure <u>intellectual notions</u>.
For these cannot be <u>pointed</u> at when I hear the word, ..."[91]
And yet in fact, Norris continues, children learn the meaning of
words such as "virtue", which apply to purely intelligible concepts,
almost as quickly as they do that of those which refer to material
things. The only explanation, he concludes, is that they see this
meaning in the Intelligible World, since God is present to them.

There is no doubt that Norris intended to maintain this distinction between two different sources of knowledge in the Second
Part of his <u>Theory of the Ideal or Intelligible World</u>. Thus, in a
passage part of which has already been quoted, he affirmed that
"We discover Ideal truths by the sole operation of the mind: for
thus we know and can demonstrate that the three angles of a triangle
are equal to two right ones, not by measuring them (for that way
would be as unaccurate as 'tis unartificial), but from an intellectual
view and consideration of the Ideal natures of these things." But on
the other hand "These are the <u>only</u> truths which we can so discover:
in all other truths our senses are concerned, and we must be beholden to our eyes, and to our ears, and to our hands for the knowledge we have of them; and a man would be ridiculous that should go
to prove by mere reason that such a one won the plate at a horse-
race."[92] And in his "Explanatory Account" of his theory he made
it clear that, in his view, in our knowledge of the material world,
it was only what was immutable and necessary in nature that was
known in the divine Ideas.

But if this was and always continued to be Norris's view, it
is clear that our "ideas" of material things must for the most part
be mental images which give us no knowledge of the inner natures
of things but are based on sense impressions. This is evidently true
of the ideas of tables and stools to which he refered in his account

of a child learning a language. In his <u>Cursory Reflections</u> on Locke's <u>Essay</u> (1690), Norris had agreed that most of our ideas of material things represented no more than "nominal essences" in Locke's sense, though he had insisted that bodies also had real essences, mostly unknown to us.[93] And in the Second Part of his <u>Theory</u> he declared explicitly that "the inward essences of bodies" were amongst the things which, though intelligible in themselves, were unknown to us in this life.[94] In this case it is clear that our sense knowledge cannot involve a vision of the Ideas of the different objects that we see, if the word "Idea" is used in the sense in which Norris normally used it for the definition of the essence of a thing. God has Ideas of trees and rocks and horses, Ideas which define their internal structure and organisation, and which are the exemplars according to which the created things are made; but these Ideas are unknown to us. The only Idea in this sense that can be involved in our empirical knowledge is the Idea of extension or of material being in general, with the laws and characteristics which that implies. For these are applicable <u>a priori</u> to all possible material beings, whereas our knowledge of particular material things is <u>a posteriori,</u> and our ideas of them can only be a combination of sense images with the Idea of extension or of material being.[95]

Such was the view that Norris's principles necessarily implied. As has been seen, it is very similar to that which Malebranche seems to have held; but it was to some extent obscured for Norris in the Second Part of his <u>Theory of the Ideal ... World</u> by what he took Malebranche to say on our "seeing" the Ideas of sensible objects. This confusion, whose sources we have examined, accounts for the unsatisfactory theories of imagination and vision which Norris proposed in this work, and for his resulting uncertainty about the details of his account of our knowledge of the material

150

world. Norris's difficulty on this point was due to the fact that the theory he was expounding was not so much his own theory as that of Malebranche, and that he himself did not fully understand it. It was no doubt his deference for Malebranche that led him to try to incorporate in his system the latter's complex theory of intelligible extension, but he would have done better not to do so.

It is possible in fact to distinguish several strata in Norris's theory of knowledge as expressed in the Second Part of the Essay towards the Theory of the Ideal or Intelligible World. There is, first, his original doctrine according to which the divine Ideas are immediately present to the human mind and are the foundation of the eternally valid truths which impose themselves on everyone who considers them attentively. This view goes back, by implication at least, to Norris's earliest writings, and particularly to his translation of Hierocles upon the Golden Verses of the Pythagoreans; it is clearly implied by the teaching of his Metaphysical Essay, which was taken up and completed by the First Part of the Theory. As has been seen, it was this fundamental conviction of Norris that the Ideas or essences and truths that we know have characteristics which can only be divine that formed the essential ground of his rejection of all alternative theories of knowledge. A second stratum of Norris's thought consists of elements which he had derived in the first place from Malebranche, but which formed a natural complement to his own theories and had long become integral parts of his system. In this category must be included the attribution of judgement to the will rather than to the intellect, and the occasionalist account of sensation which regards sense impressions as subjective and as imprinted in the mind by God on the occasion fo the presence of appropriate bodily objects. Finally a third stratum comprises the new theory of the "vision" of the Ideas of bodily objects which Norris

151

derived from a misunderstanding of Malebranche's teaching on intelligible extension. In all Norris's writings, this last element is found only in the Second Part of the <u>Theory</u>; it does not fit in naturally with the rest of his theory of knowledge, and confuses his account of empirical knowledge. But as has been seen, Norris remained more certain of the truth of his own fundamental teaching than he was of this additional theory.

The Second Part of Norris's <u>Theory</u> is often of great eloquence,[96] and it contains a number of discussions of considerable value and penetration, some of which remain to be examined in a later chapter. But taken as a whole it was not an entirely satisfactory work. Not only did it include the unsatisfactory theory of the vision of the Ideas of empirical objects, the uncertainty of which Norris acknowledged with characteristic honesty, but even apart from this its reasoning was unnecessarily diffuse. Norris seems almost to have lacked confidence in his own thought, with the result that he wanted to follow Malebranche as closely as possible, and to gather together all possible arguments in support of his conclusions. Consequently, especially in his later chapters, he included many reflections taken from Malebranche which did little more than duplicate his own arguments. Furthermore, as has been seen, there was something artificial about the way in which Norris followed the framework of <u>La Recherche de la Vérité</u> in his exposition of his theory of knowledge. This framework expressed the way in which Malebranche had come to his theory by the elimination of all alternative hypotheses, but it did not naturally fit Norris's approach; for it was essentially because he was convinced that the eternal necessity and validity of truth and of the ideas or essences whose relationships it expressed was immediately and inescapably known that he concluded that "the ideas whereby we understand are the divine Ideas." This basic certainty of Norris's thought is expressed again and again in the Second Part of the Theory, which in this respect is notably more independent of Malebranche than Reason and Religion had been. But it is a pity that Norris did not go further, and lay the framework of La Recherche entirely aside. If he had done so, his work would probably have been both clearer and less repetitious, and might well in consequence have had a greater influence.

Norris owed many important points of his theory of knowledge to Malebranche, particularly the attribution of judgement to the will and the occasionalist explanation of sensation. But his fundamental certainties of man's direct contact with the divine Ideas and of the contrast between this strictly intellectual knowledge and sense experience were attained independently, though they were of course rooted in the whole Platonic background of his thought. It is unfortunate that he was so impressed with Malebranche's exposition of the views which they largely held in common that he followed it so closely, when his theory could have been expressed more simply and more cogently if he had developed and expressed it in his own terms.

CHAPTER VI THE THEORY OF LOVE

Like the theory of knowledge and of the "Ideal World", the
analysis of love was a subject that had interested Norris from the
beginning of his literary career. His earliest published work, it
will be remembered, was a translation of Waring's Effigies Amoris,
and since then he had developed his own ideas on various aspects
of love in his Letter on Platonic Love and Discourse concerning
Heroic Piety (both in Poems and Discourses, 1684), and in his
Letter concerning Love and Music, Letter concerning Friendship,
and Contemplation and Love, in the Miscellanies of 1687. In these
writings he had developed his ideas in two main directions: on the
one hand he had made a sharp distinction between the loves of desire and benevolence, while on the other he had emphasised the
reasonableness of making God the centre of all one's desires.
Norris's later studies of love served mainly to develop these two
points and to give them a new precision.

It was only a year after the publication of the Miscellanies
that Norris's next work, The Theory and Regulation of Love, appeared. This was dedicated to Lady Masham, who seems to have
written to him to express her appreciation of his earlier works.
In a preface addressed to the reader, Norris declared his intention
to be that of laying down the general principles on which a system
of ethics based on the various modifications of love could be built.
Such a way of writing ethics, he declared, was "entirely new and
unblown upon", and accordingly he had been forced to use un-
familair terms in order to express his meaning clearly. But, he
continued in the first section of the book itself, the proper direction
of love was the central concern of morality. It was what a man

154

loved that made him what he was, as St. Augustine insisted,[1] and
therefore "he ... that shall rightly state the nature, and prescribe due measures for the regulation of love, not only serves
the cause of morality, but may be truly said to discharge the
whole province of a moralist."[2]

The word "love", Norris declares, is used in various senses,
a fact which makes its analysis important, but all ideas of love
have this in common, that they represent a movement of the soul
towards good. In this movement, two moments can be distinguished.
"For as in the motion of bodies we first conceive gravity or a con-
naturality to a certain term of motion, and then the motion itself
which is consequent upon it, so also in love (which is the motion
of the soul) order requires that we first conceive a certain con-
naturality or coaptation of the soul to good, whence arises all the
variety of its actual motions and tendencies toward it."[3] In this
distinction, which derives essentially from Aristotle and the Scholastics, the "gravity" of the soul is its natural tendency towards
the good in general, towards universal goodness: in other words,
towards God. It is from this connatural tendency of the soul towards good that all its actual movements or choices derive. But
God's goodness is unfolded or reflected in all created things, which
are therefore also capable of attracting man in their various different ways.

In a subsequent chapter Norris goes on to draw out the analogy between love and motion. This discussion does not add much
to our knowledge of his theory of love, but it is interesting as including his first reference to Malebranche. "The excellent Monsieur Malebranche", he writes, has drawn a parallel between the
properties of spirit and those of matter, comparing the understanding with the property that matter has of receiving figures,

and the will with that of motion or mobility. "The first of these parallels he pursues and illustrates in many particulars, but when he comes to the last he gives only this one instance of resemblance, that as all motions naturally proceed in a right line unless by the interposition of external and particular causes they are otherwise determined, so all the inclinations which we have received from God are right, and would tend only to the true good, were they not turned aside to ill ends by the impulse of some foreign cause."[4] But although Norris welcomed Malebranche's support on this point, the rest of his argument was hardly affected by it, for the further analogies which he drew were based on the most diverse physical theories, taken indiscriminately from Aristotelian, magnetic, and Cartesian theories of motion. His interest was centred on his conception of love as a continual endeavour or attraction towards God, and he seems simply to have chosen whatever analogies seemed helpful to illustrate it from the various physical theories that were current in his time.

Although Norris held that the various types of love could be distinguished in different ways, he was convinced that the fundamental and most important distinction was that which distinguished the love of concupiscence or desire, on the one hand, from that of benevolence or charity on the other. "For when I consider the motion of love, I find it tends to two things, namely to the good which a man wills to anyone, whether it be to himself or to another, and to him to whom this good is willed. So that the motion of love may be considered either barely as a tendency towards good, or as a willing this good to some person or being. If it be considered in the first way, then 'tis what we call concupiscence or desire, if in the second, then 'tis what we call benevolence or charity."[5] The distinction between desire and benevolence, taken in this

156

sense, was of course traditional, but Norris was to develop it in a way which differed from that of the Scholastic tradition.

The love of concupiscence or desire, Norris holds, is "a simple tendency of the soul to good,"[6] abstracting from the question to whom this good is willed. The primary and adequate object of desire is the good in general, which can ultimately be identified with God, for we desire particular goods only to the degree in which they seem to participate in the general nature of goodness. Our love towards the good in general is necessary, natural, and unavoidable. Particular goods, on the other hand, do not determine the will in the same way, though Norris insists that there is a sense in which they too determine it. Particular goods necessarily attract us to the extent that we apprehend them as good, but since they can enter into competition with other goods and thus become relatively bad, we are not determined to choose them. However they still continue to have a certain attractiveness to us in themselves, so that we continue to have a certain necessary inclination or velleity towards them, even though we are free to refuse to choose them.[7]

After examining at some length the various distinctions that can be made within the love of desire, Norris goes on to examine the second "branch" of love, as he calls it, the love of benevolence or charity. He had already defined this as the willing of good to some person or being, and he now divided it into self-love (the willing of good to oneself) and charity (the willing of good to another). Charity could be further divided into common charity, the willing of good to all men, and friendship, a specially intense mutual benevolence between a few people, mutually known. But Norris was well aware that many philosophers held that the distinction between self-love and charity was a superficial one only, since they considered that all charity was rooted in self-love. This was the view of the Epicureans, and even Plato in some of his writings derived love from indigence. Norris for his part conceded that "all love of concupiscence does proceed from indigence, and ends in self-love. For all desire is in order to further perfection and improvement, and did we not want something within, we should not endeavour towards anything without. And accordingly God, the self-sufficiency of whose nature excludes all want of indigency, is by no means capable of love of concupiscence".[8] But this, he held, was not true of benevolence or charity. We often do good to others, he agreed, merely in the hope that they will one day return the favour, and we also find our own pleasure in doing good to others, but he strongly opposed the view that all benevolence depended on self-love. On the contrary, he held, we can love our neighbours without any concern for our own interests.

Norris used several arguments to prove the possibility of disinterested benevolence. He argued first from the nature of the case: "I consider that the good of another considered as another's may be the object of volition as well as one's own. For the object of volition is good in common, or that which is agreeable to any intellectual being, whether oneself or any other. But now good as another's, or to another, is good as well as one's own, and therefore may be the object of volition, and consequently we may will good to another independently of our own interest."[9] But Norris's principal arguments in favour of the possibility of disinterested benevolence are a posteriori. We know from experience that we sometimes choose to do good to people who can never requite us, and rejoice in the happiness of people with whom we are entirely unconnected. But the example on which Norris primarily bases his case is that of God. God is entirely self-sufficient; he stands

in need of nothing, and thus cannot be moved by the love of concupiscence; yet he is the most communicative and beneficent of
beings. Benevolence, therefore, does not depend on self-love.

Norris developed this argument more fully in his Discourse
concerning Divine Providence, which was published in 1691 in the
second volume of his Practical Discourses. Here he presented his
proof as the exact retorsion of the Epicurean argument against the
possibility of divine providence.

"The falseness of this Epicurean principle is put out of all
question to us who believe a creation; for if that love proceeds
from want be an argument that a Perfect Being can have no
love, then we may argue as well the other way, that if a Perfect Being does love then love does not proceed from want.
And we have sufficient discovery of this in the creation, which
considering the self-sufficiency of the Divine Nature, must
needs be the effect of a pure, unselfish, and distinterested
love." [10]

One can hardly fail to notice that, in the course of Norris's
discussion of benevolence, a certain change came over his understanding of the terms he was using. At the beginning of the discussion the loves of desire and benevolence were taken simply for
different aspects that were to be found in every love: one desires
a good (desire) for someone (benevolence). The two aspects could
be considered in abstraction from each other, but they could not
be really separated. But by the end of the discussion desire and
benevolence are taken for really distinct types of love: desire is
born of the indigence of the lover who seeks a good that he lacks;
it is founded on self-love, whereas benevolence includes not only
self-love but also a charity which can be entirely disinterested.
God, who lacks nothing, cannot be moved by desire, but he is the

159

perfect example of disinterested benevolence. But this change of terminology does not involve any real inconsistency in Norris's theory. Every desire continues to imply benevolence (either towards oneself or towards someone else), and all benevolence continues to imply a desire for good. But the desire which is common to all love is a simple tendency towards the good in general, abstracting from the question for whom this good is desired. The fundamental distinction for Norris, it might be said, is that which separates self-love from disinterested charity. In future he reserves the expression "love of desire" (or "of concupiscence") for the desire of the agent's own good, while distinguishing this from the "love of benevolence" which can be entirely disinterested.

This terminological difficulty seems to be the result of the fact that Norris originally derived the distinction between the loves of desire and benevolence from the Scholastic tradition. In that tradition, the two loves were merely two aspects that were present in every love. For Aquinas, for instance, there was no such thing as strictly disinterested benevolence, save in the sense that one could so identify oneself with someone else as to feel his good as one's own.[11] Norris took this traditional terminology and adapted it to his own doctrine, according to which one could desire good for someone else without any reference to oneself.

The originality of Norris's theory of love at this point lay in his view that the good which was the object of desire need not be conceived as the good of the agent himself, and that consequently there could be a genuinely disinterested benevolence. In taking this view Norris differed both from the Scholastics and also from Malebranche. According to Malebranche, God could not have created man out of benevolence towards him, since this would imply that God acted for an end outside himself. This argument clear-

160

ly supposes that benevolence implies a desire for something that one lacks, as otherwise it would have no force. For Norris, on the contrary, it was evident that, since God lacks nothing, he cannot have created for his own advantage, but must have done so out of pure benevolence. In his later writings, influenced no doubt by Malebranche, Norris sometimes affirmed that God created the world for his own glory; but he did not regard this statement as contrary to his view of the divine benevolence. For Norris, the glory and the benevolence of God were closely linked. God could receive nothing from his creatures, and his glory consisted in giving himself to them. In Norris's view benevolence is a pure perfection. In saying this he followed the teaching of the neo-Platonists that it is the nature of goodness to wish to communicate itself to others. This view goes back to Plato's Timaeus, but it was especially clearly enuntiated by Hierocles in the work which Norris had himself translated into English. It was always to remain fundamental to Norris's thought on love.

This radical division of love into desire for a good that one lacks and a benevolence that can be entirely disinterested is the most important part of the Theory and Regulation of Love. It represents something permanent in Norris's thought on love, whereas the discussion which follows on the "regulation" of the two "branches" of love is far from expressing his final opinion on the subject. Passing to the "measures" which ought to be observed in the regulation of desire, Norris begins by pointing out both the difficulty and the importance of regulating it properly. Man's desire for the good in general is so impetuous that he is apt to reach out after everything that at first sight seems good for him without pausing to consider how this good may, in its concrete circumstances, run counter to some higher good, and thus become bad.

161

"For to observe how things are in <u>combination</u> requires <u>thought</u> and <u>reflection</u>, which in this hurry we are not at leisure to make; but to find how things are <u>singly</u> in themselves there needs nothing but <u>direct taste</u> and <u>natural sensation</u>. Whence it comes to pass that we more readily do the one than the other, and so are very apt to transgress order and to <u>love irregularly</u>."[12] This difficulty, he continues, is accentuated by Original Sin, which has the effect of making us more susceptible to sensual than to intellectual goods. And yet, he insists, "as the good state of the natural world depends upon those <u>laws</u> of <u>regular motion</u> which God has established in it, ..., so does the welfare and happy state of the intellectual world depend upon the <u>regularity</u> of <u>love</u>."[13] To prescribe what love is obligatory and what is permitted is the essence of the moral law.

According to the <u>Theory and Regulation of Love,</u> there are three goods which the moral law commands man to desire: God, the good of the community, and whatever has a natural and necessary connection with the common good. When Norris speaks of the love of God in this context, he means an explicit love of God above all things, since the implicit love of God is identical with the love of the good in general which, being natural and unavoidable, cannot form the subject of a moral duty. Indeed the only love of God to which man can be obliged is one of explicit and free desire, for we cannot love him with a love of benevolence since he already possesses the fulness of all good.

"I know very well that I am singular in this point," Norris writes, "and that nothing is more common, among those that treat of the love of God, than to talk of it as of a love of <u>bene-volence</u>, and accordingly they always express our love to God and our love to our neighbour under the same common appellation of charity, as if they were both one and the same love whereby we love God and whereby we love our neighbour. But there is, I remember, an old rule, that we may talk with the many but must think with the few, and I think 'tis very applicable in this case. For however we may use the word Charity in respect of God to comply with popular modes of speaking, yet I cannot see how, in strictness and propriety of notion, God may be loved with love of benevolence. For certainly, as indigence in the lover is the ground of his loving with love of concupiscence, so indigence in the person loved is the ground of our loving him with love of benevolence. But now, what can we wish to God that he has not already? ... To speak truly, we can no more love God with love of benevolence than he can love us with love of desire. God is as much above this our love as he is above our understanding. He can indeed wish well to us, but we can only desire him."[14]

The love of God that is commanded, then, is one of desire. And God ought to be desired above all things, for there is no common measure between his goodness and that of created things. At this time, however, Norris still considered that there were other goods which we were obliged to desire: the good of the community and whatever was necessary for the attainment of this. The good of the community, he declares, consists in the harmony and order of society. This harmony is what God himself chiefly regards in the creation and government of the universe, and no man ought to seek his own private good except insofar as it is conducive to, or at least consistent with, the good of the whole community. And since the desire of the end implies that of the means which are necessary to attain it, we must also desire whatever is needed for the common good. God could have created a different world

163

from this one, and in that case different actions might have been necessary for its well-being from those which are required in this present world; but in any case certain actions would have contributed to the common good, the harmony of the whole creation, and these would still have been obligatory.

It is not always clear whether Norris, when speaking of the common good, is thinking of the good of human society here and now, or of the harmony and perfection of the whole created universe. The former way of looking at it would be a reflection of the views of Cumberland and the other "more modern masters of morality", while the latter would be closer to the conception which Marsilio Ficino expressed in passages which Norris later quoted.[15] But in either case it seems that the love of the common good would be more suitably regarded, according to Norris's own definitions, as part of the love of benevolence; for to love the common good is to wish good to the whole community. In the Theory and Regulation of Love Norris already sees in the common good the principle which ought to regulate the duties of benevolence or charity, and in his later writings he does in fact treat the love of the common good as part of the love of benevolence.

Norris concludes his treatment of the love of desire by declaring that "we may desire anything that is not contrary to what we must desire."[16] We may, for example, desire sensual pleasure, provided that it does not conflict with the order and good of the created world.[17] He then goes on to consider the regulation of the love of benevolence, the regulation of self-love, common charity, and friendship. Norris's treatment of these subjects at this time is not especially original, and need not detain us long. Self-love,he declares, is usually the most "irregular" of all forms of love, and the root of all our other irregularities, but neverthe-

164

less "self-love is never culpable when, upon the whole matter, all things being taken into the account, we do truly and really love ourselves."[18] Self-love, the wishing of good to oneself, is never blameworthy provided we do not mistake our true selves by prefering the good of our bodies to that of our souls, provided we do not mistake our true interest by prefering an immediate advantage to our long-term good, and provided we do not seek our private good at the expense of that of the community as a whole.

Common charity ought to be extended to all beings who are in any way capable of receiving any benefit: to all mankind, but also in their measure to the beasts and even to the angels. The only beings who can be excluded from it are those who are incapable of any benefit: God, who already is and possesses all good, and the damned, who cannot receive any blessing. As to the order that ought to be observed in charity, Norris takes the common good as his chief criterion. "Thus had I the disposal of an ecclesiastical benefice, which is a thing wherein the good of the public is highly concerned, I ought certainly to bestow it upon him who I thought would do most good in it, though at the same time I had never so many friends or relations that wanted it. For this is a sure and never failing rule, that the good of the public is always to be prefered before any private interest whatever."[19] Only when the public interest is not involved, or when it would be served equally well by either of the candidates, ought one's choice to be determined by the personal need of the recipient; and only when the needs of both are equal, finally, ought one to help one's friend, relative, or neighbour in preference to a stranger. In any case, Norris insists, one ought always to consider the real need of one person before the mere convenience of another; and one must consider the real good of others, not merely what they themselves may want at the

165

moment. Like self-love, the love of one's neighbour must be based on truth.

On the subject of friendship, Norris does little more in the Theory and Regulation of Love than to repeat and expand what he had said in his Letter concerning Friendship, which formed part of the Miscellanies. Friendship is "a sacred enclosure of that benevolence which we owe to all mankind in common, and an actual exercise of that kindness to a few which we would willingly show to all, were it practicable and consistent with our faculties, opportunities, and circumstances."[20] Norris then discusses the contracting of friendship, the behaviour which conduces to its maintenance, and the conditions under which it may cease, but he does so, he declares, only in order to make his analysis of the various forms of love complete: true friends themselves do not need to be instructed in the art of friendship.

The Theory and Regulation of Love was only a step towards Norris's final teaching on this subject. It expressed clearly his sharp distinction between desire and benevolence, but its teaching on desire was far from his final position. Although it contained Norris's first references to Malebranche, it was in fact but little influenced by him, and Georges Lyon was far from justified in calling it "un ouvrage tout inspiré de Malebranche."[21] Not only did Norris's teaching on benevolence differ from that of Malebranche, as has been seen, but his whole analysis of the divisions of love was notably simpler. Malebranche sometimes spoke in terms of a division similar to that of Norris, but he also spoke of a "love of order" and of a "love of esteem" or "complacence", an esteem which ought to be given in proportion to the perfections of the beings which are loved.[22] Norris on the other hand restricted himself entirely to a distinction between the loves of desire and bene-

166

volence which he regarded as exhaustive. It is possible to consider that Norris's analysis of love was too simplified, but it must be remembered that, while Malebranche confessedly followed the common usage of words in moral matters,[23] Norris was explicitly seeking a new clarity of thought and was conscious of using words in an unusual sense.[24] Norris wanted his definitions to be taken literally, and if love is defined as the "motion of the soul towards good"[25], then it can be adequately divided into movement towards a good which one desires and movement towards the person for whom one desires it. In this context esteem and complacence must be regarded as intellectual acts which give rise to the movement of the will but which do not form part of it, as causes of love rather than as aspects of it.

In The Theory and Regulation of Love Norris specifically declares that our complacence or rejoicing in the divine perfections does not involve any movement of the will. But it is in his Discourse concerning the Excellence of Praise and Thanksgiving, a sermon originally preached before the Fellows of All Souls and published in the second volume of Practical Discourses (1691), that he most clearly expresses his view of esteem or complacence. In this sermon Norris declares that to praise God is a nobler activity than to love him. Since God lacks nothing, he cannot be the object of our benevolence; the only love that we can have for him is one of desire, and desire is inevitably egoist. "He that loves God, loves him for his own good, in order to his happiness and well-being; but he that praises him (so far as he does so) does it not upon any self-end, but merely because he thinks it just and equitable that a creature should acknowledge and adore the excellency of his creator; which certainly is the noblest as well as the justest thing a creature can do."[26] The only merit of love is that of being an indirect tribute to the divine perfection. "And yet even here praise will have the preeminence, because this acknowledges the divine perfections directly and expressly, which the other (i. e. love) does only implicitly and by consequence."[27] For Norris, then, esteem is not a part of love. It is not a movement of the soul towards good, but a value judgement to which the movement of love bears witness. The terminology of Norris's analysis of love was often to give rise to misunderstandings in the course of his life, but in itself it was strictly logical and consistent.

Reason and Religion, published in 1689 one year after The Theory and Regulation of Love, marked a notable development, under Malebranche's unfluence, of Norris's theory of knowledge, but it did not mark any change in his views on love. In this work Norris repeated his former teaching on the subject of desire in its relationship to God, though he now illustrated this teaching with different physical analogies, drawn from the Cartesian and Gassendist theories of motion instead of from the theories of gravitation and magnetism and from the Aristotelian theory of natural motion. The new analogies were less helpful as illustrations of his teaching on love than his previous ones had been, but that teaching itself remained unchanged.

It was not until 1693 that Norris again returned to this subject, but when he did, in A Discourse concerning the Measure of Divine Love,[28] his views had undergone a decisive development and had, indeed, attained what was to be essentially their definitive form. This Discourse is in the form of a sermon on the text "Thou shalt love the Lord thy God with all thy heart, and with all thy soul, and with all thy mind" (Matt. 22, 37), though it seems probable that it was never preached but was written specifically for publication. In his earlier writings, Norris had interpreted this commandment

168

to mean that one must love God above everything else, but he had admitted, in common with the great majority of other interpreters, that one could legitimately desire created goods provided they did not conflict with the love of God above all. Now, however, Norris pointed out that such an interpretation did not do justice to the literal meaning of the text. "Can he be said with any tolerable sense to love God with all his heart, all his soul, and all his mind, that only loves him above other things, at the same time allowing other things a share in his love? Can he be said to love God with all his love, that loves him only with a <u>part</u>? What though that part be the larger part, 'tis but a part still; and is a <u>part</u> the <u>whole</u>?"[29] The literal sense of the commandment requires that God should be the only object of man's desire, but if this sense is to be maintained, Norris declares, a firm philosophical basis must be found for it.

In Norris's view, the proper object of one's desire was whatever caused one's pleasure or did one good. But according to the generally held opinion, with which the traditional philosophy agreed, created things acted on man and were thus the causes of his pleasure. If this were so, Norris considered, the call to reserve all one's love (of desire) for God alone could not but appear chimerical.

"It is most clear and certain that God only is to be loved, if God be the only proper object of our love; and 'tis as clear that he is the only proper object of our love, if he only be our good; and 'tis as clear that he only is our good, if he only does us good, if he only betters and perfects our beings; and 'tis as clear that he only does so, if he be the only true cause of our pleasure, of all those grateful sensations whereof we are conscious and wherewith we are affected. I say, if he be: but here lies the point to be debated. And 'tis a great point indeed; for upon this hinge the whole weight of the present theory turns."[30] Norris accordingly proceeded to examine the whole question of the source of our sensations. The arguments which he used to establish, in agreement with Malebranche, the occasionalist theory of sensation, have already been examined in our previous chapter. It was this acceptance of occasionalism, so far at least as related to the action of matter on spirit, that enabled Norris to conclude that God was the sole cause of man's sensations, and thus of his pleasure, and that he was therefore the only proper object of his love of desire. Those who saw in bodies the causes of our pleasure and pain might think it right to love and fear them, Norris continued. They might even think it right, with the pagans, to sing hymns of praise and worship to the material world. But we who knew that material things had no power of themselves to benefit or harm us would reserve our love, fear, and adoration for God alone, and would recognise that the literal sense of the great commandment to love God with one's whole heart was also a strict demand of reason. "By which you may see", Norris concluded, "what noble divinity may be dug up out of the mines of philosophy, and how necessary it is to have a right system of nature in order to the thorough comprehension of Christian Morality, which has its bottom and foundation in the nature of things, and is accordingly as capable of demonstration as any theorem in that science whose character is evidence and certainty."[31]

Having thus established his thesis on the love of God alone, Norris proceeds to examine the objections to which it might be liable. It might be objected, first, that his interpretation of the first great commandment of the gospel leaves no room for the second: "thou shalt love thy neighbour as thyself." But this objection, in Norris's view, confounds two distinct kinds of love: "We do not love God by wishing any good to him (whereof he is not capable) but by wishing him as a good to ourselves. On the contrary, we do not, or at least should not, love our neighbour by wishing him as a good to ourselves (for he is not our good) but by wishing good to him. That is in short, we love God with love of desire, and we love our neighbour with love of benevolence or charity."[32] On this point Norris does no more than apply the fundamental distinction that he had already established in his Theory and Regulation of Love.

A further objection could also be made: may one not love a delicate fruit, for instance, or a rich wine? Even if it is conceded that such bodies are only the occasions and not the causes of our pleasures, it remains true that agreable sensations are attached to the use of created goods. Why then should one not desire them? To this very natural objection, Norris replied with what was essentially the Augustinian distinction between frui and uti, traditional in Christian spirituality. "We may seek and use these sensible things," he wrote, "to which by the order of nature pleasure is annexed; as on the contrary, .. we are to shun and avoid those sensible things to which is annexed the opposite sentiment of pain. But it will not hence follow that either the former is to be loved or the latter to be feared ... The short then of this matter resolves into this, that we may seek and use sensible things for our good, but we must not love them as our good."[33]

Apart from a conclusion in which Norris exhorts his readers to practise that love of God whose reasonableness he has shown, this examination of possible objections concludes the Discourse concerning the Measure of Divine Love. In further developing and explaining the teaching of this Discourse, however, Norris was

171

greatly assisted by Mary Astell, an admirer of his writings who first wrote to him on 21 September 1693, telling him of an objection to his reasoning which had occurred to her and which she had been unable to answer for herself. This letter initiated a correspondence which lasted for a year and which was published, at Norris's suggestion, in 1695 under the title of Letters concerning the Love of God. A second edition, revised by the two authors, appeared in 1705, a third in 1730, and Mary Astell always remained a friend of Norris and a strong defender of his teaching.[34] In her first letter, after excusing herself for writing to Norris who, she feels sure, will not be so narrow minded as to condemn a woman for interesting herself in such serious subjects, Mary Astell brings forward her difficulty. She is ready to agree that God alone is the efficient cause of our sensations, and also that he ought to be the sole object of our love, but she does not agree that Norris's argument is sufficient to prove this conclusion. For if God is the sole cause of our sensations, then he is the cause of pain as well as of pleasure; if it is argued that he should be loved as the cause of our pleasure, could it not be argued a pari that he should be hated as the author of our pain? Ought one not rather to say, she asks, that it is because he alone does us good that God ought to be the object of our love, and that he does us good as much by causing our pain as by causing our pleasure?

Before answering Mary Astell's objection, Norris began by affirming, following Malebranche,[35] that the formal object of man's love was not the good in itself but relative good, good for man. The consideration of the infinite perfection of God in himself should inspire one with an infinite esteem for him, but it would not necessarily suffice to make one adore, fear, and love him, unless one saw that he was also good for oneself. But although

Norris at first rejected Mary Astell's reasoning, insisting that pain was a real evil and that God was to be loved in spite of, and not because of, being its author, he came in the course of their correspondence to accept her basic point. If God were the cause of pain and evil in the same sense as he is of pleasure and good, he conceded; if he created some men on purpose to damn them, as Calvinists thought; then it would be as appropriate to hate as to love him. But in truth God desired only good for his creatures, and the pain which he inflicted was either (after death) a punishment for sin which justice demanded, or else, in this life medicinal, and a result of his mercy. The sufferings of this life were for men's own good, and were indeed such as they would choose for themselves if they could see the whole picture. Norris's correspondence with Mary Astell is an excellent example of his willingness to learn from sympathetic criticism, and although in the course of it Mary Astell came to accept on every point Norris's analysis of the soul and its activities, yet on the essential point at issue it was Norris who accepted her insight. The fact that God was the only cause of the sensations that man underwent meant that he alone was the reasonable object of man's fear and hope, but it was because of the benevolence that was the mainspring of his actions towards us that he ought precisely to be loved rather than hated.

Letters concerning the Love of God, then, ended in the complete agreement of the two correspondents. In some respect, indeed, Mary Astell carried Norris's principles further than he had done himself, as when she pointed out that the first commandment of love was so far from contradicting the second that, on the contrary, it alone made the latter possible. It was only if one's heart and desires were set on God alone that one became free to love one's neighbour objectively, as oneself, for only then would one's

173

desires not come into conflict with those of others. Six weeks after the close of the correspondence, however, a further difficulty occurred to Mary Astell, and her letter was incorporated, with Norris's reply, in the published version of Letters concerning the Love of God under the heading Two Letters by way of Review. If God was the proper object of our love not simply because he was the cause of all our sensations but rather because he willed our good and could alone produce it, she asked, was occasionalism really essential to Norris's teaching on the love of God? Might one not admit that bodies contributed by some sort of "natural efficacy" towards our sensations? For if there was no natural connection between bodies and sensations, if God could produce sensations equally well without bodies being there at all, was not the material world entirely superfluous? Such a conception, she suggested, need not undermine Norris's teaching on the love of God, since the bodies which contributed towards our sensations would be no more than mechanical causes, mere involuntary instruments in the hands of God. Norris's reply to this objection has already been examined from another point of view. He was so firmly convinced of the truth of occasionalism that he hardly replied to her suggestion that the admission of a certain subordinate causality in bodies would not invalidate his argument for the love of God alone, except by saying that the surest way to exclude all desire of creatures was to deny any causality on their part with regard to sensation. There seems no doubt, however, that Mary Astell was right in suggesting that it was not the exclusion of effecient causality as such, but rather the denial that bodies had any independent or deliberate rôle in the production of sensation, which was important for Norris's thesis on the love of God. The fact remains, however, that it was Malebranche's occasionalism which originally led Norris to his conviction that the love of desire both could be and ought to be reserved for God alone.

Norris's writings on love were not in any way polemical, but the publication of Letters concerning the Love of God was followed by that of two sharp attacks on his theory. An anonymous Discourse concerning the Love of God appeared in 1696, while a year later Dr.Daniel Whitby, precentor of Salisbury and thus Norris's close neighbour, published another Discourse of the Love of God. The first of these books was printed for Awnsham and John Churchill, who were then Locke's publishers, and was thought by Norris and others to be Locke's work. But in fact it was the work of Lady Masham, who thus fulfilled, in a very different way from what he had hoped, the wish that Norris had expressed (in the dedication of The Theory and Regulation of Love) that she should write a book which would be a monument of her "extraordinary genius".[36] Lady Masham's book showed evidence of considerable personal ill-feeling against Norris, whom she accused of a fanatical enthusiasm similar to that of Catholic mystical writers. If Norris denied that it was right to love anything on earth, she claimed, he ought to have urged the austerities of the "Papists" and an entire withdrawal from the world; but instead he proposed a quite unreal distinction between loving something as one's good and seeking it for one's good. Lady Masham regarded this distinction as unreal because in her own view nothing could be sought without being loved. She rejected Norris's division of love into the loves of benevolence and desire, and instead identified all love with complacence or liking. "When I say that I love my child or my friend, I find that my meaning is that they are things that I am delighted in; their being is a pleasure to me .... To say one loves a thing, and that it is that which one has complacency in, is just

175

the same: love being only a name given to that disposition or act of the mind we find in ourselves towards anything we are pleased with."[37] Benevolence and desire are acts which follow love, and one cannot wish well to or desire anything which does not please one.

The tone of Daniel Whitby's Discourse of the Love of God was less sharp than that of Lady Masham's book, but his argument showed even less understanding of what Norris meant than hers did. In his introduction, Whitby tells his readers that he had communicated most of his criticisms to Norris privately after the publication of the latter's Discourse concerning the Measure of Divine Love and before that of Letters concerning the Love of God, and that only the fact that Norris had paid no attention to them had decided him to publish them. But the reason why Norris had paid little attention to Whitby's criticisms is not far to seek, for the precentor's argument was largely an ignoratio elenchi. Whitby pointed out that Norris's new teaching on the love of God alone differed from what he had said in his earlier works (the Miscellanies and The Theory and Regulation of Love), a fact which Norris had never denied,[38] but devoted most of his book to proving that one could legitimately desire one's food and drink and other earthly goods. However, Whitby used the terms "love" and "desire" in a much broader sense than did Norris, with the result that his book was spent labouring the proof of things that Norris never intended to deny.

The Discourses of Lady Masham and Whitby were not works of great weight or value, so it is not surprising that Norris replied to them only briefly. He himself answered them only in An Admonition concerning two late Books called "Discourses of the Love of God" which he appended to the fourth volume of his Practical

176

Discourses, published in 1698. After protesting at the tone of personal animosity in which these books (particularly that of Lady Masham, which he attributed to Locke) were written, Norris declared that "a kind pen" had undertaken to reply to Locke's arguments (i. e. those of Lady Masham), so he himself concentrated almost entirely on Whitby's book, pointing out that the views expressed there differed only verbally from his own. He would have no scruple, he affirmed, in conforming to the popular way of speaking by saying that he desired food or drink, or that he loved "a pen that writes well, or a knife that cuts well, or a horse that goes easy, or an adversary that reasons closely and to the purpose. There is indeed", he continued, "a sense wherein I cannot allow the love of these things, but sure not in that popular sense which is pleaded for, which, as my Discourses do not condemn, so I can safely say it was never in my thoughts to deny."[39] "In short then, I allow the loving of creatures as that signifies at large the willing the use of them, but I deny the loving of creatures, more strictly speaking, as meaning by it the uniting our souls to them as our true goods or beatific objects. Which will resolve at last into that maxim of St. Austin, Utendum est hoc mundo, non fruendum, that the world is to be used, not enjoyed."[40] All that he had done, Norris declared, was to give a new philosophical justification to this ancient Christian principle, but neither of his adversaries had attempted to disprove his philosophical argument, that God alone was the true cause of the good that we experience in the use of earthly things.

The "kind pen" which undertook to reply to Lady Masham's criticisms was none other than that of Mary Astell, but her reply was not published until 1705, when it formed part of her longer book, The Christian Religion as professed by a Daughter of the

177

Church of England. In her reply to Lady Masham, Mary Astell went over to the offensive, and attacked Lady Masham's conception of love as liking or complacence. Such an understanding of love, she declared, was not consistent with the Christian commandment to love one's enemies. If love was "that disposition or act of the mind we find in ourselves towards anything we are pleased with", as Lady Masham affirmed, then either we must be pleased with our enemies or we cannot love them; reason and experience show that we cannot be pleased with them, so it followed that, on Lady Masham's terms, the love of one's enemies was impossible. But in fact, Mary Astell continued, one could go further: "Indeed if their account of love be right, it is ridiculous to give any precepts concerning it. For it is certain that we shall be pleased with that which pleases, whether or no it be commanded; and though we are enjoined ever so often, it is not possible to be pleased with that which does not please". [41] In short, Lady Masham had removed love from the moral sphere altogether, making it something anterior to reflection and therefore not subject to voluntary control, whereas for Mary Astell and Norris love and its proper direction were the very heart of the moral life.

Passing from the love of benevolence to that of desire, Mary Astell gave the same reply to Lady Masham as Norris himself had already given to Whitby. She showed also that she now accepted without reserve Norris's views on occasionalism and on the importance of this theory for the working out of a theory of love. Finally she affirmed that Christianity enjoined us to set our hearts on things above, not on things on the earth, and to love God with our whole heart; it enjoined us to love our enemies and to do good to those who persecuted us, even though they did not please us at all. All these commandments were difficult, and had always been

178

difficult to fallen man. But the characteristic mark of Lady Masham's teaching was to cut down the ideals of Christianity to the level of fallen man's performance.

The replies of Mary Astell and Norris to the critics of the latter's theory of love were both fair and, from their point of view, conclusive. But Norris's reply to Whitby showed that there was no fundamental difference between his new theory, according to which the love of desire ought to be reserved for God alone, and Whitby's view, which had also been that of Norris in his earlier writings, which allowed a certain love of earthly things provided one did not rest in them as one's final good. The divergence was more verbal than real. Nevertheless Norris's new formulation was not without a real value and importance. In his works on the love of God, Norris sought to show that the full demands of Christian perfection in the matter of love were not chimerical, but were firmly based in the nature of reality, and he expressed those demands in terms that were close to those of the gospels. Although it differed from common usage, Norris's way of speaking, reserving the word "love" (of desire) for the desire of one's ultimate good, was justified, it may be thought, as a means of underlining the very real difference between the love by which one seeks God, the supreme Good, and the "love" by which one seeks one's food and drink. It is clear, however, that Norris's unusual use of language laid him open to misunderstanding. [42]

Norris's teaching on the love of God encountered a much more vehement opposition than might have been expected. Dr. Whitby and in particular Lady Masham saw in Norris's teaching, less a philosophical theory which ought to be discussed in order that its merits and its weak points should be brought to light, than a manifestation of religious fanaticism which needed to be stifled.

179

To some extent, no doubt, this was due to a misunderstanding of Norris's meaning; but it was also a manifestation of the then widespread attitude which abhorred every expression of religious fervour as "enthusiasm". Mary Astell was right when she discerned in Lady Masham a desire to cut religion down to a purely human level. Norris and Lady Masham were both Arminians; both had their roots in Christian Platonism, and both believed in the rationality of Christianity. Their different views mark the divergent directions in which an originally shared religious attitude could develop.

At the beginning of The Theory and Regulation of Love, Norris affirmed that to prescribe the proper measures for the regulation of love would be to fulfil the whole duty of a moralist. In its final form his teaching can be summed up in terms of the two commandments, to love God with one's whole heart (desire) and to love one's neighbour as oneself (benevolence), commandments which, in his view, do no more than express the strict demands of reason. But these two commandments themselves could, in Norris's view, be summed up in one duty which he regarded as the fundamental principle of ethics: the duty of loving as God loves, or willing as he wills. Norris first enunciated this principle in a Post-script that he added to his Discourse concerning the Measure of Divine Love. [43] He did not hold that things were good only because God willed them, any more than he considered that they were true only because God chose to conceive them in a certain way; but he did consider that God's will, though not the cause of good, was the perfect measure of it. It would be inconsistent with the divine perfection for God to will otherwise than in accordance with the real values of things, and so the perfection of man's will must lie in its perfect conformity with the will of God. When ascet-

180

ical writers speak of conformity to the will of God, they usually mean the acceptance of whatever may befall one under God's providence, but Norris meant something much more fundamental. For him, willing what God wills meant loving as God loves, making the divine will the rule of one's love; and this was the same as loving according to the order of reason, since God's love was perfectly conformed to his infinite understanding. In this sense, he wrote, "Idem velle quod vult Deus is the sum and abridgement of all morality".[44]

Now if this rule, idem velle quod vult Deus, is applied to the matter of love, we find, in Norris's view, that the love of desire must be reserved for God alone, while the love of benevolence must be extended to all creatures in their different degrees; for God, being entirely self-sufficient, can desire nothing outside himself, but wills good to all his creatures in accordance with their place in the whole scheme of things. Norris appreciated that the differences between God and man were such that man could not love precisely as God loves. God does not desire himself in the same sense in which man desires him, and finite man cannot love with an infinite love; but if he concentrates all his desire on God and wills good to all his neighbours, he will in his own measure be following the rule of the divine will.

Since he considered that God's love is always conformed to the order of justice, Norris's principle idem velle quod vult Deus amounts to the same thing as Malebranche's amour de l'ordre, the love of order which forms the centre piece of his ethics.[45] And it is in this context, too, that the common good fits into Norris's mature thought: it is no longer seen as one of the objects of the love of desire, but rather as a principle which ought to regulate the love of benevolence, and which is not finally to be distinguished from that order of perfections which exists in the mind of God and which is the ordering principle of God's own benevolence. In this matter, as in his restriction of the love of desire (in his strong sense of the term) to God alone, Norris's final theory of love owed much to his reading of Malebranche, though the latter's theories formed the natural complement to his own earlier conceptions; but Norris's theory as a whole was far from identical with that of Malebranche. As has been seen, Norris's analysis of the divisions of love was notably simpler than Malebranche's; and it was also expounded at greater length. But the fundamental difference between the two theories was in the matter of benevolence. Unlike Malebranche, Norris held that man was capable of disinterested benevolence, and was indeed morally obliged to it, though he could not love God in this way since God already possessed all good. And the possibility and obligation of human benevolence was rooted in the benevolence of God; for God had created the world out of pure benevolence, and willed good to all his creatures. On this point Norris always remained faithful to his own early thought, which in this respect was based on neo-Platonism.

As has been seen, Norris's teaching on the love of God was regarded by his opponents as an expression of religious enthusiasm, but Norris himself always insisted that his theory was a philosophical one, based on reason, though he agreed that it entailed religious consequences. And there can be no doubt that Norris's claim that his theory was a rational one was justified. When Norris demanded that one should set one's heart on nothing short of God, he was not, as Lady Masham asserted, calling for a withdrawal from the world; on the contrary, he was asserting the claims of reason at their fullest extent. For his conception of God was not in any way a sectarian one. God, he believed, was known, not primarily by any special revelation, but as the Truth, Justice, and Beauty that was immediately present to the mind of every man; and to seek God alone was to seek Truth and Goodness, and to set one's heart on God was to expect one's ultimate satisfaction from nothing short of the source of all truth and being. It may be thought that such a programme claims too much for human reason, but it is certainly not an irrational ideal. Norris and his opponents had different conceptions of religion and morality; but these different conceptions were rooted in different ideas about the nature of reason and its relationship to God. The centre of Norris's thought was his theory of knowledge as an immediate experience of God.

CHAPTER VII   THE PRACTICAL TEACHING OF NORRIS

Norris's teaching on God and human knowledge and his analysis of love were the central points of his speculative thought. But his most popular and influential writings were of a more "practical" sort, and these were in many cases particularly characteristic of his turn of mind, and throw considerable light on his more speculative works. The most important of Norris's "practical" works was his Reflections upon the Conduct of Human Life, with reference to the Study of Learning and Knowledge. In addition to this, the following can perhaps be classed in this category: Spiritual counsel: or, The Father's Advice to his Children (1694); the four volumes of Practical Discourses published in 1690, 1691, 1693, and 1698 respectively;[1] A Practical Treatise concerning Humility (1707); and A Treatise concerning Christian Prudence (1710), Norris's last work.

Reflections upon the Conduct of Human Life was first published in 1690. A second, greatly enlarged edition appeared the following year, and it was this second edition whose text was followed in all subsequent editions.[2] It was one of Norris's most influential works, written in a lively and eloquent style, and was republished in Treatises upon Several Subjects (1697). As a separate work it attained its fifth edition in 1723, while John Wesley, who greatly admired it,[3] republished it in a shortened form. It consisted of three "reflections", in the first of which "the general Conduct of Human Life is taxed for placing Learning and Knowledge in such things as are little or nothing perfective of the Understanding", in the second "for using undue and irregular Methods in prosecuting what is really perfective of the Understanding", while in the third "the general Conduct of Human Life is taxed with a too importunate and over-earnest Pursuit after Knowledge in General."

In his first reflection, Norris began by considering what knowledge was really perfective of the human mind. The formal perfection of the human intellect, he held with the Scholastics, like that of any other faculty, consisted in its exercise, but its objective perfection, that which fulfilled and satisfied it, was truth. Truth however was divided into necessary truth, "that which cannot but be true, that which is always and immutably true", [4] and contingent truth which concerned matters of fact which might have been other than they were. It was only the knowledge of necessary truth, Norris then affirmed, that perfected the intellect; knowledge of contingent facts contributed to this perfection only to the extent that it included or led to a knowledge of unchanging essences and their necessary relations. Norris advanced several arguments to show that it was the knowledge of necessary truth only that constituted the perfection of the intellect, but the fundamental reason that led him to this view was the consideration that knowledge of necessary truth was knowledge of the divine Ideas, and that the Ideas were God himself in his "omniformity", [5] that is, insofar as he represented all possible essences. Only God, in fact, could perfect the mind, but the necessary truths, of geometry for instance, were aspects of the divine essence whereas contingent truths were not.

But the world in general, Norris recognised, was far from identifying science and learning with the knowledge of necessary truths alone. On the contrary, knowledge was generally confused with erudition, and it was the man who knew many contingent truths or who understood many languages who was taken for learned.

Norris agreed that the knowledge of languages was important as a means of learning or communicating truth; he himself elsewhere urged the importance of learning French in order to read Descartes and Malebranche.[6] But languages were a means to knowledge, and to know them ought not to be an end in itself.

The consideration of history, which, Norris declares, is also generally taken for an important branch of learning, brings him to an important distinction. "A thing may deserve to be known, not as perfecting the understanding, but merely as touching upon our interest. I grant therefore that it may be of consequence to know some historical passages, if we are in any way concerned in them, and so it may be to know the clock has struck one, if I have appointed an assignation at that time; but sure the bare naked theory of the clock's having struck one can add but little to the stock of my intellectual perfection. The most trivial matter of fact in the world is worth knowing, if I have any concern depending upon it; and the greatest, without that, is utterly insignificant."[7] It may be important to know the facts of history, but this knowledge does not in itself contribute to one's intellectual perfection.

Norris gives two further examples of studies which were generally taken for important branches of learning, but which did not really contribute to the perfection of the understanding. He criticises the affectation which identifies learning with erudition, taking pride in knowing obscure and useless facts, and he strongly attacks the Scholastic disputations which were still practised at the universities, declaring that they were little more than "mere quibbling and jesting, not arguing but punning",[8] since they depended on the use of partly ambiguous middle terms. He brought quotations from Gassendi and Rohault in support of his criticisms of Scholastic disputation, declaring it to be a mere waste of time,

186

concerned neither with necessary nor with contingent truth. Norris's denunciation of Scholastic disputation was not a criticism of the Scholastic method as such or of syllogistic reasoning, which he always held in high esteem. But it is interesting to observe that later, in the preface to the Second Part of his Theory of the Ideal ... World (1704), Norris undertook the defence of Scholastic disputation against the criticisms of Locke, although these criticisms were less severe than those which he himself had proposed in Reflections upon the Conduct of Human Life. By 1704 Norris had long been absent from Oxford and the actual practice of disputation, and had acquired a new respect for the Scholastic authors from his reading of them in preparation for writing his Theory; but his change of mind on Scholastic disputation must probably be seen primarily as a reaction against Locke.

It is clear that, from a Christian point of view, it could be objected that Norris's theory, by identifying the perfection of the intellect with the knowledge of necessary truth only, entirely excluded the biblical history of salvation from the sphere of those truths which perfected the understanding. Precisely this objection was made by W. Duncombe in reply to a letter from Henry Needler, an admirer and follower of Norris, on this subject. And there is no doubt that Needler's reply to Duncombe's objection was the same that Norris himself would have given.

"It do not conceive that it is either false or impious to assert that the knowledge of any miracle or other matter of fact contained in the Gospel-history adds no real perfection to the rational faculties of him that knows it; if by rational faculties be understood the same as understanding. But if that phrase be taken to denote the whole reasonable soul as indued with the faculties of understanding and will, or as a moral agent, (in which sense you seem to understand it), I am far from denying that the knowledge of the Gospel-history has a direct

187

tendency to perfect the <u>rational faculties</u>. The case is really this. Man may be considered in a two-fold capacity: either as an <u>intelligent being</u> or as a <u>free agent</u>; and accordingly he is capable of a double perfection, <u>intellectual</u> and <u>moral</u>; his <u>intellectual</u> perfection consists in science or the clear knowledge of truth; his <u>moral</u> in virtue, or the constant choice of good. Now the knowledge of the Gospel-history does not perfect the soul in the first sense, any more than the knowledge of any other matters of fact; and for the same reasons; nor indeed was revelation intended to give man that kind of perfection. But however, it directly tends to perfect the soul in the second sense, that is, <u>morally</u>; for the very aim and design of the gospel is to regulate men's wills and affections."[9]
The first of Norris's three <u>Reflections upon the Conduct of Human Life</u> gives two distinct criteria for deciding what is worth knowing. Necessary truths alone, being identified with the divine Ideas, perfect the mind, and knowledge of the contingent facts, say of history, contributes to this perfection only to the extent that it leads one to the knowledge of necessary truths; but on the other hand certain contingent truths deserve to be known, not because they perfect the intellect, but because the knowledge of them is useful or necessary with regard to our interests either in this life or in the next.

Before going on to consider how these two criteria were related to each other and what considerations ought to regulate man's search for knowledge in general, Norris next turned, in his second reflection, to examine the methods which were and which ought to be followed in seeking to know necessary truth, the true perfection of the intellect. But he disclaimed the intention of writing a complete treatise on this subject, for the adequate treatment of which

188

he referred his readers to Descartes and Malebranche. Echoing his early works, particularly his translation of Hierocles and his sermon on The Root of Liberty, Norris affirmed that the Ideal World was present to every mind and thus potentially illuminated everyone, but that our effective illumination depended on our attention to this light. In this context the way in which Norris spoke of "the Light within" led Quakers to think that if he understood their teaching he would find himself in agreement with it, and it was this misunderstanding which led to Norris's controversy with them, which will be examined in a subsequent chapter.[10]

In general, then, it was by turning to the Word, the Ideal World, present to every mind, that knowledge of necessary truth must be sought. More particularly, the Ideal World could be consulted in three ways: by attentive thought, by purity of heart and life, and by prayer. It was the first of these to which Norris gave by far the most attention. Quoting Malebranche, he described attention as the soul's natural prayer to God for illumination; and he reaffirmed what he had already written in the Miscellanies, that is was by dint of careful thinking that all advances in knowledge had been made. Coming to the method that ought to be followed in thinking, Norris declared that he could do no better than to translate the rules which Malebranche had given in La Recherche de la Vérité, [11] and which in fact Malebranche had himself for the most part adopted from Descartes. The essence of these rules was that evidence must be maintained in all one's reasonings and that, with this in view, one ought to reason only about things of which one had clear ideas. Above all Norris followed Malebranche in insisting "that we should beware lest we should sit down contented with a false light or appearance, and so be deceived. And that therefore our collations in order to the finding out of the truth we look after be so often repeated till we can no longer withhold our assent without being secretly chid and reprehended by a certain Master answering from within to our questions, that is, to our labour, application of mind, and desire of heart."[12] The Master who answered from within was of course, for Malebranche as for Norris, God, the Ideal World. Norris thus followed Descartes and Malebranche in insisting that one should assent to no proposition that one found oneself able to doubt; one should give one's assent only when one could not withhold it without suffering the reproaches of reason itself. This essentially Cartesian view of course fitted in very naturally with the attribution of judgement to the will which, as has been seen, Norris adopted from Malebranche. It seems to be reflected in the increasing reticence which he showed, as time went on, in attributing certainty to his various theories.

Apart from careful and attentive thinking, Norris affirmed that purity of heart and prayer were also means to the attainment of truth. He did not regard them as alternatives to rational thought: no truth could be attained without careful attention and methodical thinking. But prayer was appropriate since truth was in the end identical with God, while purity of heart and life calmed one's passions and restricted one's desires, thus enabling one to seek the truth disinterestedly, in peace, and with an undivided mind.

After this examination of the methods to be employed in seeking necessary truth, Norris finally examined, in his third reflection, the measures by which man ought to regulate his search for knowledge in general. He began this examination by considering the present state of human knowledge. Man can know necessary truth, but nevertheless, Norris affirms, "the utmost pitch of knowledge man by his utmost efforts can arrive to in this world is very

inconsiderable."[13] Doubtless there are almost an infinity of creatures whose very existence is unknown to us, and even those who
devote their time to the study of one particular substance never
attain to an exhaustive knowledge of it, as Boyle admitted in the
case of the metal antimony. As particular examples of our ignorance even in the clearest and most advanced branches of knowledge, Norris quoted the insoluble problems of whether the extension of the universe was finite or infinite, of whether or not matter and time were infinitely divisible, and of whether or not there
were ultimate degrees of speed and slowness. Norris regarded
these paradoxes, on either side of which, he declared, there were
insoluble difficulties, as evidence simply of the imperfection of
human knowledge; but it is interesting to observe that Collier,
who was greatly influenced by Norris, later took them up
and saw in them, by an argument which anticipated the antinomies
of Kant, a proof that no real extension existed.[14]

Although man, then, could attain true and certain knowledge,
the extent of knowledge that he could attain in this life was severely
limited. Furthermore, Norris continued, the little that man did
know served rather to destroy than to increase his happiness. In
any case, life was short, while the road to knowledge was long,
painful, and laborious. Finally, the future life rendered a feverish
striving for knowledge here below superfluous, since once one had
attained the beatific vision of God one would see the whole of truth.
The most important thing, accordingly, in this life was to follow
the path of virtue and religion in order to get to heaven, for there
alone could even one's intellectual perfection be attained. Man
therefore "ought to busy himself in the study of learning and knowledge no further than as 'tis conducive to the interest of religion
and virtue."[15]

Mankind in general, however, Norris observed, was far from accepting this measure for the conduct of its intellectual life. Moralists were quick to condemn those who wasted their time seeking advancement at court, but Norris asked "whether a man that loiters away six weeks in court attendances for a place of honour be not every whit as accountably employed with respect to the end of man in the other world and his business in this, as he that shall spend so much time in the solution of a mathematical question as M. Descartes, I remember, confesses of himself in one of his Epistles."[16] The waste of time in useless studies was not generally condemned, but Norris considered that it was blameworthy.

If Norris's rule for the measures that ought to be observed in the pursuit of knowledge was not generally accepted in theory, still less was it followed in practice. In Norris's view, little of what was generally studied was any aid to virtue or religion, and it was precisely the most useless studies that absorbed the most time. At this point Norris gave a trenchant criticism of the classical education which was universal in the public schools of his time, and which he himself had received at Winchester. This criticism was greatly expanded in the second edition of the Reflections. Norris criticised the public schools on two counts: considering the short span of human life they spent too long on education; but, above all, what they taught was largely frivolous and useless, for to fill the mind with the fancies of the pagan poets did not help to perfect it. "How many excellent and useful things", he asked, "might be learnt in the mathematics and other ingenious and profitable sciences, while boys are thumming and murthering Hesiod and Homer, which then they do not understand and which, when they do, they will throw by and despise?"[17] Such studies, he continued, were not only useless: they were often positively harmful. A work

192

such as Ovid's De Arte Amandi could do nothing but harm to those
who studied it. "I do not condemn this sort of learning out of ignorance", he concluded, "for I myself had my education in a very
eminent school, that of Winchester, where I made no small proficiency in classic learning, as 'tis called; and I have since plied
it very hard, and run through all the criticsms of it. But upon a
serious review I take no satisfaction either in those studies or in
those acquirements."[18] Yet these studies occupied the greater
part of one's time at school, and some people kept them up throughout their lives.

Despite the vigour of Norris's attack on classical education
as then practised, his attitude to classical studies was not one of
overall condemnation. He never discouraged the learning of Latin
and Greek or the study of the ancient philosophers; in the course
of these Reflections upon the Conduct of Human Life he quoted
Hierocles with approval, and in his actual attack on the public
schools he quoted St. Augustine and referred to Plato in support
of his criticisms. His criticism was in fact reserved for the study
of the pagan poets, which he regarded as useless, time consuming,
and often corrupting. It was these studies which, he considered,
ought to be replaced by the study of useful sciences such as mathematics.

Norris's attitude to mathematics also showed a certain am-
bivalence. As has been seen, he criticised Descartes for spend-
ing so much time working on the solution of a mathematical problem, but he recommended mathematics as a useful branch of study.
In fact Norris considered that the study of mathematics was useful
in that it accustomed the mind to abstract reasoning and to the
"Ideal World"; being concerned with necessary truth, it perfected
the intellect. Moreover, like the knowledge of many contingent

193

truths, it could also be useful on account of its practical applications. Its study was blameworthy only when it came to occupy an undue proportion of someone's time, to the detriment of more essential matters. The force of Norris's criticism was reserved for studies which, in his view, served neither to perfect the mind nor to aid man in his moral and religious life or in his daily life on earth.

For Norris's Reflections upon the Conduct of Human Life, taken as a whole, taught that there could be three valid reasons for studying something. Something could be worth knowing either because, being a necessary truth, it perfected the mind, or because it was useful or necessary for the moral or religious life, or because it contributed to the fulfilment of man's needs in this present life. Since man was destined for an eternal life, however, and since the attainment of the beatific vision, which was also the vision of all truth, depended on the fulfilment of moral and religious conditions, the second of these criteria was the most fundamental one, and should be taken as a measure to regulate the other two.

Reflections upon the Conduct of Human Life has been described as a profoundly anti-intellectual book.[19] And it is true that Norris did not regard intellectual activity as the principal end of human life on earth. In that sense, however, even Descartes was no intellectualist. But although Norris considered that the good moral conduct of life must be man's principal aim on earth, he did not in any sense subordinate truth to religious sentiment. In his own time he was criticised from the opposite point of view by Edmund Elys, an Anglican clergyman who sympathised with the Quakers. Elys considered that the only truth which perfected the intellect was "the practical understanding of true goodness",[20] and he left no place for intellectual values as such. This was of

194

course the opposite of Norris's view, according to which only necessary truth, which included not only the truths of morality and natural theology but also those of metaphysics, geometry, logic, and so-on, perfected the intellect. Norris did not subordinate truth to any other consideration, and it was for strictly rational reasons that he put his first emphasis on the attainment of the beatific vision.

In the closing pages of his Reflections, Norris spoke of his own life in the light of the principles that he had enunciated. He declared that he had directed his studies at Oxford not so much to his own satisfaction and the pursuit of truth as to achieving a reputation with others, and that much of his time had been spent on "unconcerning curiosities". [21] He now had greater need of heat than of light, and had determined to restrict his studies in future to "only such things as make for the moral improvement of my mind and the regulation of my life". In fact, however, if his publications before and after 1690 are examined, no significant change of their subject matter can be detected. His writings, with the possible exceptions of his translation of Waring's Effigies Amoris and some of his poems, had never been frivolous, though his translation of Xenophon's Life of Cyrus would doubtless fall under his condemnation of vain classical studies. But most of his writings had always upheld serious Christianity, and his departure from Oxford did not, as has been seen, mark any break in the development of his philosophy. But what is probably true is that the younger Norris had often written with an eye to fame and reputation, or simply for the pleasure of expressing his ideas, whereas from this time onwards he became more conscious of his duty to expound or defend truths which he regarded as important for man's moral and religious life. Norris grew more serious in the purpose of his writing; at the same time he became more careful of truth in accordance with the Cartesian principles that he had enunciated in the second of his Reflections, and more fair in controversy. But the subjects of his writings did not change.

When Norris wrote that he was determined to confine himself in future to subjects which were important for morality and religion, he did not mean that he intended turning to the reading or writing primarily of works of piety. He was convinced that the will followed the intellect and that, if one wished to promote the practice of virtue, the most important thing was to show that the path of virtue was also that of reason. Accordingly even his most "practical" works continued to appeal primarily to reason. As he wrote in the "Epistle Dedicatory" of the third volume of his Practical Discourses (1693), "I think we cannot do better service to religion than by resolving the practical duties of it into principles of philosophy, or make a better use of philosophic notions than to employ them in the service and for the interest of religion."

The views which Norris expressed in Reflections upon the Conduct of Human Life reflected his own combination of a Platonic and Cartesian philosophy with a serious acceptance of the fundamental doctrines of orthodox Christianity. Some of his criticisms of the false attitudes of the learned men of his day were borrowed from Malebranche,[22] but all the essential arguments of this work had already been expressed or implied in the Miscellanies, particularly in the poetical part of it. Probably no other of Norris's works expresses so fully his fundamental interests and cast of mind, and he would doubtless have been delighted that it became, through Wesley, one of the most influential of all his writings.

Reflections upon the Conduct of Human Life was the most

characteristic of Norris's "practical" works, and the most important from a philosophical point of view. Nevertheless his other writings on the practice of the religious and moral life cannot be passed over in silence in any survey of his thought as a whole, particularly as some of them were amongst his most popular works. Norris's spiritual teaching was contained mainly in Spiritual Counsel, or The Father's Advice to his Children, which was published in 1694. This little book of fifty pages was written primarily for Norris's own children, but was published, he declared, both because it might prove useful to other people and also in order that, if he should die before his children were old enough to understand his advice, this should be available for them, not in a manuscript that would probably be lost, but in a printed book that would always be accessible.[23] It proved in fact a very popular work.[24]

In this work, Norris insisted that religion was the principal business of life, and that it must be the affair of every day. We cannot here follow the details of Norris's advice, which was a fine expression of his own deep and rational piety. But while he insisted on the importance of reverent prayer and particularly of the habitual thought of God's presence and of one's dependence on him, he emphasised even more that a just and honest life was the best form of devotion, mercy and goodness the best prayer. Norris did not feel that it was necessary to detail the different aspects of a holy life, since "they are so plainly and so fully laid down in the Holy Scriptures, and so largely commented on and explained in those many excellent Practical Treatises which by the good providence of God we of this age and nation enjoy",[25] but he did suggest means to help one to fulfil one's duties. "The first great and general instrument of a holy life", he wrote, "is consideration".[26] By "consideration" Norris meant attentive meditation and reflection on truths

197

that one already knew, the truths, for instance, that sin was the greatest of evils, that one would inevitably live to regret every sin that one committed, and that the path of virtue was uniquely reasonable. This teaching exactly expressed the view that Norris had held ever since his sermon on The Root of Liberty and his correspondence with Henry More on the central importance of attention to truth as the source of right conduct.

But what was one to do if one was not sure from general principles whether or not one ought to perform a certain action? For such doubtful cases Norris suggested a double rule. First, one should consider whether the proposed action was one that one could refer to the glory of God; an action that one could not sincerely offer to God could not be virtuous. If this consideration left one still in doubt, one should ask oneself this further question: "whether or no you do in your conscience really think that the holy and blessed Jesus, according to that character and representation you have of him and his way of living in the Gospel, would, if now again upon earth, do such an action."[27] For this consideration to be real one must of course have a genuine understanding of and feeling for the character of Jesus Christ, and accordingly it is not surprising that Norris urged his readers to be assiduous in reading the New Testament, and to learn the Sermon on the Mount, in particular, by heart.

After these more fundamental suggestions, Norris went on to make some more concrete suggestions. One ought to learn self-control and avoid worldly conversation. With regard to reading, one ought not to waste one's time with novels and comedies, while works of religious controversy were generally based on the equivocal use of terms, and made one lose more in charity than one gained in truth. Apart from religion, the only subject which Norris urged his

198

readers to study was philosophy, which, he declared, "will open and enlarge your minds, give you true and thorough views of things, bring you acquainted with yourselves as well as with external nature, and lay an excellent ground for morality and religion."[28] The philosophy in question, he emphasised, was not Scholastic philosophy, but that of Descartes and Malebranche, and he commended with great enthusiasm the study of La Recherche de la Vérité. Finally he concluded his book with the general advice to his readers to form, from reading the gospels, as true an idea of the spirit and life of Christ as possible, and then to form their own lives on this model, "ever remembering that he is the best Christian, not that knows most, or that believes most, or that can talk most of Christianity, but who is, in the heart and life, the nearest follower of Christ."[29]

Spiritual Counsel, as one would expect in a book of this kind, makes no reference to most of Norris's distinctive theories. In its emphasis on the importance of attentive thought, however, and in its whole rationality, it is characteristic of his outlook. Although its emphasis on following the example of Christ may seem somewhat remote from Norris's usual purely rational approach to morality, the divergence is probably less than appears at first sight. Norris was convinced that natural and Christian morality were in complete accord. Reason consulted the divine Word, the Logos, and the Word was incarnate in Jesus Christ. Accordingly the moral duties which reason enjoined were perfectly mirrored in the human life of Christ. Norris's moral teaching in its developed form was summed up in the duty of loving as God loved, modelling one's love on that of God; his spiritual teaching was summed up in the imitation of Christ. He was convinced that these two principles coincided; and although the former was theoretically the more fundamental, the latter was often in practice easier for fallen man who lacked the unimpeded and clear use of reason. Spiritual Counsel also emphasised both the unique reasonableness of virtue and man's dependence on grace for attaining it. Like his other writings it bears witness to his belief that the work of grace was to enable fallen man to live according to reason.

Very shortly after his arrival at Newton St. Loe, Norris preached the Visitation Sermon in the presence of Bishop Ken in Bath Abbey on 30 July 1689. This was a vigorous sermon on the duties of the parish clergy, and an attack on the practice of non-residence, and was published as an appendix to Reflections upon the Conduct of Human Life. Apart from this and his early sermon on The Root of Liberty, Norris published four volumes of Practical Discourses, which appeared in 1690, 1691, 1693, and 1698 respectively. The first of these volumes, originally entitled Christian Blessedness: or, Discourses upon the Beatitudes, was in essence a straightforward exposition of the beatitudes from the Sermon on the Mount; the remaining volumes were collections of sermons on various subjects, those in the third volume being on the whole the most philosophical. Some of the more important of these sermons are discoursed elsewhere in this book, [30] and it will be necessary to do no more here than to touch on the teaching of the rest. Norris himself warned Mary Astell not to look in his sermons for an exact exposition of his speculative thought; but the Practical Discourses nevertheless give ample evidence of the identity of his fundamental preoccupations in the religious and philosophical spheres.

Norris saw the Christian life in primarily moral terms. God required man to live in accordance with the Natural Law, which was essentially knowable by reason. A partial revelation of this law had been given to Moses, and it had been more fully revealed by Christ. Men however had not obeyed this law, and in his benevolence and mercy God the Son, the Word, had become man in Christ, both in order to give the perfect pattern of human life and, above all, in order to offer his life as a sacrifice for sin. The redemption which Christ's sacrifice won, however, was not applied to man automatically; it was conditional on man's repentance and his sincere effort to live virtuously in future. The path of virtue, which was summed up in the two commandments of setting one's heart on God alone and of loving all one's neighbours with sincere benevolence, was strictly reasonable, but fallen man could live reasonably only with the help of grace, which, however, was offered to all men.

Norris's Practical Discourses frequently emphasise man's direct relationship with God and immediate responsibility to him. In practical morality as in speculative thought, Norris holds, the common example of the world is one of error and vice; in action as in thought one must be prepared to follow one's own insight into what is right. "Let us be sure by doing our duty to satisfy our own consciences, whatever others do or think ... Let us for once dare to be wise, and be guilty of the great singularity of doing well, and of acting like men and Christians."[31] Norris quoted Luther as an example of someone who dared to stand by his own conscience and his understanding of the Bible against the whole weight of authority and tradition, and it seems clear that in his view the Protestant insistence on following one's own conscience and the philosophical duty of seeking truth independently for oneself, a duty which he had learned especially from Descartes and Malebranche, were closely related. In fact they were virtually one principle in his mind: one must always act in accordance with the truth that one saw for oneself, whether in the "Intelligible World" or in the Bible, and to follow human authority was always a snare.

The direct dependence of every creature on God was the root of the respect that one owed to everything that existed. "It must be a great affront to the infinite majesty of God to despise any part of the natural creation", [32] since all creatures were modelled on the divine Ideas. Most of all one must respect human beings. Man's relationship to God was the most intimately personal thing about him, and accordingly Norris now affirmed that "'Tis great profaneness to despise anything that never so remotely relates to God, and carries in any degree the face of religion; (upon which account by the way, I think it a very unjustifiable practice to ridicule or make a mockery of what the most mistaken sect of men calls divine worship)..."[33] In his youth Norris had sometimes been far from observing the spirit of this precept,[34] but in his later writings he showed himself a fair and courteous adversary, and was recognised as such by Quakers, by nonconformists, and in particular by Henry Dodwell in the controversy on the immortality of the soul. And although he was a strong supporter of the Established Church and considered that political power should be reserved to its adherents, he was opposed to persecution for religious beliefs.

Norris's identification of truth with God and his view that absence of attention to truth is the root of sin find frequent expression in his sermons. In A Discourse of Practical Atheism[35] he examines the case of a man who says that he believes in God but acts as if God did not exist. Such a man, he suggests, may in reality not believe in God at all, although he claims to do so; alternatively he may have a wrong conception of God; but he may have an orthodox belief to which he does not attend in the daily conduct of his life. Norris notes that a man of evil life is called in English an "ungodly" man, and that this word, translated into Greek, means "atheist". This English term expresses a deep truth in Norris's view, for the evil man effectively denies God by his actions. In particular, those who love creatures in such a way as to make them the final objects of their desires make them their God and effectively deny the true God. Norris's teaching on "practical atheism" exemplifies the doctrines of his sermon on The Root of Liberty and of his writings on the love of God. The same principles which led Norris to speak of a practical atheism in the evil lives of some professing Christians might also lead one to recognise a "practical theism" in the good lives of some professing atheists, though this what not a consideration that Norris himself suggested.

The Practical Discourses show Norris to have been a man of sincere compassion towards the poor. One can speak of "the love of God", he declares, in three senses: God's benevolence towards us, our desire for God, and a benevolent compassion on our part towards one-another similar to that which Christ exercised towards us. But the rich man who refuses to help his poor neighbours shows them no benevolence; he shows no real desire for God either, since a genuine desire for God would imply the fulfilment of the commandments which he has assigned as conditions for attaining to him, and mutual charity is one of these conditions; and he can be sure in consequence that God has no love for him. Riches and the possession of property carry with them the duty of relieving those in need. And if this is true, Norris continues, of those who refuse to help their neighbours, what is to be said of those who go further and act against strict justice? "Those particularly who defraud poor labourers of their hire, who oppress and grind the poor instead of relieving them, and above all those who corrupt and abuse public benefactions and places of hereditary charity, such as hospitals and almshouses - I say, what shall we say of those birds of prey which turn these public benefactions into private advantages, and raise ample preferments for themselves out of a common charity?"[36] Norris's protest against the abuse of public charities was so ardent that one wonders whether he had a particular case in mind. He emphasised further the respect that one ought to have for the poor, who might be people of more worth than those whose help they sought, and urged that, where possible, one's help for them should be such as aided them to provide for themselves. One should live at all times for the glory of God, "wherein is also apprehended the good and welfare of human society, it being for the glory of God that his creatures, whom he made for the greatest and supreme happiness, even the enjoyment of himself, should be as prosperous and happy as may be, both in this life and in the next".[37] As can be seen, Norris showed himself in the Practical Discourses to be a vigorous exponent of Christian morality in both its individual and social aspects.

In the preface to the Second Part of his Theory of the Ideal ... World, Norris wrote that, if that work had a favourable reception, he might be encouraged "to trouble the world once more, upon a subject of more general concernment". This was an allusion to his project of writing a series of works on the Christian virtues. The first of these works appeared in 1707 under the title of A Practical Treatise concerning Humility. The project was then interrupted by Norris's interventions in the controversy on the immortality of the soul,[38] and it was not until 1710 that A Treatise concerning Christian Prudence, his last work, appeared. These were both "practical" works in Norris's sense, and they add comparatively

204

little to our knowledge of his distinctive ideas. They will be analysed here only insofar as they cast new light on Norris's thought.

A Practical Treatise concerning Humility begins by defining that virtue in terms which reproduce unchanged the doctrine of the sermon on The Root of Liberty. Humility is the virtue which leads us "to think truly and justly of ourselves, to think of ourselves as we ought to think, to think of ourselves as we are, neither higher nor lower, neither better nor worse."[39] There is no virtue in denying the excellences that one possesses; indeed it is one's duty to recognise them, but to recognise also that they are gifts from God. As in his other writings, Norris insists again that "consideration", that is, careful attention to the truth, is the great remedy against sin, and in particular, he now declares, against pride. On all these central points the Practical Treatise concerning Humility expresses views which Norris had held since his earliest writings.

The passage of this work in which Norris treats of humility as the necessary disposition for receiving the help of divine grace is interesting as it afforded him the occasion of expressing his understanding of the nature and rôle of grace more fully than he had done elsewhere. By grace Norris understood "the inward operation of God's Spirit supernaturally assisting our natural faculties, so as to enable them to act for and attain a supernatural end. Or (in plainer and more familiar words), that divine assistance whereby we are disposed and enabled to keep God's commandments, and to lead good and Christian lives."[40] This view was of course traditional, but when he went on to describe the ways in which grace worked he adopted Malebranche's division into graces of light and of sentiment:

"Since there are but two principles or motives of action, viz.

either the <u>reason</u> which we perceive why a thing should be
done, or the <u>sense</u> of <u>pleasure</u> which we find in the doing of
it, I further think that the manner of that divine operation
which we call <u>grace</u> cannot be more rationally and intelligibly
explained than (according to the hypothesis of a modern philosopher) by the way of <u>light</u> or by the way of <u>sentiment</u> ..."[41]
The "grace of light" illuminated the mind, while the "grace of
sentiment" was necessary in order to counterbalance the weight
of concupiscence in fallen man. Norris took this division from
Malebranche's <u>Traité de la Nature et de la Grâce</u>, but both he
and Malebranche rightly pointed out that it was also the doctrine
of St. Augustine. [42]

Although Norris adopted Malebranche's view of grace up to
this point, he did not follow the rest of the teaching of the <u>Traité</u>
<u>de la Nature et de la Grâce</u>. Where Malebranche affirmed that
graces were distributed to men in accordance with the passing
thoughts and desires of the human soul of Christ, Norris preferred, in agreement with virtually the whole of Christian tradition,
to admit his complete ignorance of the principles according to
which this distribution took place, affirming only that God could
not, in this or any other matter, act arbitrarily or without reason.
Norris's reticence on this point was certainly closer to the Bible
than was Malebranche's theory, but there is no doubt that his
adoption of the latter's theory of the grace of sentiment marked
a real advance in his teaching on this subject.

In the preface to his <u>Treatise concerning Christian Prudence</u>
Norris declared that he would never be able to complete his plan
of writing a series of works on the Christian virtues; his "little
health and less abilities" would not allow him to do so. Nevertheless he hoped that this book on prudence would "in some measure

answer the design of such an undertaking in the general, by treating of that virtue which sits at the helm and governs all the rest, conducts the whole movement of life, and is as it were a kind of universal virtue." Norris in fact identified prudence with rational consideration and attention to the truth; prudence was the proper use of reason regarding things to be done, and in this sense, which reflected his thought ever since his sermon on The Root of Liberty, it was the sole true cardinal virtue. More exactly, prudence was attention to truth only insofar as this attention was effective in producing a right choice, so that Christian prudence in particular was "a practical knowledge of that good which Christianity requires and of that evil which it forbids, actually directive of the will in the choice of that good and the refusal of that evil."[43]

After pointing out that prudence, because of its immediate reference to action, was not identical with knowledge, Norris added that it could also not be identified with wit or policy. Locke had opposed wit to judgement, but Norris, interestingly, did not agree: "There are a great many useful and severe truths that are capable of a very ornamental dress, ... so that the truth shall neither spoil the wit nor the wit the truth, but rather serve to recommend it with the greater grace and advantage. Or else truly I should have a much meaner opinion of oratory and poetry than I have ..."[44] Norris agreed that wit and prudence did not always go together: "There are a great many witty men ... of whom one may say what was once said of an eminent person, that he never said a foolish thing, nor ever did a wise one";[45] but nevertheless this defence of wit in Norris's last work is interesting as showing that he did not repudiate his own earlier devotion to poetry. If prudence could not be identified with wit, still less was it the same as policy, which Norris identified with practical astuteness, the art of choosing means to attain an end without regard either to the rightness of the end or to the moral status of the means. The Scholastics held that prudence was concerned only with the choice of the right means to attain the end of human life, but Norris insisted that it concerned both the identification of the proper end of human life and the choice of the right means to attain it.

The only proper end of human life, Norris declared, was God, who contained all goodness and all truth; and the means to be adopted in order to attain the vision of God were those which God himself had laid down. These means, however, the commandments, were not arbitrary: without charity, for instance, which God commanded, one could not enjoy God in heaven. Norris further considered that to consult one's own eternal interest by the prudent choice of end and means was also one's duty. And in a passage which foreshadowed Butler's Analogy he added that one ought not to neglect so great a stake even if one thought the truth of Christianity doubtful and eternal life uncertain. Even the possibility of eternal life made it the most important of considerations. [46]

Passing on to consider the question of how one ought to observe the commandments, Norris affirmed that one ought to fulfil them as perfectly as possible. In his earlier writings he had defended the view that there were certain good actions which were counselled but not commanded by God, but he now left this disputed question on one side, declaring that he was not now concerned with what was strictly commanded as a duty, but with what prudence recommended. However since he held that prudence was enjoined on man as a duty, it seems to follow that there would logically be no place left for "works of supererogation". This same conclusion also seems to follow from Norris's developed teaching on the love of God, but it is not a conclusion that he himself ever explicitly drew.

208

After this appeal for a vigorous and whole-hearted fulfilment of one's moral and religious duties, Norris went on to examine the position of those whom he called "half-Christians" or
"almost Christians". These were the people who had enough religion to render them uneasy in their sins, but not enough effectively
to reform their lives. Such people had the worst of both worlds,
and their position was peculiarly unreasonable. "If we think there
is no truth or reason in religion, why do we do anything; but if we
think there is, why don't we do enough? Either we should do nothing,
or we should do more."[47] Norris urged such people to pray the
Holy Spirit to eclipse the attractions of this world by those of grace,
so that they might become new people, made in the image of Christ.
Norris's discussion of "half-Christians", which was a favourite
passage with John Wesley,[48] combines a rational appreciation of
the importance of the truth or falsehood of Christianity with an
appreciation of the rôle of grace, understood in Malebranche's
sense, in any thorough-going conversion. In accordance with his
invariable view, Norris saw the Christian life in essentially moral
terms. God's commandments, he continued, should be observed
as perfectly as possible, either by innocence or by repentance;
for under the Christian dispensation repentance was also acceptable with God. By repentance Norris understood "such a change
in a man's mind as effectually turns a man from sin to righteous-
ness".[49] Looking backwards it implied a sincere sorrow for sin
and a retractation of one's former choice; looking forwards it
implied a sincere endeavour to keep God's commandments in future. Such repentance was a part of wisdom, since it was the re-
versal of the false judgement which had been at the root of one's
sin. Thus in his last work Norris continued to uphold the view
which he had first expressed in his sermon on The Root of Liberty,

according to which a false judgement, resulting from insufficient attention to truth, was always at the root of sin.

When he had thus examined the moral substance of the Christian life, Norris went on to treat of the means which God had provided to aid man to fulfil the commandments. These means included faith, prayer, the reading of the Bible, the hearing of sermons, the sacraments, and ecclesiastical communion. After considering these, he then examined the prudent conduct of life in terms which largely repeated Reflections upon the Conduct of Human Life. The knowledge which one needed was primarily that which was useful for the moral life: knowledge above all of God and of oneself. However, he added, all true knowledge was valuable, and Boyle had shown in his Christian Virtuoso that the study of nature, for instance, could lead one to knowledge of God. The essential thing, however, was to acquire a stock of solid and rational principles by which to guide one's life, and then to think about them frequently and put them into practice. Any man could become wiser: he might come to see reasons to change some of his principles. But one should never change one's principles in accordance with fashion or with other people's ideas or preferences.

The Treatise concerning Christian Prudence, Norris's last work, was fully in accordance with the lines of his other "practical" writings. Norris showed in it, however, a tendency to use the term "prudence" in two distinct ways. Strictly speaking he regarded it as the attentive consideration of moral truth leading to action in accordance with that truth; but at times he spoke as if it was solely concerned with identifying the right end for human life and the means for attaining that end, and with effectively choosing that end and these means. Norris did not hold the Aristotelian view that one could act only for one's own interest. On the contrary, he held that benevolence was strictly altruistic. Yet at times he wrote as if "securing one's eternal interest" was the whole of morality. In this emphasis he was of course typical of his time. It should be remembered, however, that the Treatise concerning Christian Prudence was a "practical" work in which he did not aim to express his understanding of the moral life as a whole.

Norris's writings on practical morality were probably the most influential of all his works, pointing forward in different ways both to Pietism and Methodism and to the prudential morality of Enlightenment Christianity.[50] They show him to have been a man who took Christianity absolutely seriously, and they reflect many of his philosophical convictions without for the most part insisting on the more controversial details of his speculative theories. It has been said that Norris's religion had little connection with his philosophy, and even that the two were barely compatible, but his "practical" writings show their fundamental unity. The rational and moral element in Norris's religion was very strong, but he held that reason was in immediate contact with God and that even the most exigent Christian commandments were part of the natural law. Norris's interests and preoccupations were the same in his more speculative and more practical writings. In the next chapter we shall examine his specific teaching on the relationship of reason and faith, with reference in particular to the mysteries of Christianity. The unity of his thought as a whole will be considered in the final chapter of this book.

CHAPTER VIII REASON AND FAITH

As has been seen, Norris was convinced that Christianity
was in entire accord with Natural Religion. In particular he considered that the Christian moral law, including even its most exigent precepts, coincided with the Natural Law and was in principle
capable of being known by natural reason without any special revelation, though in practice the example of Christ might in certain
cases be an easier way for fallen man to discern his duty than rational consideration. The existence of God was of course the fundamental truth of philosophy, and the immortality of the soul, though
not strictly proved, was at least strongly suggested by rational
considerations. But on the other hand he also considered that the
possibility for sinful man to attain God's forgiveness through repentance depended on God's gracious intervention in Christ, who
by his death had made up for human sin. Fallen man, furthermore,
could not live virtuously and reasonably in a consistent way without
the help of grace, which was the work of the Holy Spirit in the soul.
The doctrines of the Trinity and the Incarnation were thus essential
to Christianity. As a strongly rational thinker who was at the same
time a convinced Christian, Norris was well qualified to intervene
in the controversy with the Socinians and Deists.

Norris's intervention in this controversy was occasioned by
the publication in 1696 of John Toland's Christianity not Mysterious.
Norris first thought of writing a direct reply to Toland's book, but
on reflection he "judged it better to give an absolute account ot the
positive side of the question";[1] in other words he decided to examine
in itself the whole question of the credibility of the mysteries of the
Christian religion. This decision resulted in the writing of An Ac-

count of Reason and Faith, which first appeared in 1697 and was deservedly popular. Norris's work entirely eschewed personalities, and examined the problems at issue in a dispassionate way. As a result in rose above the level of ephemeral controversy, and became a work of permanent value on its subject. It attained its twelfth edition in 1724, its thirteenth in 1740. A fourteenth edition was published in 1790, introduced by a letter from H. Croft commending it to the Unitarian Joseph Priestley, while the final chapter was re-edited in 1795 in the collection The Scholar Armed against the Errors of the Time and was reprinted with this collection as late as 1800. No other work of Norris's continued in circulation so long. An Account of Reason and Faith was Norris's principal work on this subject, but in order to get a complete picture of his teaching one needs also to take account of what he wrote on the relative certainties of reason and faith in the course of his treatment of our knowledge of the world of sense in the First Part of his Theory of the Ideal or Intelligible World.

Norris began his Account of Reason and Faith with two chapters in which he defined what he meant by reason and by faith. His account of reason followed the teaching of all his works on the subject, and need not be repeated here. By "reason" he did not mean the activity of reasoning, but rather the simple power of knowing truth. Man, he declared, is not always thinking, nor does he always possess habitual knowledge, but the possession of reason or intellect, the power of knowing truth, is essential to him. When the Socinians affirmed that there could be nothing in religion which was above reason, they meant that there could be nothing which was beyond the power of man's mind to understand.

Turning to faith, Norris defined this as "an assent grounded not upon the internal reason and evidence of the thing, but upon the

213

bare testimony and authority of the speaker."[2] It was thus to be distinguished on the one hand from assent to complete internal evidence, which was knowledge, and on the other from assent to incomplete evidence, which was opinion. Faith could be divided into human faith and divine faith, according to the source of the testimony on which it was based. Human faith often did not get beyond the status of opinion, but divine faith could in principle be as certain as any knowledge. From the logical point of view it was founded on a syllogism such as this: "Whatever is revealed by God is true; but (this proposition) is revealed by God; therefore (this proposition) is true." In such a syllogism, Norris held, the major premiss was absolutely certain. The minor premiss could also be evidently true, though, as he later declared in the First Part of the Theory of the Ideal ... World when explicitly considering the relative certainties of reason and faith, it was more often only morally certain.

Faith, then, was acceptance of something as true because of someone's testimony to it, and not because of internal evidence of its truth. Propositions which were believed must indeed be understood to some extent, since if one had no idea what one believed one would in fact believe nothing. And further, in Norris's view, the same proposition could in certain cases both be known by natural reason and believed by faith. Norris knew that Augustine and Aquinas disagreed with him on this point, but he insisted that "'tis not the absolute nature of the thing believed, but the quality of the motive, that specifies faith and distinguishes it from other assents. So that 'tis no matter what the absolute nature of the thing be in itself, whether it be evident or not evident, knowable or not knowable, provided it be assented to upon the proper medium and motive of faith, that is, upon authority, without any respect had to

214

the natural evidence of the thing."[3] Accordingly to seek rational proofs for truths of faith, such as the creation of the world, did not take away from faith: one could both know from natural reason that something was so and also believe it because God had revealed it. Faith itself was a reasonable assent, founded not upon the internal evidence of the proposition believed, but upon the (external) evidence that God had revealed it.

Having thus defined what he meant by reason and by faith, Norris was ready to consider the specific Socinian objection that Christianity could not contain mysteries which were beyond man's comprehension. The essence of the Socinian position, he declared, was the denial of the distinction between what was above reason and what was contrary to reason. Robert Boyle had examined this distinction at some length, and had taken "things above reason" for things which reason could not find out for itself, whether or not it could understand them once they had been revealed;[4] but Norris was not content with this presentation of the distinction, since the Socinians did not reject truths which reason could not have discovered for itself provided they were fully understandable once they had been revealed to it. Norris accordingly formulated the distinction as follows:

"By things above reason, ... I conceive to be meant, not such as reason of itself cannot discover, but such as, when proposed, it cannot comprehend. And by things contrary to reason, I conceive such as it can and does actually comprehend, and that to be actually impossible. Or in other words, a thing is then above reason when we do not comprehend how it can be, and then contrary to reason when we do positively comprehend that it cannot be."[5]

When Norris declared that a proposition which was above reason

215

was one that reason could not comprehend, he did not mean that reason could not understand its meaning. As he had already affirmed, a proposition to be believed must be understood to some extent. What he meant was that the proposition in question was such that reason could not perceive whether or not it was true, either for lack of sufficient clearness in the ideas involved or for lack of a proper means of comparing these ideas. Just as one could talk intelligently about space or movement while lacking a complete understanding of their nature, so the Christian could believe the mysteries of his religion and talk about them in a meaningful way although he did not have sufficiently clear ideas of them to perceive their truth by internal evidence.

Taken in this sense, Norris suggested, the distinction between what was above reason and what was contrary to reason was an evidently valid one. "This immediately appears", he wrote, "from the very direct view of the ideas themselves. For what can be more plain than that not to comprehend how a thing may be, and to comprehend that it cannot be, are two different things? And what better way have we to know the distinction of things, but only that the idea of the one is not the idea of the other?"[6] Furthermore, to declare that a proposition was above reason was a relative thing: it did not mean that it was above all reason, but only that its truth could not be directly apprehended by human reason at present. Indeed Norris did not consider that the mysteries of Christianity would necessarily remain always beyond the power of human reason to understand. With the advance of human knowledge, some mysteries might become rationally explicable.[7] Even now, some things which were above the reason of most men were not above that of experts in the field in question. But to be contrary to reason was something absolute, not relative; what one saw clearly to be false

216

was contrary to all reason, and could never be true.

After this examination of the distinction between what was above and what was contrary to reason, Norris next approached the problem from another angle: is human reason the measure of truth? Norris fully agreed that there is a sense in which it is. He agreed with the Cartesians that whatever one clearly saw to be true was true, and that any proposition that one saw clearly to be false was false in reality. But he pointed out that it did not follow from this that man saw the whole of truth, or that what he did not perceive to be true could not be so. Norris considered that it was obvious that man did not know everything, and thus that he was not the final measure of all truth, but he nevertheless undertook to prove this by an examination of the nature of truth.

In accordance with his invariable view, Norris distinguished between necessary and contingent truth, and argued that necessary truth could not ultimately be distinguished from God. From this identification of truth with the divine nature it followed that truth in its full extent was infinite. In An Account of Reason and Faith, however, Norris did not confine himself to this metaphysical argument for the infinity of truth, but added that our own intellectual experience should also convince us of it. "Do we not find, as in a spacious campaign, so in the immense field of truth, that our eye wearies and our sight loses itself in the boundless prospect, and that, besides the clear view which we have of a few things at a little distance from us, there lie all round us vast tracts unmeasurably diffused, whereof we have only confuse and indistinct images, like the faint blue of the far distant hills?"[8] The more one knew, the more one was conscious of what one did not know. Faced with the boundless extent of truth one realised the finite nature of one's own understanding.

Norris seems to have realised, however, that few if any thinkers would suggest that the human mind was in this sense the measure of truth. More serious from his point of view was the suggestion that though man, being finite, could not know the whole extent of truth, nevertheless there was no particular truth that he could not understand if it was proposed to him. In this case man could know the whole of truth in a distributive though not in a collective sense. To this objection Norris replied in two ways. On the one hand, one's lack of knowledge of the whole extent of truth was a handicap even for the understanding of particular truths. We know many particular truths, he declared, but we cannot know the full significance that these truths may have in other connections. Many truths can indeed be understood without all their implications being known, but there are others, such as the conduct of divine providence, which cannot be understood in isolation and which therefore remain largely mysteries for us. [9] And on the other hand there were some truths that were strictly infinite. In accordanc with the distinction which was to play a considerable rôle in the First Part of his Theory of the Ideal ... World, Norris affirmed that, while all the Ideas are infinite in their esse reale since this is identical with the divine essence, many are finite in their esse repraesentativum, since they represent creatures. These Ideas, and the truths which express their relationships, are in principle proportioned to the human intellect. But the Ideas which represent God's absolute perfections are infinite in their esse repraesentativum too, and are thus incapable of being adequately understood and exhaustively known by us. Our knowledge of the infinite God must contain an element of mystery.

In fact, however, there were many finite ideas too that were unknown to us, or whose relationships we could not grasp. "And

218

indeed when it shall be considered how many things surpass our conception when we are children which yet we are able well to comprehend when we are men; how many things again are beyond the ken of ignorant and illiterate men which are yet very intelligible ... to the men of art and learning; and how many things again, even among the learned, are now discovered and well understood by the help of algrebra, which were mysteries to former ages,"[10] one would have to be very lacking in intelligence to make one's own reason the final measure of truth. And yet, Norris claimed, this was precisely what the Socinians were logically obliged to do if they claimed that what was above reason was also necessarily contrary to reason.

But in this case, if human reason was not the final measure of truth and if there could be mysteries which one should believe because God revealed them, even though they remained obscure to us, what was to become of the Cartesian principle according to which one ought to accept nothing but what was clearly and evidently true? The Socinians took this Cartesian maxim as favourable to their position, while many Christians condemned Descartes for the same reason, holding not only that he had opened the gates to Socinianism and pure rationalism but that he himself was a concealed Socinian or Deist. This question was of personal importance for Norris, who was committed to the principle of clear ideas and of evidence as well as being a believer in the mysteries of Christianity. Norris was of course opposed to Descartes on the question of the created nature of truth, but he firmly believed in the Cartesian method and approach to philosophy. The rule that one must never accept less than complete evidence for truth and that, with this in view, one must reason only on clear ideas, was adopted from Descartes by Malebranche as the first of his rules of philosophical method; Norris had translated these rules in his Reflections upon the Conduct of Human Life, and he now insisted afresh on the importance of this principle, neglect of which, he considered, was at the root of the errors of the Aristotelian and Scholastic philosophy. But how was this rule of philosophical method to be reconciled with the acceptance of the Christian mysteries? In answering this question Norris was able not only to defend Descartes against the accusation of exaggerated rationalism but also to explain his own view of the proper use of reason in relation to Christian faith, and thus to formulate his final answer to Socinianism.

The usual answer to this difficulty, Norris declared, was to distinguish between matters of reason and matters of faith, and to affirm that, while in the former one should admit nothing to which one was not constrained by the evidence, in matters of faith one should submit one's mind to the authority of God and believe without understanding. Descartes himself did not in fact extend his rule of evidence to matters of faith,[11] and Malebranche on occasion explicitly made this very distinction;[12] but Norris was not satisfied with this way out of the problem. In his view, nothing should be admitted without evidence, even in the sphere of faith. The proper distinction was not between the domains of reason and of faith, but between different kinds of evidence. The assent of faith was based on the external evidence of God's testimony to the proposition in question.

If man's whole conduct ought to bear the mark of reason, this was especially true, in Norris's view, of the most important of all his activities: religion. If the fact that a certain proposition was above reason did not prove its falsity, still less did it prove its truth. While one might expect that, in a religion revealed by an infinite God, there would probably be mysteries beyond the power of our finite minds fully to understand, nevertheless no mystery should be accepted as true without sufficient reason. One must always suspend one's assent until it was determined by the evident light of truth; to act in any other way would be unreasonable, and God could never wish one to act against reason. Accordingly, in Norris's view, the true meaning of the Cartesian maxim was that one should give one's assent only to what one clearly saw to be true, either through the internal evidence of the proposition in question or through external evidence.

In Norris's view this was not only the true sense of the Cartesian maxim; it was also the meaning which Descartes himself attached to it. Accordingly it was entirely false to claim that the Cartesian philosophy was favourable to Socinianism or Deism, or that Descartes himself was a Socinian in disguise. "The truth is," Norris concluded, "the Cartesian philosophy leads just as much to Socinianism as philosophy in general does to atheism, and I will venture to say, and be bound to make it good, that as no good philosopher can be an atheist, so no good Cartesian can be a Socinian."[13]

Norris seems to have been fully correct in holding that Descartes was neither a Socinian nor a deist, and that his philosophy was not inimical to belief in the mysteries of Christianity. Descartes had too lively a sense of the infinity and incomprehensibility of God and of the finitude of human reason to affirm that what one could not clearly understand could not be true. And in fact a considerable part of the argument by which Norris proved that human reason was not the final measure of truth was directly inspired by Descartes. Nevertheless it seems true to say that Norris's application of the rule of evidence to the sphere of faith was not strictly Cartesian. As has been seen, Descartes seems rather to have limited his de-

mand for evidence to the truths of the natural order, leaving revealed truths to a faith the grounds of whose certainty he never examined, while Malebranche wrote that "to be faithful one must believe blindly but to be a philosopher one must see evidently."[14]
Elsewhere however Malebranche wrote that "our faith is perfectly
reasonable in its origin. It does not in the least owe its establishment to prejudices, but to right reason."[15] Although Malebranche
never spoke expressly of the external evidence of the truths of faith,
he seems therefore to have held a view which did not differ fundamentally from that of Norris, save to the extent that, as a Catholic,
he demanded implicit faith in whatever the Church taught, whereas Norris considered that every doctrine must be examined in the
light of the Bible and of one's own reason. Malebranche and Norris agreed, however, on the fundamentally reasonable nature of
faith.

Norris's view of the proper rôle of reason in matters of faith
can be summed up in three propositions. No doctrine that implies
a contradiction either in itself or with any known truth can be true:
if we see that some doctrine is in this sense contrary to reason,
we must reject it.[16] But a doctrine may be above reason, in the
sense that we cannot tell, by examining it in itself, whether it is
true or false. In this case we must seek to find out by an attentive
examination of the evidence whether or not God has revealed it.
The rôle of reason in religious belief is thus a central one, and
Norris considered that Christianity was well able to stand this
test. "Certainly there is not anything, neither doctrine nor precept, in that true religion which is revealed by God, in evangelical
Christianity, that need fly the light of reason or refuse to be tried
by it. Christian religion is all over a reasonable service, and the
Author of it is too reasonable a master to impose any other, or to

require (whatever his Vicar may do) that men should follow him blindfold, and pull out their eyes to become his disciples."[17] Norris was convinced that there was nothing in the mysteries of Christianity that was evidently contrary to reason, and he had now shown that the fact that they were not fully comprehensible did not render them incredible, provided there was sufficient evidence that they had really been revealed by God. He now added that the fact of their revelation was "obvious to every eye that can but read the Bible."[18] Noone who read the New Testament without prejudice could deny, he affirmed, that the doctrines of the divinity of Christ, the Trinity, and the redemption were taught in its pages.

Since the Socinians claimed to accept the Bible as a divine revelation, Norris did not find himself obliged to prove the divine origin of the teaching that it contained or implied. If he had had to deal with this question, he would no doubt have replied, as he had in The Christian Law Asserted and Vindicated,[19] by appealing to the Old Testament prophecies and prefigurations which were fulfilled in Christ, to the sublimity of Christ's teaching, to his miracles and particularly his death and resurrection, and to the mutual harmony of the gospel records, together with the luminous but superhuman character of the teaching of the Bible as a whole. Such arguments, he considered, coalesced to give a moral certainty of the divine origin of the biblical revelation. It is clear, however, that they do not amount to a strict or metaphysical proof, and Norris had to take this fact into account when he came, in the First Part of his Theory of the Ideal ... World, to consider the relative certainties of faith and reason.

In the final chapter of An Account of Reason and Faith Norris turned to address the Socinians more directly. The Socinians did not deny that there were many things in nature that they did not understand. In that case, Norris asked them, "since there are so many inconceivable things, or if you please mysteries, in the works of nature and providence, why not in religion? Nay, where should one expect to find mysteries if not there, where all the things that are revealed are revealed by God himself, and many of them concerning himself and his own infinite perfections?"[20]

After this reflection, which interestingly anticipates one of the main arguments of Joseph Butler's Analogy of Religion, Norris proposed an argumentum ad hominem. The Socinians declared that they accepted the New Testament as a divine revelation, and they had no doubt of the existence of God: but Norris urged them to examine their position and see whether their principles would not logically lead them to deism and even to atheism. He pointed out that eternity, infinity, and immensity are also mysteries that surpass our clear understanding. If the doctrine of the Trinity is to be rejected because it cannot be fully understood, may one not find oneself obliged for the same reason to reject the existence of God himself, since his whole nature is mysterious? More immediately, Norris suggested, the Socinians might find that their views would lead them to reject the whole Christian revelation and to become pure deists. For if one removes from Christianity the mysteries of the Trinity, the incarnation, and the redemption, all that is left is Christian morality. The moral teaching of Christianity is indeed perfect, but one cannot say with certainty that it would have been impossible for men to have discovered it for themselves, and in fact a great part of it was already known and accepted before the time of Christ. To identify Christianity in this way with Christian moral teaching alone would easily lead one, Norris declares, to reject the miracles recorded in the Bible, for stories of miracles are always suspect if the purpose for which they are said to have been performed seems insufficiently important to justify them. If God only wanted to reveal a moral law which it was possible for men to discover for themselves, the whole biblical history tends to appear superfluous, and thus incredible. In any case, Norris concludes, all that can remain of Christianity will be its moral teaching; the Christian gospel of forgiveness will disappear, since this depends on the redemption worked by Christ, and presupposes his divinity. Shorn of its mysteries, nothing can remain of Christianity but a purely natural religion.

As Croft pointed out in his 1790 edition of An Account of Reason and Faith, Norris's criticism of the Socinians was distinguished by its politeness and fairness. But it was all the stronger for that. It seems undeniable that Norris was right in holding that the Socinianism of Christianity not Mysterious could only be a temporary position on the way to pure deism,[21] and the later writings of Toland showed that he was indeed a deist or free-thinker rather than a Socinian who accepted the authority of the Bible. But, as has been seen, apart from this final chapter An Account of Reason and Faith was concerned less with the immediate controversy with Toland than with the analysis of the relationship between reason and faith for its own sake. Norris held that faith was an assent based on evidence external to the proposition believed; divine faith was based on evidence that a certain proposition was revealed by God. In this work, however, Norris did not examine in any detail the nature of this evidence, or the related question of the relative certainty attaching to matters of natural knowledge and matters of faith. But he subsequently considered this question explicitly in the course of the First Part of his Theory of the Ideal or Intelligible World, which thus completes his teaching on reason and faith.

In the First Part of his Theory, it will be remembered, Nor-

225

ris had argued that the ideal or intelligible world was known with greater certainty than was the natural or external world. The latter was known only through sensation, and to those who replied that it was known also by faith Norris added that one's knowledge of revelation itself depended on sensation. This admission that the existence of the external world was known by faith and yet was less certain than that of the world of Ideas or eternal essences clearly posed the problem of the relative certainties of faith and reason. In An Account of Reason and Faith Norris had already affirmed that faith could not be more certain than knowledge. Some theologians held that faith was more certain than science or knowledge, but, Norris declared, "'tis for want of the latter that these men so excessively extol the former."[22] Now in the First Part of his Theory he examined the question more thoroughly.

As has been seen, Norris held that faith was based on an implicit syllogism of the form "Whatever is revealed by God is true; but (this proposition) is revealed by God; therefore (this proposition) is true". In this syllogism, the major premiss was a metaphysical truth, a proposition of science or knowledge in the strict sense. This very fact, Norris pointed out in passing, proved that faith could not be more certain than natural knowledge, since no conclusion could be more certain than its premisses. But the key question, for the certainty of faith, was the degree of certainty attaching in each particular case to the minor premiss, that a certain doctrine had actually been revealed by God. To this question, Norris gave a gradated reply. If God wishes, he can "accompany the outward revelation of his word with such a brightness of internal light and evidence that a man may as certainly know and be as well assured that this or that in particular is revealed by God as he is in the general that whatsoever is revealed by God is true."[23]

226

But it is certain, Norris continues, that God does not ordinarily
give such a special illumination of grace.[24] We are normally led
to believe that a particular doctrine has been revealed by God,
not by any metaphysical or absolute evidence, but by "a collection
of rational considerations which, fairly laid together, are sufficient
to convince and satisfy an indifferent mind of the truth proposed,
so far, as to exclude all reasonable doubt concerning it, which is
what, in contradistinction to the other, we call a _moral_ certainty,
and that because it is founded upon moral evidence such as has
force enough to persuade, tho' not enough to extort the assent.
This certainty", Norris continues, "is indeed of an order inferior
to the other, but as great as the present case will ordinarily admit. For sure no man can now be well presumed able, with any
reason or modesty, to pretend that he is as certain that the Scripture is the Word of God as he is of the other general principle that
whatever God has revealed is true."[25]

This being so, Norris gave a double reply to the original
question. If someone knew with absolute certainty that a particular
doctrine was revealed by God, the truth of the doctrine in question
was as certain for that man as any truth known by reason. But this
was not normally the case: in all normal cases, faith had only a
moral certainty. "So then," Norris concluded, "faith can never
exceed the certainty of science, but may very well come short of
it, and ordinarily does so, as having only a moral certainty, and
that because one of the grounds on which it rests ordinarily has no
greater."[26] If the evidence for faith were strictly compelling, he
added, it would be impossible to account for the prevalence of un-
belief. Norris recognised that his conclusion that faith normally
had no more than a moral certainty might offend some zealous partisans of faith, but he insisted that moral certainty was "sufficient

227

for all the purposes of Christian life, to persuade a man to re-
nounce the present world for the glories of the next, and to make
it such a faith as shall work by love. And", he added, "they do
no real service to the interest of religion, but rather expose it to
the ridicule of the more philosophic libertines, who go to strain
the matter any higher."[27]

In order to see Norris's teaching on the relative certainties
of faith and reason in perspective, it must be remembered that he
considered that the whole of natural religion was known by reason.
The existence of God, man's dependence on him, and the obligations of the Natural Law were thus known with strict or metaphysical certainty. And on the other hand the moral certainty of faith
was the same type of certainty as that on which most of the ordinary
activities of life were based, the same type of certainty as that of
any historical fact, and indeed of all contingent knowledge. Norris's
analysis of faith and reason fitted in precisely with his conception
of contingent and necessary truths. Certain articles of faith, such
as the doctrine of the Trinity, were indeed in themselves necessary truths, but being in Norris's sense above reason they were
known only through revelation, and revelation was contingent.

Norris's teaching on reason and faith was thus in full accordance with his whole theory of knowledge. But it did not necessarily depend on it, and writers such as Waterland, Croft, and
van Mildert, who rejected Norris's metaphysics, praised An Account of Reason and Faith.[28] In this they were surely right. And
although the development of biblical criticism since then has added
a further dimension to the discussion, the problems which Norris
considered remain even today of fundamental importance. In any
discussion of the logical status of Christian belief and of the rôle
of reason in religion, Norris's examination of the distinction be-

tween the concepts of what is contrary to reason and what is above reason, his analysis of faith and of the rôle of reason in religious belief, and his sober evaluation of the degree of certainty that attaches to faith, remain of permanent value.

CHAPTER IX   ESSENCE AND SUBSTANCE, AND THE IM-
MORTALITY OF THE SOUL

At the beginning of the Second Part of his Theory of the Ideal
or Intelligible World, Norris examined the question, raised largely
by Locke, of whether matter could think, and the related question
of the souls of animals. Norris's views on this subject were criticised by Anthony Collins in a letter to Locke, and especially by
Samuel Bold, a strong defender of Locke. Norris never replied
directly to Bold's Remarks on what Mr. Norris hath said in his
First Chapter of the Theory of the Ideal World, Part 2, to demonstrate the Immortality of the Soul, though Mary Astell wrote in
defence of his teaching; but in 1708 he wrote A Philosophical Discourse concerning the Natural Immortality of the Soul in answer
to the views of the non-juror Henry Dodwell who held that the human soul was naturally mortal, but that the souls of those who had
had knowledge of the gospel were immortalised by God, either to
glory or to damnation. Dodwell replied to Norris's very courteous
criticism in A Letter to the Reverend Mr. John Norris of Bemerton,
which Norris answered with A Letter to Mr. Dodwell concerning the
Immortality of the Soul of Man (1709), in which his views on the
spirituality of the soul received their final and clearest expression.
The difference between Norris and his adversaries lay fundamentally in their different conceptions of substance. In this chapter we
shall examine successively Norris's theory of substance and of our
knowledge of it as illustrated by our knowledge of the soul and the
body, his views on the souls of animals, and his teaching on the
immortality of the human soul.

Norris began the Second Part of his Theory with a "Prelimin-

230

ary Consideration concerning the Principle of Thought, or what it is that thinks in us. With a full Discussion of that great Question, Whether Matter can Think?"[1] At the outset he declared that "though the understanding seems to promise a discovery of itself by its own light, yet it has a dark side to us-ward, and that which perceives all other things cannot so easily perceive itself."[2] Norris held that the soul did not have a direct view of its own essence or Idea, but only a conscious sentiment of its being and of its operations. In taking this view Norris followed Malebranche, but the resultant theory was not in fact very different from Locke's view which he had criticised, without fully understanding it, in his Cursory Reflections.[3]

If the soul has no direct intuition of its own essence, the only means of discovering what it is that thinks in man will be to examine the nature of matter. Several authors, of whom Locke was the most important, had suggested that it was not impossible that matter might be given the power of thinking. Norris pointed out that, if thought could indeed be an attribute of matter, it would be impossible to prove that there was a soul separate from the body, still less that the soul was immaterial and naturally immortal. One might still believe in an immortality resulting from a positive decree of God, but one could not prove that the soul was not naturally corruptible and therefore mortal. However, he did not imagine that reflections of this sort could decide the issue of whether matter could think; they merely served to indicate the importance of the question at issue.

Since Norris held that man can know the nature or essence of things only by examining the ideas that he has of them, his examination of the nature of matter takes the form of a study of the idea of material being, which he identifies with extended being.

231

Can a being whose essence is to be extended think? Norris affirms that it is immediately apparent that the ideas of extension and thought are entirely distinct. Further, the ideas of extended being and thinking being are no less distinct. Does it not follow, then, he asks, that an extended being is not a thinking being, and that matter, therefore, cannot think? Norris held that such an argument, which was basically that of Descartes, was fundamentally valid, but that, in this summary form, it gave occasion to serious objections, so that it needed to be carefully examined. For though it was clear that extension was not thought, might not both extension and thought be inadequate conceptions, ideas abstracted from different aspects of one same substance or reality? Figure and motion, for example, he points out, are entirely distinct ideas, and yet the same substance can be both figured and movable. For the modes of a substance are really distinct from each other, but they are only formally distinct from the being whose modes they are. Before one can be sure, therefore, that the same substance cannot be both extended and thinking, one must first be sure that extension and thought are adequately distinct ideas representing different essences, and not merely ideas of modes obtained by abstraction from the same reality.

Norris undoubtedly saw this difficulty very clearly, and he admitted that "'tis sometimes pretty hard to know whether our ideas are complete or incomplete, abstract or entire, and consequently whether things are really distinct or indistinct from one another, by the formal conceptions which we have of them."[4] Nevertheless he considered that though it was difficult it was not impossible to distinguish ideas of modes from those of substances. In the example already given, for instance, while one can think of a figured substance without thinking of a movable substance, one cannot conceive

232

a figured substance existing without a movable substance also existing, since figure and the possibility of motion are both modes or aspects abstracted from extended being. Accordingly Norris formulates the general principle that, while the mere distinction of two ideas does not of itself prove the distinction of the realities they represent, nevertheless, where one can clearly and distinctly conceive one thing existing without another, there the ideas involved are complete and adequately distinct, and accordingly represent distinct substances. Norris's solution to this problem agreed in essence with that formulated by Descartes and Malebranche, but Norris discussed the question with particular thoroughness.

Applying this rule to the ideas of extended being and thinking being, Norris declares that it is evident that one can conceive the existence of a thinking being while supposing that no extended being exists, since one knows one's own existence as a conscious being even while one doubts the real existence of material things. Accordingly the ideas of a thinking being and a material or extended being are entirely distinct, and so must be the beings which they represent. An extended being, therefore, cannot think.

As has been seen, Norris had taken from Malebranche the principle that we have no clear idea of the essence of the soul. It was for this reason that he proved the real distinction of the soul from the body by the roundabout means of examining the essence of matter as extended being. But there was something artificial about Norris's adoption of this principle, since all his writings show that he in fact felt more confident in his knowledge of spiritual than of material reality. Accordingly it is interesting to see that, in his last work of this subject, A Letter to Mr. Dodwell concerning the Immortality of the Soul of Man, he suggested a more direct means of knowing the essence of the soul, and hence its dis-

tinction from the body. Starting from the cogito he suggests that
perhaps this proves not only that we are, but also what we are.
"I can separate all things from me but thought, and yet find that
I remain in being. But that I cannot separate from me; and if I do,
I presently lose myself and am no more. But then from the absolute inseparability of thought, and its necessity and sufficiency to
my existence, it seems again to follow that this is that wherein my es
sence does consist .... Then 'tis plain that a thinking being is an
idea by itself, and consequently has nothing to do with extension
or body as to any ideal or essential communication, however it may
by the divine power be otherwise vitally united to her, as we find
in fact it is. But that's nothing to their real distinction."[5] In this
reflection Norris followed Descartes rather than Malebranche. It
would be wrong to emphasis this late development of Norris's
thought, since he himself proposed it only as a suggestion; but it
must be admitted that this argument seems more in keeping with
his fundamental turn of mind than does Malebranche's line of reasoning which he generally followed.

Throughout his discussion of this subject, as has been seen,
Norris presumed that our knowledge of ideas was a knowledge of
real essences. It was for this reason that he could argue from a
distinction of ideas to a parallel distinction in the things which they
represented. In the Second Part of his Theory of the Ideal ... World
he pointed out the connection of this principle with his theory of know
ledge as a whole. "The real distinction of ideas argues the like distinction in the things, because indeed ... it is the ground of it.
Things were made according to their Ideas, and therefore if the
Ideas are really distinct, 'tis impossible but that the things must
be so too. And hence it is that we can justly argue from the one to

234

the other, from the distinction of Ideas to the distinction of things, which yet would be no consequence if either there were no such Ideas, or if we did not see things by the same Ideas whereby they were made. For as for Ideas that are <u>modalities</u> of our own souls (as some are pleased to dream) I see no reason why any distinction in <u>them</u> should argue any distinction in things. For what connection is there between my being variously modified and made different from myself, and other things being really different from one another?"[6] As has been seen, Norris's theory of knowledge was based on his conviction that Ideas and truths are directly experienced as eternal and necessary, and impose themselves upon the mind as such. But he also held that his theory of knowledge alone provided a justification for assuming that things corresponded to our ideas of them, an assumption which in some degree was essential to all thought. In this reflection Norris followed Malebranche, who had made this same point in his <u>Conversations Chrétiennes.</u>[7]

As Norris pointed out, referring to Locke's <u>Reply to the ...</u> <u>Bishop of Worcester's Answer to his Second Letter</u>, Norris agreed that thought was not included in the essence of matter. But Locke then had recourse to the omnipotence of God, declaring that God could endow matter with the power of thinking although this power was not included in its essence. To this suggestion Norris replied "I have, I hope, a due reverence for the power of God, and would be as far from setting any undue limits to it as he can be. And yet I must needs say that to assign the power of God <u>instead</u> of a natural reason, or to fly to the power of God <u>against</u> clear reason, appear to me equally unphilosophical."[8] God, Norris continues, can endow matter with any perfection that is contained even by implication in its essence: he can endow it with motion, and even with

235

life insofar as this is a phenomenon of the physical or mechanical order. But if he adds to matter a perfection which is not even virtually contained in its essence, he changes the essence. God can add a thinking substance to an extended substance, but it will not then be matter that thinks. To say that matter thinks is to say that it is no longer matter.

The fundamental distinction between the views of Norris and Locke on this matter lay in their different conceptions of the nature of substance. Locke himself expressed his point of view in a letter to Anthony Collins which he wrote only seven months before his death. Collins had written to tell Locke of the passages in the Second Part of the Theory of the Ideal ... World which contained references to his views, and had criticised Norris's arguments on the subject of whether matter could think. In his reply Locke wrote: "Extension, and solidity, we have the ideas of; and see, that cogitation has no necessary connection with them, nor has any consequential result from them; and therefore is not a proper affection of extension, and solidity, nor doth naturally belong to them: but how doth it follow from hence, that it may not be made an affection of, or be annexed to that substance, which is vested with solidity, and extension? Of this substance we have no idea, that excludes cogitation, any more than solidity."[9] This comment reflected Locke's view of substance as the unknown substratum behind appearances; but Locke never replied publically to Norris's argument. His views were, however, expressed clearly by his faithful disciple Samuel Bold in an essay entitled Remarks on what Mr. Norris hath said in his First Chapter of the Theory of the Ideal World, Part 2, to demonstrate the Immateriality of the Soul, dated 7 September 1704 and published in the following year as an appendix to his Discourse concerning the Resurrection of the same Body.

236

Bold sums up Norris's argument under three headings: "First, that if matter be capable of thought, then the natural immortality of the soul cannot possibly be proved. Secondly, that the ideas of an extended being and of a thinking being are distinct ideas. Thirdly, that if God should superadd a power of thinking to matter, the species would thereby be changed, and so it would not be matter, but something else, that would think."[10] For several pages Bold writes as if Norris regarded the first of these points as a proof that matter could not think, but finally he admits that Norris did not regard it in this way. But Bold's essential argument is based on Locke's conception of substance as the unknown substratum or support of qualities. The experience of thought, he declares, proves that we are substances having the capacity of thought· but it does not at all resolve the question of what other properties our substance may possess. "We have no other idea of the substance of one thing than we have of the substance of another; nor can we regularly infer a diversity of substances from the diversity of things or the diversity of ideas we have of them."[11] In accordance with this view of substance, the affirmation that matter may be able to be endowed with the power of thinking means merely that a substance that has the property of being extended may also have the property of thinking; such a substance would be "matter" and "spirit" at the same time.[12] Locke's teaching, followed by Bold, is therefore not materialist; but it makes both thought and extension properties of a substance whose nature is unknown to us.

Norris never replied explicitly to Bold, but Mary Astell, in her book The Christian Religion as Professed by a Daughter of the Church of England replied amongst other things to those who denied the necessarily immaterial nature of thinking substance. Mary Astell did not add anything to Norris's doctrine, but she treated

the theory of thinking matter with a fine humour. Locke agreed,
she declared, that God could not change the essence of a thing
without destroying it, and yet he affirmed that it was not clear
that a merely material being could not think. He agreed that God
could not make a triangle the sum of whose angles did not equal
two right angles; but could God, she asked, make a triangle that
was capable of talking, walking, or dancing? "Let us see", she
wrote, "whether it be possible for Omnipotency to make a triangle
equal to a square, and that can eat and speak; since I should be as
glad to dine and to discourse with a triangle as Mr. L. would be to
get a demonstration of the soul's immateriality."[13] Mary Astell's
raillery did not, of course, touch the real meaning of Locke's
theory, since he held, not that a substance whose essence was to
be extended might be able to think, but that a substance which possessed the property of being extended might also possess the property of thinking. But in this case his affirmation that "mere material being"[14] might have the power of thinking was indeed a misleading one, since, as he himself admitted, such a substance would
be "spirit" as well as "matter". Mary Astell's humour aimed to
show that it was illegitimate, even on Locke's principles, to affirm
that "mere matter" could think. But she did not throw any light on
the fundamentally different conceptions of substance that divided
the view of Locke and Bold from that of Norris and herself.

It was not until 1709, in his Letter to Mr. Dodwell concerning the Immortality of the Soul of Man, that Norris explicitly formulated his conception of substance in a way which implicitly replied to Locke and Bold, and which at the same time showed precisely where the difference between his view and that of Locke on this
matter lay. "'Tis plain", Norris writes, "that the word substance
is not taken here a substando, but a subsistendo, and denotes only

238

such a being as is subsistent by itself, as that signifies independently upon any other as a subject."[15] Norris in fact took substance
for "real thing", an essence or real being existing in itself, as
distinct from a mere aspect of something, whereas Locke and his
followers took it for an unknown substratum of the properties of
things. Both these meanings had in some degree been present in
the Scholastic idea of substance, but they had now become dissoci-
ated. It is hard not to think that Norris's conception, which agreed
with that of Malebranche, was a more realistic one than Locke's.
Bold had accused Norris of basing his views on the immateriality of
the soul on pure speculation without any basis in experience, but in
fact it seems truer to say that it was he, following Locke, who in-
voked an entirely occult entity, a "substance" which could not be
known. Norris on the other hand held that careful examination of
an idea can show whether the idea in question is one of a thing, a
substance, or whether it is one of a mode, an aspect of a thing
separated by abstraction from the totality. In detail, of course,
Norris's doctrine of substance shared in the uncertainty which,
in the Second Part of his Theory, surrounded his understanding of
the Ideas or essences of particular material beings. But this element of uncertainty did not extend to the essence of matter or extended being as such; and Norris was convinced that our ideas of
"thinking being" and "extended being" were ideas, not of modes,
but of complete essences which were hence exemplified in really
distinct beings or substances.[16]

This clear teaching that all thought, including all consciousness, is derived from an immaterial soul, and that consciousness
is foreign to matter, necessarily raises the question of the nature
of animals. Whenever he had referred to this subject prior to writing his Theory of the Ideal ... World, Norris had followed the tra-

239

ditional Scholastic view which attributed a certain sense consciousness to animals while denying that they possessed reason or
self-consciousness. But when in the Second Part of his Theory he
had specifically examined the question of whether matter could
think, he recognised that he would have to choose between two
alternatives. Either animals were purely material beings, in
which case they had no consciousness at all, or else they had an
immaterial soul. Placed by Descartes before this same dilemma,
Henry More had preferred to affirm that animals had immortal
souls rather than to regard them as inanimate machines. Norris
on the other hand adopted the view of Descartes and Malebranche,
though only as the more probable solution of the question. He examined this question in the second chapter of the Second Part of his
Theory of the Ideal ... World.

In this chapter Norris first examines the theory according
to which animals have consciousness and hence are endowed with
immaterial souls. He agrees that this theory is logically coherent,
but declares that it raises serious difficulties and is supported only
by "the confuse appearances of sense."[17] Amongst the difficulties
attending this hypothesis Norris mentions those of determining the
upper limit of the type of thought or consciousness that is to be attributed to the beasts, and of the lower limit of the types of creature to whom an immaterial soul is to be conceded. Furthermore
it seems that, if animals have immaterial souls, these must be
immortal, but it is difficult to envisage what sort of immortality
would be suited to them. These and other difficulties would not be
sufficient, however, to disprove the theory if there were convincing
arguments on the other side. But in Norris's view there are not.
The only reason that makes us suppose that animals have the power
of sensation and consciousness is the fact that we observe them

240

acting in ways which, in human beings, are the expression of consciousness. It is by analogy with our own behaviour that we conclude that the actions of animals express conscious thoughts or feelings. But this analogy, Norris holds, is far from decisive.

Norris fully agrees that the actions of animals bear the mark of reason, but declares that it is not necessary to suppose that the reasonable principle from which their activity springs is intrinsic to them. The actions in question could be the effects of mechanical causes, if these were disposed and arranged by the wisdom and power of God. Norris takes the examples of watches and of the "grottos and fountains of great men's gardens"[18] to show that even man, with his limited knowledge of the laws of nature, can make machines which anyone who did not understand them would take for living things. If man can do such things as this, is it not clear, he asks, that God can produce all the effects of nature by mechanical means. And indeed, the extreme complication of animal bodies suggests that they are very perfect machines. This is particularly true, he declares, of the human body; and we find in fact that there are many movements in our bodies over which we have no control, while others, which are usually conscious reactions to sensation, are on occasion performed mechanically and unconsciously, and yet with complete perfection.

In Norris's view, however, the clearest example of what purely mechanical causes can do is found in plants. Almost everyone, he declares, admits that plants have no thought or consciousness, and yet "whoever shall attentively consider how a plant draws the juices of the earth to itself, works and elaborates those juices till it converts them into its own juice, then of that juice ... turns some into wood, some into leaves, some into blossoms, some into fruits, some into beautiful flowers, etc.",[19] cannot but admit that their activities are as wonderful as those of animals. Both plants and animals, then, show evidence of reason in their construction and their activities; but there is no more ground for thinking that this reason is intrinsic to animals than it is to plants. Norris points out that, if animals performed their actions as a result of conscious thought, if birds, for instance, built their nests or bees extracted honey from flowers as a result of thinking about these tasks, one would have to credit them with a high degree of intelligence; and yet, he argues, they show no signs of this intelligence in other contexts, and the fact that they always perform their activities in the same way strongly suggests that these actions do not spring from a principle of reason within the creatures themselves, but from instinct. And instinct, he declares, "can signify nothing intelligible but a certain specific contexture of parts, determining animals of the same kind to the like actions upon the like occasions".[20]

In Norris's view it follows from these considerations that the activities of animals can be explained without supposing that they have any power of thought. Their activities can be explained by a mechanical causality directed by God, and in many cases this is the only possible explanation of how they act. But the argument from animals' activities is the only one proposed by those who consider that animals can think. Accordingly Norris concludes that, bearing in mind the difficulties that are involved in the view that animals have immaterial souls, the Cartesian theory that animals are inanimate machines is much more probable than the rival hypothesis. He did not however consider that this view was altogether certain. Even Descartes had written that "Although I regard it as demonstrated that it cannot be proved that there is any thought in beasts, I do not for that reason think that it can be demonstrated that there

is none, because the human mind cannot penetrate their hearts."[21]
Norris did not consider it impossible that animals might be similar to human babies that never grew up, but he was convinced that
they did not think in such a way as could explain their activities.
He concluded his examination of this subject with a rather charming reflection on how animals ought to be treated:

"Though it is my opinion, or if you will my fancy, that reason
does most favour that side which denies all thought and perception to brutes, ... yet after all, lest in the resolution of so
abstruse a question our reason should happen to deceive us, as
'tis easy to err in the dark, I am so far from encouraging any
practices of cruelty upon the bodies of these creatures which
the Lord of the creation has (as to the moderate and necessary
use of them) subjected to our power, that on the contrary I would
have them used and treated with as much tenderness and pitiful
regard as if they had all that sense and perception which is commonly (though I think without sufficient reason) attributed to
them. Which equitable measure they that think they really have
that perception ought, in pursuance of their own principle, so
much the more <u>conscientiously</u> to observe."[22]

It will be remembered that the Cambride Platonists had objected against Descartes that a mechanistic explanation of nature
was favourable to materialism. If animals were regarded as purely
material, might not the same mechanistic explanation be extended
to man as well? Norris specifically envisaged this objection to his
own adoption of the Cartesian hypothesis, and replied that it was
entirely misconceived. He pointed out that the Cartesian theory was
based on the principle that matter was incapable of thought. Man
however knew himself by immediate experience to be a thinking being, so that on this view it was impossible to regard him as merely

material. On the contrary, Norris declared, it was the view which suggested that matter might be capable of consciousness and thought that opened the way to materialism by rendering any proof of man's spirituality impossible. There is no doubt that Norris was right on this point. It was not the Cartesian dualism but the denial of any clear distinction between matter and spirit that opened the way to materialism. The view that the reason manifested by animals is external to them furnishes a strong argument for the existence of a God, and Kemp Smith was doubtless right when he affirmed that it was the Cartesian view of matter which gave belief in God so firm a hold even on the most sceptically inclined minds of the eighteenth century.[23]

Having seen Norris's views on the nature of substance and the distinction of the soul from the body, and on the related question of the souls of animals, it remains for us to examine his teaching on the immortality of the human soul. In his earlier works Norris had always affirmed that the probability of immortality was known by reason, but that certainty on this point was derived from the Christian revelation. This view was expressed more particularly in his Discourse of Walking by Faith, in the fourth volume of his Practical Discourses. In the Second Part of his Theory of the Ideal ... World he pointed out the relevance of the question of whether matter could think to the problem of immortality. But it was not until 1708 that he examined this question in detail, and explained in what sense he regarded the soul as naturally immortal and in what respects he considered its immortality knowable or not knowable by reason.

The question of the nature and immortality of the human soul was very much under discussion in the early years of the eighteenth century, and was conducted largely with reference to Locke's sug-

244

gestion that matter might be capable of being endowed with the
power of thought. Locke himself did not question the immortality
of the soul, though he held that it was purely gratuitous and known
only by revelation; but his tentative suggestion that matter might
be capable of thought was taken up enthusiastically by explicit adversaries of immortality such as William Coward, to whom Norris referred in the Second Part of his Theory.[24] Norris's entry
into the controversy, however, was not occasioned by Coward or
by any direct adversary of immortality, but by the theory of Henry
Dodwell according to which the soul was naturally mortal, and the
souls of pagans, unbaptised infants, and idiots actually ceased to
exist at death, while the souls of those who had knowledge of the
gospel were immortalised by the "divine baptismal spirit" either
to glory or to damnation. Various authors, including Samuel
Clarke, replied to Dodwell, often with some acerbity. Norris's
Philosophical Discourse concerning the Natural Immortality of the
Soul, wherein the great Question of the Soul's Immortality is endeavoured to be rightly Stated and fully Cleared; Occasioned by
Mr. Dodwell's late Epistolary Discourse, on the other hand, was
in essence an attempt to clarify the issues involved in the controversy, and made only occasional references to Dodwell's particular theories. In this work Norris achieved a clear statement of
his own views on immortality, while entirely avoiding personal
attacks on Dodwell or other adversaries. He did not aim to prove
the immortality of the soul, which, he declared, could be shown
by philosophy to be probable, and which was taught categorically
by revelation. His aim was rather to explain in what sense the soul
could be described as naturally immortal, and he achieved this
limited aim with considerable success.

Norris begins his analysis by declaring that nothing exists

by nature except God; all creatures exist only because they are willed by God, and accordingly their existence is merely positive. Once a created thing exists, however, certain properties follow necessarily from its nature, and these properties are called natural in contrast to positive properties which do not flow from the essence of the thing but are joined to it merely by the agency of an external cause. To declare that immortality is a natural property of the human soul means, therefore, that it follows immediately from the essence of the soul once this has been posed in existence by God. But this raises a problem: if existence is always a positive gift of God, its continuance will also be merely positive; the activity by which God holds his creatures in existence depends, not on the natures of the creatures in question, but on the divine will. In what sense, then, can one speak of a natural immortality of the human soul? Is there any sense in which immortality follows from the nature of the soul, once this has been posed in existence by God?

In replying to this question, Norris distinguishes two senses of the word "immortality". "Immortal", he writes, "may signify either the same as <u>indissolvible</u>, in opposition to corruption, or else the same as <u>unperishable</u> . . ., in opposition to cessation of being. And the same in proportion is to be applied to <u>mortal</u>, by which may be understood either what may be dissolved or corrupted, or what may absolutely perish or cease to be."[25] In terms of this distinction, he continues, the soul is naturally immortal in the sense of being indissoluble or incorruptible, though it is not by nature imperishable since only God exists necessarily. The soul is "a simple, spiritual, and immaterial being";[26] accordingly, "incorruptibility necessarily and immediately follows from the very nature of the soul, and is as essential a property of it as that

246

its three angles be equal to two right ones is the property of a triangle."[27] Since the soul is a simple substance, not made up of parts, it is not conceivable that even the infinite power of God should be able to dissolve it. But though the soul is naturally incorruptible, it is not naturally imperishable, since the action by which God preserves creatures in existence does not differ from a continuous creation, and if he ceased this activity every created being would cease to exist.[28] God alone, then, Norris concludes, is naturally imperishable; but there is no reason to think that God will ever annihilate his creatures by withdrawing his creative power from them. Being by nature incorruptible, the soul is naturally immortal in the only sense in which a creature can be, and this fact is known by reason. By God's positive will it is also imperishable. This being so, Norris declares in one of his few references to Dodwell's book, it would be wrong to say that the soul is naturally mortal, since such a statement would entirely neglect the soul's incorruptibility. Norris's teaching on this subject follows in general that of the Scholastics, but he distinguishes more clearly between the two senses of immortality than they had usually done, so that his presentation is particularly clear.

Later in the same year, Dodwell replied to Norris in A Letter to the Reverend Mr. John Norris of Bemerton which, together with An Expostulation relating to the late Insults of Mr. Clark and Mr. Chishall, was published as an appendix to a book entitled An Explication of a Famous Passage in the Dialogue of St. Justin Martyr with Tryphon, concerning the Immortality of Human Souls ... In this Letter Dodwell thanks Norris for the courteous tone of his Philosophical Discourse, which he contrasts with the "insults" of Samuel Clarke and Edmund Chishall.[29] But the reasoning of Dodwell's Letter is confused, and adds little to the views that he had already expressed. He begins by saying that, if Norris admits that the soul could be reduced by God to nothingness, he has conceded the essential. If the soul can cease to exist, it does not matter whether its end comes by natural dissolution or by annihilation, and there is no reason why God should not annihilate the souls of unbaptised infants, idiots, and pagans. Nevertheless, however, Dodwell devotes the greater part of his Letter to the attempt to prove that the soul is in reality material, and hence corruptible. Man is a mere sublunary being, unless he is vivified by the "divine baptismal spirit" who is in reality the Holy Spirit, who gives immortality to those who receive him by faith, and an eternity of punishment to those who refuse him.

Norris replied to Dodwell's Letter in A Letter to Mr. Dodwell concerning the Immortality of the Soul of Man (1709), in which he dealt with two main subjects. In the first part of his Letter he set out to prove, against Dodwell, that it is not reasonable to think that God will annihilate any human souls; in the second part he aimed to prove the spirituality or immateriality of the soul, which he had simply presupposed in his Philosophical Discourse. Norris's teaching on this last subject has already been examined earlier in this chapter; it remains only to see his direct reply to Dodwell.

Norris began his Letter to Mr. Dodwell by recalling that philosophers as different as Aquinas and Malebranche agreed in holding that the annihilation of any creature would imply inconstancy and changeableness in God. Norris himself recognised the strength of their argument, but did not find it entirely convincing; strictly speaking, he considered, God could have willed, from all eternity, that a creature should exist for a certain time and then return to nothingness. However, if one remembered that all things were created in accordance with the divine Ideas and were therefore reflections or images of God, that they formed a world of order and beauty, and that they all glorified God, it was difficult to see why God should choose to annihilate any of them, let alone so considerable a part of his creation as the souls of all unbaptised infants, idiots, and pagans. Turning then from the general question of annihilation to Dodwell's specific hypothesis, Norris points out that this theory implies that the great majority of human beings do not have immortal souls, but are similar to the animals. And yet, he continues, the souls of pagans, amongst whom were all the great authors of antiquity, are in no way inferior to or different from those of Christians. Pagans are moral beings in the same way as Christians are, and many of them anticipated an immortality with rewards and punishments. Turning to the Bible, Norris points out further that St. Paul declares that pagans have the law written in their hearts, and makes no distinction between pagans and Jews in respect of God's judgement. Neither reason nor revelation, he concludes, authorises us to make any distinction between Christians, Jews, and pagans in the matter of immortality.

Norris points out further that we have no experience at all of annihilation. In our experience no simple substance ceases to exist. Material things are made up of parts which in due course fall apart, but the elements of which they consist do not disappear, but are re-formed into other aggregates. According to Descartes the total amount of matter and motion in the universe always remains the same, and we have no reason to think that God will ever annihilate anything that he has made. It is for these reasons, Norris declares, that opponents of immortality have always concentrated their attacks on the notion that the soul is a simple spiritual substance and is therefore not capable of being dissolved into parts.

249

As has been seen, however, Norris held that, while the bare possibility of annihilation could not be excluded by natural reason,
though revelation removed all doubt on this score, the spirituality
of the soul, and therefore the impossibility of its natural dissolution, was known with certainty.

Norris's two works on the immortality of the soul do not
add greatly to our knowledge of his teaching as a whole. But they
show him, near the end of his life, as both a clear thinker and a
notably courteous controversialist. The nature of the soul, its
natural contact with God and direct responsibility to him, had
been amongst his foremost preoccupations since the beginning of
his literary career. His first philosophical publication was a translation of Hierocles upon the Golden Verses of the Pythagoreans,
and it is appropriate that his last speculative works should have
been devoted to the defence of the natural dignity of the human
soul against a theory that would restrict immortality to those who
had come into contact with Christianity. Norris's views on this
subject were not peculiar to himself, and they did not necessarily
depend on his philosophy as a whole, except to the extent that, as
has been seen, his doctrine of substance, which was essential to
his proof of the spirituality of the soul, was an essential part of
his theory of knowledge. But his teaching on immortality fits very
naturally into the whole pattern of his philosophy and shows him,
even in highly controversial matters, to have been a balanced and
careful thinker.

CHAPTER X   CONTROVERSIES WITH LOCKE AND WITH THE
QUAKERS

In the course of his life, Norris was involved in many controversies. Apart from his early attack on Calvinism, we have seen that he wrote against the Dissenters, against Toland and the Socinians, and against Dodwell on the immortality of the soul. We have seen too the controversies to which his theory of the love of God gave rise, and the differences that separated him from Locke on the subject of thinking matter and the related question of the nature of substance. But though Norris's writings on these subjects were in varying degrees controversial, they are of interest mainly as expositions of his views on the subjects in question. There remain however two controversies to be examined which add little to our knowledge of Norris's thought, but which are interesting precisely as controversies: the personal relations and mutual criticisms of Norris and Locke in the years 1690-3, and Norris's relations with the Quakers during the same period. These controversies will be examined in successive sections of this chapter.

1. Norris and Locke, 1690-3

It is clear that Norris and Locke were men of a very different stamp from one another. Not only were their philosophical ideas in many respects opposed, but so too were their political sympathies. Nevertheless they were personally acquainted with each other, through their common friendship with Lady Damaris Masham, daughter of Ralph Cudworth the Cambridge Platonist. It is difficult to imagine that they would ever have been close friends, but their relationship seems to have been one of mutual respect until a personal quarrel which had nothing to do with their ideas transformed them into direct adversaries and filled Locke, in particular, with bitterness towards Norris.

Norris's acquaintance with Lady Masham seems to have begun when she wrote to express her appreciation of some of his writings, and in 1688 he dedicated his Theory and Regulation of Love to her. Two years later Norris further dedicated his Reflections upon the Conduct of Human Life to Lady Masham. The preface and certain other passages of this book were the occasion of a certain misunderstanding between the two, since Norris seems to have thought that Lady Masham, who must have spoken of her failing sight, had become strictly blind, and wrote of her

"Madam, the affliction Your Ladyship is under for the loss of your sight is so great, and your complaints upon that occasion so just, that I can neither blame you for the one, nor excuse myself from pitying you for the other."[1] In fact, however, though Lady Masham's sight was poor, she was not blind, and did not like to be refered to as such. Locke later wrote of this incident to Molyneux: "She has, 'tis true, but weak eyes, which Mr. Norris, for reasons he knew best, was resolved to make blind ones. And having fitted his epistle to that supposition, could not be hindered from publishing it so; though my Lady, to prevent it, writ him word that she was not blind, and hoped she never should be."[2] But this letter was written over six years later, at a time when Locke had become very hostile to Norris, and it seems likely that Lady Masham's letter reached Norris too late for alterations to be made in the first edition. At all events, all these passages were altered in the second edition which appeared in the following year, a fact which Locke omits to mention, and all references to Lady

Masham's supposed blindness removed; and Norris and Lady Masham remained on friendly terms for a further two years.

When Locke's Essay concerning Human Understanding was published early in 1690, Norris's attention was very soon drawn to it by a friend whose identity is unknown, who asked him for his judgement on the new work. Norris was then preparing the first volume of his sermons (Christian Blessedness, or Discourses upon the Beatitudes of our Lord and Saviour Jesus Christ) for the press, and was thus able to add his Cursory Reflections upon a Book called, An Essay concerning Human Understanding as an appendix to this volume. Cursory Reflections was the first detailed criticism of Locke's Essay to be published, and it remains one of the most interesting, since Norris tried to discuss Locke's work on its own merits and not in terms of the effects that it might have on religious or ethical thought.

Norris ended his Reflections with a warm eulogy of Locke and his book, but in his actual criticism he mentioned only those passages or arguments which seemed to him to be open to objection. Some of his isolated criticisms were virtually unfounded, and seem to betray a certain lack of sympathy for the work he was examining. Thus he criticised Locke's remark, in Essay, Bk. I, Ch. I, no. I, that "the understanding, like the eye, whilst it makes us see and perceive all other things, takes no notice of itself", on the grounds that this principle would render the whole following work impossible, but he omitted to add the rest of Locke's phrase, ". . . and it requires art and pains to set it at a distance and make it its own object". In truth, Locke's view of reflection as a source of knowledge hardly differed from what Malebranche and Norris meant by the immediate consciousness of one's internal mental states, and Norris's objection was little more than a quibble. But

253

if some of Norris's objections were triftling, most were serious and important criticisms of Locke's argument.

The most important criticisms in Norris's Cursory Reflections were concerned with Locke's argument, in Book I of the Essay, against innate principles. Norris agreed with Locke in rejecting the existence of innate ideas, but he argued very cogently that Locke's arguments for rejecting them were not conclusive, and were furthermore incompatible with principles which Locke himself asserted in other parts of his work. Thus, Norris suggests, when Locke argues against innate principles on the ground that there are no principles to which mankind gives a universal consent, he implicitly denies the existence of self-evident propositions, which, however, he elsewhere admits; for are not self-evident propositions universally accepted? Locke, however, held that such propositions could not be regarded as universally accepted, since children and idiots had no knowledge whatever of them; and if anyone, even a child or an idiot, had no knowledge of these principles, then they could not be innate, since it was impossible for any idea to be imprinted on the mind without the mind being aware of it. Against this argument Norris replied that "If there may be impressions made on the mind, whereof we are not conscious, or which we do not perceive, then (by the Author's own measure) the not perception of them is no argument against such original impressions ... And now that there may be such impressions whereof we are not conscious is what the Author himself expressly does own, and what by his principles he stands obliged to own."[3]

As examples of Locke's admission that we can have ideas of which we are not conscious, Norris cites several passages in which Locke appears to concede that ideas can be impressed on us

254

by the objects round us without our being aware of them, and then goes on to argue from Locke's account of memory. While the other passages which he quotes from Locke do not seem to bear the meaning that he puts on them, Norris does succeed in showing that Locke's theory of the memory implies that ideas can be in the mind without our being conscious of them. For Locke, Norris declares, does not regard memory as "a recovery of ideas that were <u>lost</u>, but a re-advertency or re-application of mind to ideas that are actually there, though not attended to. <u>For</u>, says he, Pag. 65, Sect. 2, <u>the narrow mind of man not being capable of having many ideas under view and consideration at once</u>, it was necessary to have a repository to lay up those ideas which at another time it might have use of. And accordingly, Pag. 66, Sect. 7, he calls them <u>ideas which are lodged in the memory</u>. And Pag. 67, Sect. 8, he calls them <u>dormant ideas</u>. So that according to him to <u>remember</u> is to retrieve, not the ideas themselves (for they are supposed to lie <u>dormant</u> in the mind), but only the perception or consciousness of them."[4] In this case, Norris points out, the presence in the mind of ideas of which one is not conscious is not taken for contradictory or impossible; and accordingly, he argues, Locke is not in a position to take the absence of any perception of innate ideas in children or idiots as a proof that they have no such ideas, since he himself elsewhere admits that we can have ideas which we do not perceive. Locke tacitly admitted the validity of this criticism by amending his description of the memory in the second edition of the <u>Essay</u>, though his theory on this subject remained far from clear.

Against the existence of innate principles, Locke further argued from the late appearance in our minds of the truths, such as the principle of contradiction, that were usually taken for such:

255

if these principles were really innate, ought they not to be the first thoughts that came into the mind of a child, and ought they not to appear at their clearest in children, whose minds were not corrupted by a bad education and who were not able to conceal their true thoughts? To these arguments Norris replied that there was no reason why innate truths should necessarily be the first truths known: Locke himself admitted that the power of thinking did not enter into operation until a certain period of life; why then might not innate ideas have to wait for a certain passage of time, or other circumstances, to disclose themselves? "If nullity of perception will not conclude against innate principles, much less will the lateness of perception be able to do it."[5]

Norris's criticism of Locke's arguments against the existence of innate principles of morality followed very much the same lines as his criticism of his reasoning on innate speculative principles. Locke argued that there were no universally accepted moral principles, but Norris replied that he had already shown that the lack of consent of children and idiots was irrelevant; if however Locke denied that there were any principles of morality that were evident to everyone who thought about them, then not only was he mistaken but he contradicted what he himself elsewhere affirmed. For in Book 4 of the Essay Locke declared that morality could be placed amongst the sciences capable of demonstration, and wrote that "I doubt not but from principles as incontestable as those of the mathematics, by necessary consequences, the measures of right and wrong might be made out to anyone,"[6] who applied himself attentively and sincerely to consider them. Accordingly, Norris declares, Locke cannot consistently deny that there are self-evident principles of morality.

Locke further insisted that one could demand a reason for

256

every moral rule, but Norris replied that there was no reason why the same law should not be both innate and capable of being demonstrated, just as, in his view, the same proposition could be the object both of faith and of science. In the first edition of Considerations upon the Nature of Sin Norris had himself suggested that there were innate "rational tendencies or practical sentiments" which, however, did not exclude the possibility of the same rules being proved by reason, and though he no longer held this view he still considered that Locke's arguments were not sufficient to disprove it. To Locke's further suggestion that the fact that people could break moral laws without remorse proved that these laws could not be innate Norris replied that an innate law could be infringed as easily as a written law, since innateness would be nothing but a particular way of being known. It was by no means certain, Norris concluded, that one would be able to distinguish innate truths from those one learned some other way.

Norris's critique of Locke's argument against innate knowledge proves clearly, it seems, that Locke's reasoning is valid only against a naive and literal form of the theory, which would assert the presence in the mind from birth of explicit ideas and principles. In such a form the doctrine does not seem to have been held by any notable philosopher, and Norris showed successfully that Locke's argument was not valid against any more sophisticated form of the theory. It seems, however, that the exclusion of a naive theory of literal innateness was in fact Locke's principal object in the first book of his Essay. Locke regarded the more sophisticated theory of virtually innate ideas which, though already present, would be actualised only with experience, as an improper way of speaking, but he considered that only a theory of actual and literal innateness would be contrary to the design of his Essay.[7]

257

But though Norris denied that Locke's arguments against innate knowledge were conclusive, he fully agreed with him in rejecting the theory. "For my part, I do as little believe there are any such things as innate principles strictly and properly so called, meaning by them certain original characters written upon or interwoven with the mind in the very first moment of its being and constitution, I say I do as little believe this as the Author himself. Not for the reasons by him alleged, with the cogency of which I am not satisfied; but because I do not allow any such things as mental impressions or characters written upon the mind, which if it pretend to anything more than figure and metaphor I take to be mere jargon and unintelligible cant."[8] Norris himself, of course, explained human knowledge by the presence to the mind of the Intelligible World, and the nearest approach to a theory of innate knowledge which he accepted was to suppose "that God may and does exhibit some particular truths of the Ideal World more early, more clearly, and more constantly to the view of the soul than others, that by these she may be the better directed to the good of the reasonable life, as animals by sensitive instincts and inclinations are to the good of sense."[9] In Norris's developed thought this view took the place of the theory that he had once held of innate rational tendencies.

Apart from his criticism of Locke's argument against innate ideas and principles, Norris's other criticisms were mostly concerned with Locke's teaching, in Book 2 of the Essay, on the source and origin of ideas. But first he objected that Locke had not defined the nature of the ideas whose origin he was seeking. Norris knew that Locke described what he meant by saying that "Whatsoever the mind perceives in itself, or is the immediate object of perception, that I call idea",[10] a definition which was very

similar to that given by Malebranche at the beginning of his enquiry into the source and nature of ideas,[11] but this did not satisfy him. "Very good; so much my lexicon would have told me. But
this does not satisfy. I would know what kind of things he makes
these ideas to be as to their <u>essence</u> or <u>nature</u>."[12] Norris wanted
to know whether Locke regarded ideas as real beings, and, if so,
whether he thought of them as substances or as modifications of
substances. Norris was in fact convinced that Locke must regard
ideas as substances, and he then proceeded to ask whether they
were spiritual or material substances. If they derived from material things, he argued, they must be material; but Malebranche
had disproved the possibility of things being known through corporeal effluvia. Further, material effluvia could never represent
immaterial objects such as "truth" and "virtue", or geometrical
concepts such as a right line or a perfect circle, which were not
found in their perfection in nature. If however Locke admitted that
ideas were, as Norris himself thought, spiritual substances, then
they could not be derived from material objects.

Norris further argued that it was an impossible undertaking
to try to derive the idea of God from sensation. God "must be his
own idea, or he can have none."[13] The only possible idea of God
was the divine <u>Logos</u> or Ideal World, which could represent both
God and all possible creatures. Norris ended this part of his
criticism by inviting Locke to consider whether he could not have
avoided all his difficulties by adopting the theory that the divine
Ideas were the immediate objects of our knowledge. For a further
explanation of this theory, however, he referred his readers to
<u>Reason and Religion</u> and to his forthcoming <u>Theory of the Ideal
World</u>.[14]

Norris's criticism of Locke's views on sensation as the

259

source of our ideas is clearly of much less value than his criticism of his arguments against innate knowledge. Indeed Norris himself later modified it considerably in the Second Part of his Theory
of the Ideal ... World. It will be as well, however, to leave the
further consideration of it until we have examined Le Clerc's review of Cursory Reflections and Norris's reply to this review.
Apart from these two major topics, the rest of Norris's Cursory
Reflections consisted merely of criticisms of isolated points of
Locke's Essay. The most important of these concerned Locke's
teaching on the knowledge of essences and of truths. According to
Locke, the immutability of essences derives from the fact that we
have decided to employ a certain term to designate a certain idea
or collection of ideas; the "essences" that we know are creations
of our own understanding. Norris accepted Locke's analysis so far
as nominal essences were concerned, but insisted that "there are
also determinate essences in the things themselves, though for the
most (part) to us unknown, which have a fixed and immutable nature
without any dependence on any understanding but the divine."[15]
This distinction between nominal and real essences would have been
a help to Norris in answering the question of whether or not we
know the ideas of particular species and objects; but, as has been
seen, he did not make as much use of it in the Second Part of his
Theory of the Ideal ... World as he might have done.

Again, Locke took truth as "nothing but the joining or separating of signs, as the things signified do agree or disagree one
with another."[16] Norris accepted this as a description of "truth
of the mind or of the subject," but not of "truth of the thing or of
the object, which consists not in the mind's joining or separating
either signs or ideas, but in the essential habitudes that are between the ideas themselves."[17] Locke's words implied, Norris

suggested, that there was indeed such an agreement or disagreement between ideas or things antecedent to our thinking about them,
but Norris expressed his surprise that Locke's discussion of truth
should be confined to the truth of words and thoughts, and not extend to the more fundamental question of objective truth.

This same reflection led Norris further to criticise Locke's
conception of eternal truths. Locke affirmed that truths were called
eternal only because "wheresoever we can suppose such a creature
as man is, enabled with such faculties ... , we must conclude he
must needs when he applies his thoughts to the consideration of his
ideas, know the truth of certain propositions."[18] This, Norris
declared, was the ordinary Aristotelian account of eternal truths;
but it was inadequate because it failed to explain how these propositions were true even before man came to exist or think of them.
Truths were discovered, not made, by man. "But if they were in
being before the existence of man, then their eternity does not consist in their being understood by man whenever he shall exist, but
in their own fixed and immutable relations, whereby they have an
antecedent aptness to be understood."[19] This different conception
of the eternity of truth is of course linked with Norris's insistence
on objective truth as against subjective truth, the human understanding of truth. The ideas which Norris expressed in these criticisms were those which lay at the root of his Metaphysical Essay.

Despite these criticisms, Norris concluded his Cursory Reflections with an encomium on Locke's book. "Notwithstanding
these few erratas, I think (this) to be a very extraordinary performance, and worthy of the most public honour and respect. And
though I do not approve of every particular thing in this book, yet
I must say that the Author is just such a kind of writer as I like,
one that has thought much and well, and who freely writes what he

261

thinks ... This gentleman is a writer ... whose character I cannot easily give, but must leave it either to the description of some finer pen, or to the silent admiration of posterity. Only one feature of his disposition I am concerned to point out, which is that he seems to be a person of so great ingenuity and candour, and of a spirit so truly philosophical, that I have thence great and fair inducements to believe that he will not be offended with that freedom I have used in these Reflections, which were not intended for the lessening of his fame, but solely for the promoting of truth and right thinking ... After all, notwithstanding my dissenting from this Author in so many things, I am perhaps as great an admirer of him as any of his most sworn followers, and would not part with his book for half a Vatican. But every writer has his alloy, and I exempt not any writings of my own from the like defects ...."[20]

Norris's eulogy of Locke seems to have been perfectly sincere; but he later discovered that his hope that Locke would not be offended by his criticisms was misplaced.

In spite of Norris's praise for Locke, one can hardly help feeling that Locke must always have found some at least of Norris's criticisms irritating. Nevertheless, perhaps because of their common friendship with Lady Masham, Locke did not quarrel with Norris at the time, and did not himself publish any reply to Cursory Reflections. A reply from Locke's point of view was, however, written by Jean Le Clerc, whom Locke had got to know during his stay in Holland, and published in his Bibliothèque Choisie. Locke had spent the last two years of his exile with an English merchant at Rotterdam named Samuel Furly, and after his return to England he remained in close touch with his friends in Holland. On 1 November 1690 Le Clerc wrote to Locke to say that Furly had lent him a copy of Cursory Reflections and that he would review it unfavourably in the Bibliothèque Choisie.[21] The review in question appeared in the Bibliothèque Choisie for January 1691, where it occupied the pages 65 to 72.

At this time Norris was living at Newton St. Loe, and he does not seem to have known of this review. He saw, on the other hand, the English translation of it which appeared in the Athenian Gazette, a more popular literary journal published by the "Athenian Society" under the leadership of the littérateur and satirist John Dunton. Norris seems not to have realised that the reviews in the Athenian Gazette were translations from the Bibliothèque Choisie, even though this was stated in the English journal, and accordingly he always spoke of "the Gentlemen of the Athenian Society" as the authors of the review of his Reflections. He replied to this review with A Brief Consideration of the Remarks made upon the foregoing Reflections by the Gentlemen of the Athenian Society, in the Supplement to the Third Volume, etc, which he appended to the second edition of Cursory Reflections, in 1692.[22] Le Clerc's reply to Norris's Cursory Reflections and Norris's answer to Le Clerc can probably best be considered together.

Le Clerc introduced his critique by declaring that "Mr. Norris is a Cartesian, and as it seems of these of the Cartesians that are of Father Malebranche's opinion. This occasions that, being full of these thoughts, he seems not always to have well comprehended his meaning whom he criticises upon."[23] To this opening sally Norris replied that he did not see why his being a Cartesian and a follower of Malebranche should prevent him from understanding Locke's book, but that in any case it remained to be seen whether he had misunderstood it. In fact, many of Le Clerc's criticisms showed that he had not understood the point of Norris's arguments. Thus on three occasions Le Clerc argued as if Norris

263

held that the incontrovertible evidence of certain propositions proved that they were innate; but against this complete misapprehension of his argument Norris had no difficulty in showing that he had used the existence of evident truths, not as an argument in favour of innate ideas which he himself rejected as much as Locke did, but in order to show the insufficiency of Locke's arguments against innate knowledge.

There were two points, however, on which Le Clerc's criticisms of Norris were more to the point. Le Clerc objected that Norris's argument, inspired by Malebranche, to prove that our ideas were not effluvia or emanations from the bodies that we saw was, when directed against Locke, based on a misunderstanding; for Locke had never said that they were. When Locke affirmed that ideas were derived from the senses, Le Clerc declared, he meant only "that we could have no idea of diverse things, unless we had perceived them by means of the senses."[24] To this objection Norris replied that, if this were all that Locke meant, he himself could agree with him, since he too held that we could have no ideas of sensible objects without sensation. But it was clear, Norris continued, that Locke meant more than this; he meant "that our ideas do proceed from without, namely, from sensible objects, and are by our senses conveyed into the mind, according to the hypothesis of the vulgar philosophy."[25] On this point, modern commentators agree with Norris that Locke seems to have presupposed an Aristotelian type of explanation of sensation.[26] But Le Clerc was right in saying that Locke did not explicitly affirm this view, and that his interest in the Essay was simply to affirm that one could not have ideas of sensible objects without sensation. By the time he came to write the Second Part of his Theory of the Ideal ... World, Norris admitted that he was no longer certain that Locke in his

264

Essay had meant to affirm more than this, and in answer to a letter from Anthony Collins Locke himself agreed that no view which admitted the need of sensation was contrary to the design of the Essay.[27] Norris was probably right in thinking that Locke was inclined to accept the Aristotelian view of sensation; but Locke's aim in the Essay was not to examine the source and nature of ideas as such, but simply to investigate the source and limits of human knowledge.

But if on this point of Locke's doctrine on the source of ideas both Norris and Le Clerc were in a sense right, there was another point on which Le Clerc was certainly correct. In his Cursory Reflections Norris had affirmed that Locke held that our idea of God was derived from sensation, but Le Clerc rightly pointed out that this was not so, and that Locke in fact clearly derived it from reflection. To this objection Norris replied that "this is to set the idea of God but one remove further from the senses still, which will come to one and the same thing at long run. For these ideas of reflection are but a secondary sort of ideas that result from the various compositions and modifications of those primary ones of sensation. This is all that can possibly be understood by this second sort of ideas ... For 'tis not in the power of the soul to make any new ideas it has not received; she can only variously modify and compound those which she has."[28] The reflection of the mind on its own activities, Norris continues, cannot produce new ideas, since the understanding does not have the power to make its own objects; but even if it did have this power, it would be absurd to regard the idea of God as a creature of our own minds.

Norris's argument of course presupposes his own conception of ideas as substances, but it shows an entire misunderstanding of what Locke meant by ideas of reflection. In Locke's view

265

ideas of reflection were those which the mind formed by reflection on its own activities; the most important of these ideas were those of thinking and willing. It was from such simple ideas, joined to the idea of infinity, that Locke derived our complex idea of God. It is clear that Norris, who held that nothing created could represent God, could not have accepted this account of how our idea of him was formed, but one would nevertheless have expected him to show more understanding of what Locke meant by ideas of reflection. Not only was Locke's teaching on this subject in the Essay clear, but it agreed with what Malebranche and Norris himself understood as the soul's immediate consciousness of its own activities. It is true that Malebranche and Norris did not regard their conceptions of thinking and willing, and of the soul itself, as "ideas" in the strict sense, but they often spoke of them as ideas in a broader sense; and Locke of course always used the term "idea" in a broad sense. Locke and Norris held radically different views on the nature of our knowledge of God and on the nature of ideas, but their conceptions of our knowledge of our own conscious activities were very similar.

Le Clerc ended his review of Cursory Reflections by agreeing with Norris's closing encomium on Locke's Essay, which Norris in his reply repeated, declaring "that I both honour his person and admire his book, which, bating only some few things, I think to be one of the most exquisite pieces of speculation that is extant. And that were I in order to notional improvement to commend but three books only in the world, one of them should be this of Mr. Locke's."[29] Le Clerc's review of Cursory Reflections, which Norris attributed to the Athenian Society, was in its whole tone hostile to Norris personally, and it showed a serious misunderstanding of Norris's arguments on several points, especially re-

266

garding innate ideas; but it had the merit of drawing attention to the restricted sense in which Locke in the Essay upheld the sensible origin of our ideas, and of showing that Norris had misunderstood Locke's theory of ideas of reflection.[30]

Whatever Locke may have thought privately about Norris's criticism of his Essay, he remained at this time on outwardly good terms with Norris, and early in 1692 did him a considerable favour. In that year, it will be remembered, Norris moved from Newton St. Loe to the richer benefice of Bemerton, which was in the gift of the Earl of Pembroke. At the moment of being presented to this living Norris did not know that he owed his preferment to Locke's intervention with the Earl, but as soon as he learned of this fact he wrote a letter to Locke in which he expressed his surprise and gratitude. "Sir, I have a very grateful sense of your great generosity towards me, which indeed is of so rare and singular a nature that it surprises me no less than it obliges me, and raises my wonder to as high a pitch as it does my gratitude..."[31] Locke did indeed show real generosity in recommending the critic of his Essay to the Earl of Pembroke. In his reply he wrote of the pleasure he found in doing a service to a worthy man, and spoke of Norris as a man of reason and thought, probity and virtue, for whom he had a great esteem; and he added that Lady Masham too had wanted to find a better station for him.

But this good relationship did not last. In the autumn of 1692 an incident occurred which ended any friendship that there may have been between Norris and Locke and also, it seems, between Norris and Lady Masham. The exact details of what happened are unclear, as not all the correspondence involved has survived, and on some points the evidence is conflicting. What seems to have happened, however, is this: Norris and his wife had been staying with the Mashams at Oates, and when they left for London on the way to Bemerton Lady Masham gave Norris a letter to be delivered to Locke who was then in London. Norris travelled to London on the Friday or Saturday, and intended to give the latter to Locke in person on the following Monday. However, being asked to visit the Bishop of Bath and Wells on the Monday, and intending to leave for Bemerton on the Wednesday, he gave the letter to his and Locke's common publisher, Samuel Manship, who promised to deliver it next day. However, the letter was not delivered to Robert Pawling's house, where Locke had been staying, until the Thursday (20 October), by which time Locke had left; and the seal of the letter was cracked or broken. Pawling, who seems already to have disliked Norris, immediately concluded that Norris had opened and read the letter, and conveyed this impression to Locke. Locke wrote to Norris a letter which has not survived but was evidently indignant; but he probably confined himself to asking why the letter was not delivered at the proper time, without mentioning the broken seal, for Norris seems never to have been aware that he was accused of anything more than remissness in delivering the letter, and consequently did not understand why Locke's resentment was so fierce. Norris replied to Locke's letter that "I am sorry to see a person of your real sense and seeming civility make such haste to express a resentment upon so doubtful an occasion", and protested that "you might have thought me worthy of a more favourable construction, and not look upon yourself as affronted by me before you knew what I had to say for myself."[32] He explained the circumstances that had led him to entrust the letter to Manship, and that he thought he had taken adequate care to ensure its prompt delivery. Locke replied, in terms which betrayed considerable irritation, that he would accept Norris's apology if

268

the letter could assure him that he did indeed leave London on the Wednesday in question. In his final reply Norris freely admitted that he did not leave London till the Friday, but pointed out that, at the time when he gave the letter to Manship, he had intended to leave on the Wednesday; when his departure was postponed he did not think it necessary to retrieve the letter and deliver it in person, because he supposed that it had already been delivered. "If this will satisfy you," he concluded, "well and good, but if not, I have no more to say".[33] This unfortunate quarrel, in which Locke's friends in London seem to have added fuel to the fire of his resentment, left Norris with a feeling of injured innocence and Locke filled with a bitterness which is reflected in his subsequent writings about Norris.

The first of Locke's writings against Norris was JL Answer to Mr. Norris's Reflections 92, a manuscript which remained unpublished until 1971 when it was printed in The Locke Newsletter and which may never have been intended for publication. This short piece, the sarcastic tone of which contrasts sharply with the comparative politeness of Norris's criticisms, reflects Locke's extreme irritation with Norris at this time, but it stops short without attempting to answer Norris's serious criticisms of the Essay.[34] In the following year Locke composed two further replies to Norris, both of which were published posthumously. An Examination of P. Malebranche's Opinion of Seeing all Things in God[35] appeared in 1706 amongst the Posthumous Works of Mr. John Locke, while Remarks upon some of Mr. Norris's Books[36] was published in 1720 as part of Des Maiseaux's Collection of Several Pieces of Mr. John Locke. Remarks upon some of Mr. Norris's Books reproduced Locke's manuscript with only minor amendments, but the Examination of Malebranche, which was of course published while Norris

was still alive, omitted all the passages of the original manuscript which referred to Norris and which made it plain that the
work was intended primarily as a reply to him.

That this was the case was first pointed out by Charlotte
Johnston in 1958, in an article in the Journal of the History of
Ideas.[37] In its original form the Examination of Malebranche begins in the same sarcastic vein as JL Answer to Mr. Norris's Reflections 92. Locke quite unjustifiably accuses Norris of finding
fault with the deficiencies of the Essay "so hastily that by the
mistake of the sense and sometimes of the words of the Author
some have enquired whether the censure did not precede the perusal as others have thought it did the consideration of the treatise."[38]
He describes Norris as one of those who "with an air of infallibility
adopt what others have proposed and set themselves up for dictators
in the Commonwealth of Learning",[39] and says that "though this
pregnant author tells us .. that this is a notion which he very
early lighted upon by the natural parturiency of his own mind before he had consulted with any authors that might imbue him with
it, yet since P. Malebranche had the luck by being first in print
to rob him of the glory of this discovery, he will pardon me if I
have recourse for my information to him that is looked on as the
author of it ..."[40] Locke's sarcasm was most unfair to Norris,
who himself pointed out, immediately after the sentence quoted
by Locke, that his argument in Reason and Religion was borrowed
from Malebranche; but this passage shows beyond all doubt that
Locke's Examination of Malebranche was written as a riposte to
Norris's Cursory Reflections.

In the body of his Examination of Malebranche, Locke's main
criticism was directed against Malebranche's argument, in La
Recherche de la Vérité, Book III, Part II, in favour of "seeing all

things in God". Malebranche, it will be remembered, set out to prove his theory by the elimination of all alternative hypotheses, but Locke argued very cogently that such an argument was necessarily inconclusive since we could not know that our enumeration of the possibilities was complete. This was the strongest part of Locke's argument, since much of his more detailed criticism was vitiated by his failure to grasp what Malebranche meant, in particular, by "idea" and "sentiment" and the distinction between them. As has been seen, Norris's view that the ideas by which we knew were the divine Ideas was not in fact reached by this method of elimination, so that Locke's argument did not touch his fundamental position. But Norris laid himself open to this criticism by the prominence which he gave, in Reason and Religion, to Malebranche's argument.

Amongst Locke's more detailed criticisms there was, however, one of considerable interest. Against the occasionalist account of sensation that Malebranche and Norris present, Locke argues that, on their principles, one can never know that a material, external world exists at all. If we see nothing but God's Ideas, how can we know that it is on the occasion of the presence of bodily objects that God shows us these Ideas? Are not the supposed bodily objects, which can never be known directly, entirely superfluous? This objection, which also occured independently to Mary Astell,[41] anticipates the immaterialist position which was later taken up by Collier and Berkeley.[42]

Remarks upon some of Mr. Norris's Books is much shorter than the Examination of Malebranche, and was obviously much less fully prepared for publication. In manuscript it follows immediately after the other work, and is headed "Some other loose thoughts which I set down as they came in my way in a hasty perusal of

271

some of Mr. Norris's writings, to be better digested when I shall have leisure to make an end of this argument"; and in concludes with the words "The finishing of these hasty thoughts must be deferred to another season." In the Examination of Malebranche Locke had said that, after examining what Malebranche had to say on seeing all things in God, he intended "not to overlook what this gent tells us he has further done to establish it (the hypothesis) by other considerations of his own." [43] Remarks upon some of Mr. Norris's Books appears to be a first rough draft of this second part of Locke's examination of the theory of seeing all things in God.

Remarks upon some of Mr. Norris's Books is well described by Locke's original heading of "loose thoughts" on some passages of Norris's writings. It consists of comments from Locke's point of view on isolated points of Norris's argument rather than of a sustained critique of Norris's theory of knowledge. Locke did not really understand Norris's system, with which he had no sympathy, and his criticisms were in consequence superficial and in many cases did not deal with views that Norris really held. Thus Locke argued as if Norris's occasionalism led him to hold that the mind was "altogether passive in the whole business of thinking," [44] a view which Locke described as "the hypothesis that clears doubts, and brings us at last to the religion of Hobbes and Spinoza, by resolving all, even the thoughts and will of men, into an irresistible fatal necessity", [45] whereas in fact Norris's occasionalism was restricted to the field of sensation; Norris held that the mind was active in thinking, and he frequently emphasised the reality and importance of freedom. Locke's Remarks upon some of Mr. Norris's Books is of similar weight to the more superficial parts of Norris's Cursory Reflections on Locke's Essay; it does not ap-

proach the penetration of Norris's critique of Locke's argument
against innate knowledge. To this critique Locke never replied.

So far as is known there was no further personal contact
between Norris and either Locke or Lady Masham after the quarrel of 1692-3. As has been seen, Lady Masham later wrote against
Norris's views on the love of God,[46] while Norris in his Theory
of the Ideal ... World again examined Locke's views on the source
and origin of ideas, as well as considering his theory on the possibility of matter thinking. The different views of Norris and Locke
on this last point were rooted, we have seen, in different conceptions
of the nature of substance. These later controversies have been
examined in the context of the subjects with which they were concerned. The philosophies of Norris and Locke were of course radically different. But there seems little doubt that it was their personal quarrel that embittered Locke against Norris and led him to
wrote his three caustic replies to him, of which the Examination
of Malebranche alone can be said to contain valuable criticism.

2. Norris and the Quakers

It will be remembered that Voltaire, in the second of his
Letters concerning the English Nation (Lettres Philosophiques),
made a rapprochement between the teachings of the Quakers and
the philosophy of Malebranche. "Thou receivest thy ideas from
him who created thy soul", his Quaker interlocutor tells him;
"but as he leaves thy affections at full liberty, he gives thy mind
such ideas as thy affections may deserve; if thou livest in God,
thou actest, thou thinkest in God. After this thou needest only but
open thine eyes to that light which enlightens all mankind, and
'tis then thou wilt perceive the truth, and make others perceive
it. Why this, says I, is Malebranche's doctrine to a tittle. I am

acquainted with thy <u>Malebranche</u>, says he; he had something of
the <u>friend</u> in him, but was not enough so."[47]

Although this conversation between Voltaire and a Quaker
was an imaginary one, it had in fact good historical foundations,
for many people in England did see the philosophy of Malebranche
and Norris as a step towards Quaker beliefs. Thus on 9 May 1694
a certain Michael Geddes wrote from Salisbury (near Norris's
home at Bemerton) to Dr. Charlett, Master of University College,
Oxford, to tell him gossip about a quarrel between Norris and
Thomas Taylor, the translator of several of Malebranche's works.
Geddes informed Charlett that "I was told last week, that Mr. Norris has received a very angry letter from Mr. Taylor. But tho' I
am troubled that any difference should happen between two such
good men, yet I must own, that I shall not be sorry if the not publishing of Malebranch (sic) in English should be the consequence
of their disagreeing: for tho' I know little of his works myself, I
am strangely prejudiced against them, upon the account of the
misery the study of them has done to a merchant, a dear friend
of mine, whom, of the most sober, religious, conformable person that ever I knew in my life, they have made a brainsick
Quaker, who as he goes constantly to the Quakers meetings, so
he complains of nothing therein, but of their not being enthusiasts
enough, or to use his own phrase, of their not pretending to have
God enough in them."[48] The quarrel between Norris and Taylor
did not last long, for the work of translation was not interrupted,
and Taylor refered to Norris in glowing terms in the introduction
to his <u>Two Covenants of God with Mankind</u> (1704). [49] But Geddes's
letter is interesting as giving a concrete example of the Quaker
influence that Malebranche's philosophy could have on a reader
who was doubtless not a philosopher.

274

But if Malebranche's teaching was sometimes taken in a sense favourable to the Quakers, Norris himself had already noted elements of resemblance between the two doctrines. Thus in the first edition of Reflections upon the Conduct of Human Life (1690), when speaking of the Ideal World as present in the Logos to every human mind, Norris wrote that "This is reason, this is conscience, this is truth, this is that light within so darkly talked of by some who have, by their awkward, untoward, and unprincipled way of representing it, discredited one of the noblest theories in the world. But the thing in itself, rightly understood, is true; and if any shall yet call it quakerism or enthusiasm, I shall only make this reply at present, that 'tis such quakerism as makes a good part of St. John's gospel, and of St. Austin's works." [50] Norris did not know the Quakers only by hearsay, for his patron and neighbour at Newton St. Loe, Joseph Langton, was friendly with a learned Quaker named Richard Vickris, who lived not far off at Chew Magna. It was probably through Langton that the Quakers came to know Norris's writings, and that Norris learned that they regarded him as an adept of their ideas. Vickris recommended Langton to get Norris to read Robert Barclay's Apology for the True Christian Divinity. Norris read this work and came to have a great respect for it. But he saw very clearly the differences between his own views and those of the Quakers, and in order to make these clear he added a post-script to the second edition of Reflections upon the Conduct of Human Life in 1691. Even after the controversy which followed, this postscript remained the best summary of the differences between the two theories, and it is accordingly here reproduced in full.

"Being informed that the Quakers took great hold of the former
   edition of this book, giving out that it made for their way, I

think it convenient in a few words to undeceive them, lest they should reckon upon more proselytes than they have. I suppose, if the Quakers understood their own notion, and knew how to explain it, and into what principles to resolve it, it would not very much differ from mine. But as they usually represent it, the difference I conceive to be very great; and he that thinks I symbolise with the Quakers in my notion of the divine light understands neither me nor them, as may appear by these following instances of difference.

I. The Quakers usually talk of this Light within as of some divine <u>communication</u> or <u>manifestation</u> only, whereas I make it to be the very <u>essence</u> and <u>substance</u> of the deity, which I suppose virtually to contain all things in it, and to be intimately united to our minds.

II. The Quakers represent this Light within as a sort of <u>extraordinary inspiration</u> (whence they have the name of <u>enthusiasts</u>), whereas I suppose it to be a man's <u>natural</u> and <u>ordinary</u> way of understanding.

III. The Quakers (if I mistake not) confine their Light within to some certain objects, namely moral and spiritual truths, in order only to the direction of practice, and accordingly make it a supplement to <u>Scripture</u>, which they say is not <u>sufficient</u> without it, nor indeed any more than a mere <u>dead letter</u>. But now I do not appropriate this divine Light to moral or spiritual things, but extend it as far as all truth; yea, as far as all that is intelligible, which I suppose to be perceived and understood in this divine Light, as I have explained it.

IV. The Quakers make their Light within a special privilege of a certain order of men, their own party. Not indeed as to the <u>possibility</u>, because they suppose all men to be indifferently capable of this divine illumination, as may appear from their con-

276

tending against predestination and for universal grace. But
though they do not make it a special privilege as to the possibility, yet they do as to the act, making none but those of their
own way to be actually enlightened by it. Whereas according
to my principles this is no special privilege, but the common
and universal benefit of all men, yea of all the intelligent
creation, who all see and understand in this Light of God, without which there would be neither truth nor understanding.

V. The Quakers by their Light within understand some determinate, formed dictate or proposition, expressly and positively directing them to do so or so; whereas my Light is only
the essential truth of God, which indeed is always present to
my understanding, as being intimately united with it, but does
nor formally enlighten or instruct me but when I carefully attend to it and consult it, and read what is written in those divine ideal characters.

VI. And lastly, the Quakers do not offer any rational or
intelligible account of their Light within, neither as to the
thing nor as to the mode of it, but only cant in some loose general expressions about the Light, which they confirm with
the authority of St. John's gospel, though they understand neither
one nor t'other. Whereas I have offered a natural, distinct,
and philosophical way of explaining both, namely by the omniformity of the Ideal World or the divine Logos, who has in himself the essences and ideas of all things, and in whom the same
are perceived by us and all creatures."[51]

This post-script gave a very accurate summary of the points which
divided Norris's views from those of the Quakers. And considering
the disdain in which the Quakers were then generally held, it was
also written in a courteous tone; only the sixth article could pos-

sibly be regarded as hurtful. But this careful accuracy and politeness on Norris's part did not prevent Vickris from replying to
the post-script with an attack the language of which was so violent
as to be almost comic, at least for the modern reader. Vickris's
reply, entitled A Just Reprehension to John Norris of Newton St.
Loe for his Unjust Reflection on the Quakers, in his Book entitled,
Reflections upon the Conduct of Human Life, etc., was published
at the beginning of 1692. Later in the same year, Norris replied
with Two Treatises concerning the Divine Light, the first of which
was headed An Answer to a Letter of a Learned Quaker, which he
is pleased to call, A Just Reprehension ..., while the second was
entitled A Discourse concerning the Grossness of the Quaker's
Notion of the Light Within, with their Confusion and Inconsistency
in Explaining it. In the first of these, after replying to the personal insults of Vickris, Norris examined in detail his objections
to the first five articles of his post-script; the second of the Two
Treatises was devoted to the defence of the more general criticisms
that he had made in the sixth article of the post-script.

Vickris began his Just Reprehension by accusing Norris of
"decking thyself with thy corrupt wisdom", and by adjuring him
in quasi-biblical terms: "Canst thou by searching find out God, or
the Almighty unto perfection? I tell thee nay, but God will confound
thy wisdom, and bring to nought thy understanding, wherein it is
exalted; for he hath determined to stain the pride of all flesh, the
mouth of the Lord hath spoken it."[52] This violence of language
led Norris to ask whether this was an example of Quaker meek-
ness, and to suggest that, in Vickris's case, "the light within is
turned into a flame."[53] Reasoning, Norris declared, should be
carried on calmly and coolly, and the sincere search for truth
ought not to be denounced as "carnal reason", "corrupt wisdom",

or "vain philosophy". But if Norris complained with good reason of Vickris's lack of charity, he was far from despising the doctrine of the Quakers as such. Indeed his Two Treatises show a great respect for them, and in particular for Robert Barclay.

"That great and general contempt they lie under does not hinder me from thinking the sect of the Quakers to be by far the most considerable of any that divide from us, in case the Quakerism that is generally held be the same with that which Mr. Barclay has delivered to the world for such; whom I take to be so great a man that I confess to you freely, I had rather engage against an hundred Bellarmines, Hardings, or Stapyltons, than with one Barclay."[54]

In Two Treatises concerning the Divine Light Norris showed himself a conspicuously fair adversary. In the Answer to a Letter of a Learned Quaker he reproduced each time the article of his postscript with the full text of Vickris's objection to it, and in both Treatises he backed up his statements of Quaker doctrine with full quotations from Barclay and Keith. The fairness of this way of proceeding was specifically commented on by another of his Quaker adversaries, George Whitehead.

From the Two Treatises there emerge, apart from a number of minor divergences, two essential differences between Norris's teaching and that of the Quakers. First of all, the Quakers regarded the source of man's illumination as "not the Godhead itself, but a certain middle nature, substance, or being, betwixt the Godhead and mankind."[55] Their conception was described by Barclay as follows:

"By this Seed, Grace, and Word of God, and Light, wherewith we say every man is enlightened, and hath a measure of it..., we understand not the proper essence and nature of God, precisely taken, which is not divisible into parts and measures, as being a most pure, simple being; ... But we understand a spiritual, heavenly, and invisible Principle, in which God as Father, Son, and Spirit dwells; a measure of which divine and glorious life is in all men, as a seed which of its own nature draws, invites, and inclines to God; and this we call Vehiculum Dei, or the Spiritual Body of Christ, the flesh and blood of Christ which came down from heaven, of which all the saints do feed and are thereby nourished unto eternal life."[56]

The details of this "middle nature" are not clear in the Quaker writings. Sometimes it is represented as a sort of divine body, vehiculum Dei; often it is seen as an eternal body belonging to the Logos; sometimes it is the "lucid body" or "vehicle" of the human soul of Jesus Christ, existing before his incarnation in a terrestrial body. These different conceptions were not clearly distinguished either by the Quakers or by Henry More, who proposed a virtually identical theory in his Brief Discourse of the Real Presence of the Body and Blood of Christ in the Celebration of the Holy Eucharist.[57] Norris did not deny the possibility that such a "body of Christ" might exist; but he insisted that, even if such a "middle nature" did exist (which he neither affirmed nor denied), it could not be the source of man's illumination. Since the Quaker Vehiculum Dei was not God, it must in Norris's view be a creature; since it could be divided up, with a portion assigned to every human being, it must in his view be material. And no creature, Norris held, least of all a material one, could be the source of man's intellectual light, which involved contact with necessary and eternal Ideas which could only be in God himself. The Quaker writers and Henry More do not in fact seem to have regarded their "middle nature" as material in the ordinary sense, and they seem to have

280

thought of it as a necessary emanation of God rather than as a creature. Norris's clear dichotomies between "spiritual" and "material", between "creator" and "creature", were foreign to their thought, which on this point seems to have been influenced by theosophical conceptions. But Norris was right in identifying one essential divergence between his theory and that of the Quakers in the fact that the Quakers regarded the source of man's "inner light" as a being intermediate between God and man, whereas he held that it could be nothing less than God himself.

But if this was one essential difference between Norris's theory and that of the Quakers, the other was even more fundamental. The Quaker doctrine of the "light within" was concerned exclusively with spiritual inspiration, whereas Norris's theory was concerned with man's ordinary mode of knowledge. The Quaker doctrine was a purely religious one; they did not regard the "inner light" as the source of secular knowledge. But Norris's theory was a philosophical explanation of man's ordinary way of knowing. As he pointed out, Norris did not confuse man's knowledge of truth with the truth that he knew; he did not confuse man's mind with the mind of God. But he held that it was in God, the Ideal World, that all men saw whatever Ideas and truths they knew. And although they perceived these Ideas and truths only to the extent that they turned towards or consulted the Ideal World, yet all men did in fact consult it at least to a sufficient extent to constitute them rational, thinking beings. All men were therefore illuminated to some degree by God, and all knowledge, however secular it might be, was in a sense a knowledge of God. The Quakers, on the other hand, regarded the "inner light" as the source of spiritual inspiration only, and explained ordinary knowledge without reference to it.

Norris's Two Treatises concerning the Divine Light expressed very clearly the essential differences between his theory of knowledge and the Quaker teaching. The publication of this work did not mark the end of the controversy, since it elicited several replies from the Quaker side, but Norris himself did not write any further on this subject. Vickris, whose Just Reprehension had led Norris to write his Two Treatises, replied to it with Truth and Innocency Defended,[58] in which he attacked Norris with the same violence as had characterised his earlier work. But it is not clear why he accused Norris of misunderstanding the Quaker doctrine when in fact his own exposition of this teaching served only to underline the divergences which separated it from Norris's theory. More constructive was another Quaker reply to Norris. The Divine Light of Christ in Man, and his Mediation, truly confessed by the People called Quakers, was the work of George Whitehead, a Quaker author of considerable importance.[59] In contrast to Vickris, Whitehead's work was moderate and courteous in tone. He rejoiced that Norris accepted the divine light in his own fashion, and praised his honesty in quoting so liberally from Quaker sources. On the questions in dispute he affirmed that, according to the Quakers, God was truly present in the "spiritual body of Christ"; in this sense one could say that God himself was man's light. But the Quakers in general were simple people, he declared, who did not reflect on these abstruse questions, but were content to regard Jesus Christ as the source of all their light. Whitehead was doubtless right in saying that most Quakers were not interested in the abstruse speculations of their theorists about a "middle nature" between God and man; but it was with the theories of the educated Quakers that Norris was concerned. Their theosophical conceptions, which were remarkably similar to those of Henry More, were characteristic of much renaissance

282

speculation, but were very different from the Cartesian clarity of Norris's thinking.

The third author who entered this controversy was not strictly speaking a Quaker. Edmund Elys was vicar of East Allington, Devon, from 1659 till 1689, when he was deprived of his living for refusing the oath of allegiance to William and Mary. [60] Although he was an ardent defender of the Quakers he never seems to have joined them, but his books were published by Quaker publishers. He refered to Norris in three booklets, two of which bear the date 1693; the third, which has no date, was probably published in the same year. The first of these, A Vindication of some Sentiments of Robert Barclay, was not written against Norris. On the contrary, written in reply to other opponents of Barclay, it was dedicated to Norris; but in the course of his dedication Elys suggested that Norris was too severe in his judgement of the Quakers. Later in the same year he published a letter to Norris to defend the Quakers against the accusation of Socinianism. Norris had never suggested that the Quakers were Socinians, but Elys addressed his defence to him as being the most learned and fair of those who had written against the Quakers. Elys's third pamphlet was not directly concerned with the Quaker controversy. In his Reflections upon some Passages in a Book entitled: Reflections upon the Conduct of Human Life, Elys attacked the alleged intellectualism of Norris's Reflections, but he also criticised Norris for speaking disdainfully of the Quaker doctrine of the "light within". In view of the similarities that we have noticed between the views of Henry More and those of the Quakers, it is interesting to note that Elys was a warm admirer of More, with whom he had corresponded and whose Letters on Several Subjects he edited in 1694.

283

After 1692, as has been seen, Norris did not reply further to the Quakers. No doubt he would not have begun a controversy with them if he had not seen, through Langton and Vickris, the danger that his own ideas could be mistakenly identified with theirs. The post-script which he added to the second edition of his Reflections upon the Conduct of Human Life, together with the Two Treatises which were occasioned by Vickris's attack on this post-script, showed very clearly where the differences between his views and theirs lay. The theories of the Quakers and those of Malebranche and Norris did indeed have interesting similarities, so that the task of showing their differences, which Norris did with notable insight and fairness, led him to express his own views with particular clarity. It was for this reason that he republished the Two Treatises concerning the Divine Light in 1697, as part of his Treatises upon several Subjects.

CHAPTER XI CONCLUSION

In this book, Norris's thought has been examined as it developed from his earliest writings till the works of his maturity. It has been examined in comparative isolation, because Norris was in fact a somewhat isolated figure, living for most of his life remote from the centres of learning, and influenced more by his reading of ancient and French philosophers than by intercourse with his English contemporaries. In this final chapter, however, an attempt will be made to identify the sources of his ideas, to examine the unity of his thought as a whole, and to assess his place in the history of English philosophy.

1. Norris and his sources

It is clear that Norris was influenced mainly by three types of philosophy: the Platonic tradition, Scholasticism, and the philosophy of Malebranche. The reading of his translation of Hierocles upon the Golden Verses of the Pythagoreans at once discloses the great extent of his debt to this type of Platonism. The immediate presence of eternal truth to the soul, the identification of this truth with God, and the essential rôle of attention to truth as the root of liberty and morality, are amongst Norris's most distinctive and fundamental beliefs, and they are all to be found in this Platonic work. But if the influence of Hierocles on Norris's thought is clear, that of more recent Platonists is much less so. Norris quotes Ficinus with approbation, as he also does Plato and Plotinus, but in spite of his great respect for Henry More he does not appear to depend on the Cambridge Platonists to any large degree. He read Cudworth, but his debt to the Platonists of the period immedi-

285

ately preceding his own was mainly concerned with George Rust, Henry More, and Joseph Glanvil.[1] He may have owed to Rust his strong insistence on the uncreated nature of truth, and he certainly owed to More his distinction between the divine mind as "exhibitive" or intelligible and as "conceptive" or intelligent. He seems to have derived his understanding of the paradoxes of infinite extension and divisibility from Glanvil, who may also have influenced his strong feeling of the limitations of human knowledge. These are the only points on which a direct influence of the mid-seventeenth century Platonists on Norris is apparent, and Rust and More agreed to a great extent not only with the Platonic tradition but also with the Scholastics. But even if Norris was not greatly influenced by the specific doctrines of the Cambridge Platonists, they were no doubt largely responsible for the intellectual climate in which it was natural for Norris's thought to follow Platonist lines.

Although Norris has been classed with the Cambridge Platonists, and has even been held to be separated from them principally by his uncritical following of Malebranche,[2] he was in reality a notably more modern thinker than they. Where the Cambridge Platonists were strongly influenced by the vitalism and occultism of the Renaissance, Norris belonged to a newer age. His writings contain indeed echoes of older Platonic theories such as the pre-existence of souls and the existence of ethereal or lucid bodies, but he never suggests these as more than hypotheses; and he differs fundamentally from the earlier thinkers by his rejection of any occult sympathy between substances and by his acceptance of an essentially mechanist view of the material world. Norris was not himself a mathematician, nor was he greatly interested in the physical sciences, but he shared the new outlook on the world to

286

which they were giving rise. As time went on his mechanist interpretation of the material world grew more pronounced under the
influence of Descartes and Malebranche, as can be seen by his
late adoption of the Cartesian theory of animals as machines, but
even at the time of his correspondence with Henry More he was
not really interested in the latter's theories on the extension of
spirits. As Røstvig has pointed out, [3] even in his youthful poetry
Norris saw the world as an ordered universe functioning in accordance with law, and not as a living and semi-divine nature in
the manner of the Cambridge Platonists. Norris owed the central
convictions of his theory of knowledge to the Platonic tradition as
exemplified by Hierocles, but he never shared the tendency of the
Cambridge school to deify nature. He carried the Platonic tradition
into a new age.

Norris's relations with Scholastic philosophy are not easy
to define. This was of course the philosophy that was commonly
taught at Oxford in his time, and it is clear that he had a good
knowledge of it. In his younger days he was strongly opposed to
Scholasticism, which he describes in his Spiritual Counsel as "a
mere fantastic amusement, made up of insignificant terms, and
a company of loose indeterminate maxims, all built upon dark unintelligible principles,"[4] and he strongly criticises the practice of
Scholastic disputation in his Reflections upon the Conduct of Human
Life. But even at this period several aspects of his thought were
derived from the Scholastic tradition. In particular it was from
the Scholastics that he derived his conception of the Ideas as representing the divine essence insofar as it was able to be imitated
by possible creatures, while his view that the will always follows
the final judgement of the intellect was derived from Aquinas. In
some respects Norris later moved further away from the Scho-

287

lastics, by his acceptance for example of the Cartesian attribution of judgement to the will, but his general attitude to them gradually became more favourable, especially in matters of Logic, and he even came to defend their disputations. While his new good-will towards the Scholastics may have been partly a reaction against Locke, it was mainly the result of a renewed study of their writings, particularly of those of Suarez and Aquinas. In his Theory of the Ideal or Intelligible World Norris is always glad to adduce their authority in favour of positions on which they agree with him, regarding in particular the relationship of the Ideas with the essence of God.[5] But his debt to them is mainly a matter of logic and method; his theory of knowledge is entirely different from theirs.[6]

The influence of Descartes and above all, after 1688, of Malebranche is evident in Norris's writings, and has been analysed in many parts of this study. Indeed Malebranche's influence is so evident that it is easy to overestimate it. Norris's own theory of knowledge, based largely, it seems, on the Platonism of Hierocles, had led him independently to the conviction that the ideas and the necessary and eternal truths which we know are in God, and can hence be known only in him, and this conviction always remained the foundation of all his metaphysics. But when Norris read Malebranche, he was overjoyed to find an author whose views were similar to his own, but who had elaborated them more fully, and accordingly he adopted a considerable part of Malebranche's philosophy with great enthusiasm. Thus Norris took over from Malebranche the Cartesian attribution of judgement to the will and the theory that animals are machines; above all he adopted Malebranche's occasionalist account of sensation, which permitted him both to extend his theory of knowledge by the addition of an explanation of empirical knowledge in terms of sensations imprinted in us by God, and also to complete his theory of the love of God. And in addition, even where the views that Norris expressed were essentially his own, he often expressed them in terms borrowed from Malebranche.

Norris did not however adopt all of Malebranche's theories by any means. Thus he continued to hold that God was actuated by pure benevolence in his dealings with creatures, a view which he reconciled with Malebranche's doctrine that God can act only for himself by means of the Platonic and Scholastic principle according to which it is the nature of goodness to diffuse itself. Again, Norris never accepted Malebranche's theory on the distribution of grace, but continued to regard this as a mystery. He never accepted the view, which Malebranche had adopted from Descartes, that the soul is always thinking. And he took Malebranche's "intelligible extension" simply for the intellectual idea of matter, in the sense in which Augustine or the Scholastics accepted such an idea. It was only in the Second Part of his Theory of the Ideal ... World that he tried to incorporate the whole of Malebranche's conception of intelligible extension into his system, and this attempt, as has been seen, was not very successful.

Apart from these specific differences, there is often a difference of approach between Norris and Malebranche even where they are in basic agreement. In La Recherche de la Vérité Malebranche proposed the "vision in God" as the solution of an epistemological problem, whereas for Norris the divine character of the Ideas and necessary truths is known with certainty before any examination into how these truths are known. After the 10th Eclaircissement to La Recherche, Malebranche began to argue in the same way, but his emphasis was placed on the infinity of the world

289

of ideas, whereas Norris's attention was fixed on their eternity and necessity. In spite of his enthusiasm for Malebranche, it seems true to say that Norris's system is at bottom closer to St. Augustine than it is to him. Norris does not seem to have had much knowledge of St. Augustine's works in his youth, yet his Metaphysical Essay already proposed an Augustinian type of reasoning. Later Norris came to know Augustine's works better, but it does not seem that his affinity with him ever involved much dependence. Rather it seems true to say that Norris's philosophy is a Christian Platonism like that of Augustine, a Christian Platonism however which in his case employs largely Scholastic tools, and which is elaborated and purified with the aid of Malebranche.

From what has been said it is clear that Norris's philosophy had its roots predominantly in a Platonism such as that of Hierocles. The influence of Malebranche came only later. But Norris's own background and formation was not that which he advised for others. In Spiritual Counsel he urges his children and other readers to devote their attention in philosophy exclusively to the works of Descartes and Malebranche,[7] as being uniquely competent guides in the search for truth. Of particular interest is the letter which he wrote on 12 July (1696?) to "Corinna" (Elizabeth Thomas), who had written to ask his advice for the direction of her studies. After advising the study of Geometry and Logic, Norris continues:

"The next that I would have you read, shall I say, or study, as that which lays the foundation of all science, and will best conduct and methodize your thoughts, is Malebranche's Recherche de la Vérité. This, I say, I would commend next, but that in order to your reading him with pleasure or advantage, it is absolutely necessary you should understand the Cartesian philosophy, whereof Malebranche is a superstructure and improvement. Descartes therefore you must next undertake (after some competency in the principles of common geometry) beginning at his Metaphysical Meditations, thence proceeding to his Principles, and after that as you please in the rest of his works. When you understand Descartes thoroughly, read one or two of the best Cartesians, such as Rohault and Regis, and by that time, and truly not well sooner, you will be fit to undertake Malebranche, whom when you have made your own, you will be able to direct yourself in all your further progress."[8]

That Malebranche's philosophy is a "superstructure and improvement" to Cartesianism precisely represents Malebranche's own view of his work; but the strictly Cartesian course of study which Norris here recommends is very different from his own background, and does not adequately represent either the formative influences on or the ethos of his own thought.

2. The unity of Norris's thought

As has been seen, Norris's writings covered a wide variety of subjects. On some matters, such as practical ethics and religion, his views proved acceptable to many people who did not accept his more speculative theories. Nevertheless it is not difficult to show that, in his own mind, his different doctrines formed an essential unity.

The centre of Norris's thought is undoubtedly to be found in his conceptions of God and of human knowledge. In essence these views go back to his earliest writings, to Hierocles upon the Golden Verses of the Pythagoreans (1682), to the Letter of Ideas (1684), and to the Metaphysical Essay of 1687. God is identified with truth, and is immediately present to every soul. When one knows eternal and necessary truth one knows God, though perhaps one does not recognise him, and goodness and justice are necessary aspects of his nature. Necessary truths and the ideas or essences whose relationships they express are known directly in God, since they can exist only in him as he is the only necessary and eternal being. To this kernel of his doctrine Norris later added Malebranche's occasionalist view of sensation and his theory that even contingent things are known in God, but he remained less fully convinced of this last theory than of his own initial certainties.

Norris's theory of love fits together very naturally with his theory of knowledge. As has been seen, his views on love developed gradually. As from 1687 he upheld a radical distinction between the loves of desire and of benevolence, but it was not until 1693 that he formulated his characteristic doctrine according to which the love of desire, now defined as the desire by which the soul unites itself to an object as its real good, must be reserved for God alone. It was his adoption of Malebranche's occasionalist account of sensation that enabled him to formulate this theory, which nevertheless also represents the natural culmination of his own earlier thought on this subject.

Although Norris thus embraced Malebranche's theory on the love of desire, he always retained his own distinctive view of benevolence, according to which one may desire the good of another without regard to one's own interest. In particular Norris held, unlike Malebranche, that God loves his creatures with this disinterested benevolence. This radical distinction between the loves of desire and benevolence enabled Norris to formulate as his most general precept of morality the rule that one must will what God wills or love as he loves. God desires only himself, but he loves all his creatures with a love of pure benevolence; and man too

292

should concentrate his desire on God alone, and love all his neighbours with sincere benevolence.

This principle of desiring God alone and loving one's fellow creatures with disinterested benevolence was fundamental for the whole of Norris's moral teaching in its developed form. In his earlier writings he had followed Cumberland and other contemporaries in emphasising the good of the community as the criterion of morality in a way that hardly fitted in with some of his other doctrines, but he later came to see the common good as the realisation of the universal order that is willed by God, and love of the common good as an aspect of benevolence. Norris never elaborated a detailed system of moral duties on the basis of the two loves. His moral teaching was essentially that of the Bible. But he was convinced that even the most exigent of Christian moral precepts were strictly reasonable and formed part of the Natural Law.

To the question why one should live in accordance with the moral law, Norris gives a double reply: both our duty and our interest push us to live according to God's commandments, which are also those of reason. To oblige in conscience, a law must both be just in itself and enjoined by an authority which has a right to our obedience; but God, being our creator, has an absolute right to our obedience, and he has prescribed to us nothing but what is both intrinsically reasonable and for our own good. The moral law is an aspect of the divine nature, and obedience to it is an aspect of the respect that we owe to God.

But although Norris held that the intrinsic justice of the moral law and the fact that it was commanded by God made it our duty to obey it, he often concentrated his attention rather on the fact that such obedience was in accordance with our own interests. Man, he holds, seeks happiness, and this happiness can be finally attained only in the enjoyment of God. Accordingly man's essential interest is to please God, in order to attain to him. At this point Norris's moral theory rejoins the rest of his thought. Not only happiness but also knowledge is imperfect in this life, so that all the energies of the prudent and reasonable man must be directed to the attainment of heaven. To reach God, we must use the means that he himself has ordained: obedience to his commandments. But, as has been seen, these commandments are not arbitrary; and the basic commandments to set one's heart on nothing outside God and to love one's neighbours with disinterested benevolence, far from being mere expressions of religious enthusiasm, are the commands of reason itself. God's commands and man's interests thus coincide, duty and prudence indicate the same path, and indeed prudence itself is a duty since God has commanded us to consult our own true interest.

If the most important thing for man, even in his search for truth, is to attain to heaven, the reason is that our knowledge of truth is very imperfect in this life. From the period of his youthful poems onwards, Norris showed a strong sense of the imperfection of human knowledge. God, world of Ideas and eternal Truth, is indeed immediately present to the soul, but it is only by dint of careful attention and by affirming nothing that he is able to doubt that man can be sure of distinguishing truth from error. This conviction of the immediate presence of God on the one hand, and of the difficulty of discerning truth and following reason on the other, is at the root of what might be called Norris's practical individualism. From his earliest writings he insists on the need for each person to think for himself and not to follow the authority of other people's opinions. This is true, he considers, both in practical and in speculative matters, for the common example of the world is one of both vice and error. To live well one must follow, not the example of the world around one, but one's conscience. To attain to truth, one must follow no school or popular opinion; one must not rest on the authority of the learned, but think for oneself, admitting as certain nothing whose truth one cannot clearly see.

Norris's individualism is not confined to the practice of moral and intellectual life; it also has a metaphysical side. In his view, as we have seen, there is no necessary connection between any two distinct created substances. Each created substance depends directly and solely on God, both for its being and for its activity. It is in God alone that man can know truth. It is God alone, too, who can produce sensations in the soul. It is with God alone that each man is naturally linked. Accordingly man has nothing to seek or to fear outside God. In this sense Norris found a profoundly religious meaning in the occasionalism which he took over from Malebranche. Norris's individualism, which distinguishes him from his Cambridge Platonist predecessors, is reflected in his own intellectual development, which took place to a large extent independently of his English contemporaries.

Norris's consciousness of the limits of human knowledge was also at the root of his teaching on the relationship of knowledge and faith. Powicke held that Norris's doctrine of the immediate presence of the divine Truth to the soul logically rendered any supernatural revelation, and in particular the incarnation, superfluous, [9] but this judgement neglects the fact that, for Norris as for Malebranche, God's presence to the soul reveals only necessary truths; it gives no knowledge of God's free choices, so that man could have no knowledge of God's plan for his salvation if God had not revealed it to him by some other means. Moreover,

Norris held, the purpose of the incarnation was not primarily to reveal abstract truths, but to open the way for man to heaven. Norris's defence of the mysteries of Christianity rested on the conviction that, although God was immediately present to the human mind, the mind remained finite while God was infinite. The human mind, therefore, cannot aspire to be the measure of all truth; there may well be mysteries which surpass its clear understanding. On the other hand, of course, man must not accept any doctrine which claims to be revealed unless he has sufficient reason to believe that it really is revealed by God and is not contradictory either in itself or of other known truths. Norris's teaching on this matter was in full accord with the rest of his thought.

Norris's theological outlook and religious teaching were largely not peculiar to himself; in essence he was an orthodox Christian. We have seen that his insistence on the importance of attaining heaven and his view of the relationship of reason and faith were integral parts of his whole system, and it is clear that God occupied the centre of his interests in every sphere. But it is worth noticing at this point how well Norris's Protestantism fitted in with his theory of knowledge. Norris agreed with Malebranche in insisting that one should accept nothing on the authority of other people or of tradition but should examine everything for oneself with assiduous attention to truth. But where Malebranche distinguished between matters of reason and matters of faith, admitting for the latter the legitimacy of ecclesiastical authority and tradition, Norris made no such distinction. He agreed with Malebranche that our knowledge of God's decisions and decrees depended on positive revelation, but held that this revelation was contained in the Bible alone, which everyone must consult for himself, just as everyone must consult the Ideal World for himself in order to know matters of necessary truth. Each individual, Norris holds, is responsible to God alone, and human authority is as much a trap in matters of faith as it is in those of reason and morality. Norris shared this individualist approach with Descartes and Malebranche, but the enthusiasm with which he accepted and underlined their teaching on the importance of thinking for oneself and accepting nothing merely on the authority of others, and extended this teaching to the religious sphere, seems to show a real convergence between this aspect of their philosophy and Protestantism.

This may be one of the reasons why Malebranche's influence in England, largely through Norris, was favourable to Christianity, whereas in France, as Alquié has shown in his recent book Le Cartésianisme de Malebranche, it was more often felt in non-Christian circles. But in order to understand this contrast more fully it is necessary to see which aspects of Malebranche's thought mainly appealed to the writers of the French Enlightenment and which appealed to Norris. What mainly appealed in Malebranche to the writers of the French Enlightenment was his denial of altruism and benevolence in God and his attempt to explain the working of providence and the distribution of grace by analogy with God's way of working in the natural order.[10] As has been seen, Norris did not follow Malebranche in either of these theories. What appealed above all to him, on the contrary, was Malebranche's theory of knowledge, the direct vision of the Ideas in God, and the insistence that God is thus immediately present to every man, needing only to be recognised. This emphasis on direct and immediate contact between God and the human soul was what primarily appealed to Norris and to Malebranche's other English admirers.[11] It was also, perhaps, more fundamental to Malebranche's own thought, and more distinctively characteristic of him, than were

297

the theories whose influence was felt in the French Enlightenment.[12]

Norris's rejection of Calvinism was of course closely connected with his insistence on the realism of our knowledge of values. The goodness and justice that man knows are aspects of the divine nature, he insists, and are hence as valid for God as they are for man. In this sense his Arminianism was of a piece with his most fundamental philosophical convictions. If Latitudinarianism is taken as the view of Christianity that places more emphasis on the moral life than either on faith or on the sacraments, Norris must also be regarded as a Latitudinarian.[13] He had no doubt that God's will for man was more concerned with how he lived than with what he believed, and he did not regard orthodoxy of opinion as fundamentally important unless if affected one's practical living. He regarded faith, the sacraments, and other Christian ordinances as means rather than as ends; the substance of the Christian life was moral. But it is important to notice that Norris's conception of morality was very different from that of many of his contemporaries. The morality which Norris upheld, and on whose reasonableness he insisted, was the complete morality of the gospels, summed up in the two commandments of love. It is this fulness of moral content that gives Norris's teaching its particular flavour. Norris took the moral demands of Christianity and its teaching on eternal life absolutely seriously. As will be seen, it was this consistent Christianity which appealed so strongly to Wesley in Norris's writings, and which looked forward in a very real sense to the beginnings of Methodism.

In all these spheres, then, Norris's thought exhibits a fundamental unity. Outside this unity must be left, perhaps, his High Church reticence on toleration, and such relics of early Platonism as his acceptance even in later life of the possibility of ethereal

298

bodies, a theory which can hardly be reconciled with his generally
Cartesian understanding of the soul and the body. These points,
however, can hardly be said to affect the unity of his outlook as a
whole. A more serious weakness in his system is to be found, on
the other hand, in the uncertainty in which the Second Part of The
Theory of the Ideal or Intelligible World left his theory of knowledge. As has been seen, this uncertainty resulted from his attempt to incorporate the whole of Malebranche's teaching on "intelligible extension" into his theory, without fully understanding
that highly complex conception. More generally it is probably true
to say that Norris would have expressed his theory of knowledge
more satisfactorily if he had not tried to follow Malebranche so
closely. He owed Malebranche several important conceptions, as
we have seen; in particular he owed him the occasionalist theory
of sensation. But the close way in which he often followed Malebranche's exposition even of positions which he had reached independently seems to take away from the force both of Reason and
Religion and of the Second Part of the Theory.

　　There was one other point on which Norris's Theory of the
Ideal . . . World left an open question: the real existence of the
material world. This difficulty was common to Norris and Malebranche. Their insistence that we know the material world by
means of ideas which are in God and of sensations which are in ourselves leaves the reality of the material world doubtful. Norris
indeed goes beyond Malebranche in holding that not even faith gives
certain knowledge of an external, material world, but still he has
no doubt that such a world exists. We have suggested that Norris's
view on this question is not as unreasonable as it may appear; but
it is noteworthy that Locke in his Examination of Malebranche pointed
out the doubt in which this theory of knowledge left the real exis-

tence of the material world, and Norris's teaching in fact provided the starting point for Collier's immaterialism.

Although most of Norris's ideas were derived either from the Platonic tradition or from Descartes and Malebranche, his thought has a unity of its own and is of interest in its own right. Standing somewhat apart from the main stream of English thought, and deliberately pursuing his own reflections, he is nevertheless clearly a figure of his own age. It remains for us only to examine the influence that he had on subsequent philosophical and religious thought.

3. Norris's Influence

Many of Norris's works remained in circulation for a considerable period after his death. In 1722 the books which are listed below were advertised as "reprinted for Edmund Parker at the Bible and Crown in Lombard Street",[14] and almost all the same works were still available eleven years later.[15] In the middle of the eighteenth century Richardson in Clarissa spoke of Norris's Miscellanies as a book which would be likely to be found in a family library. As has been seen, An Account of Reason and Faith was republished as late as 1790, while the last chapter with the postscript of this same work were reprinted in 1795 as part of an anthology on the principles and evidences of Christianity. Norris, then, continued to be read throughout the eighteenth century. But a closer inspection shows that while he continued to be prized as a moralist and Christian apologist, his metaphysics had considerably less influence.

In his Advice to a Young Student (1729) Daniel Waterland recommends the reading of Practical Discourses, of An Account of Reason and Faith, and of Norris's treatises on humility and pru-

300

dence, and adds that "Norris is a fine writer for style and thought, and commonly just, except in what relates to his World of Ideas, where he sometimes trifles."[16] A similar combination of praise for Norris's religious writings and rejection of his metaphysics is found at the beginning of the nineteenth century in Van Mildert.[17] The Theory of the Ideal ... World is however found with the Miscellanies and An Account of Reason and Faith in the "List of Books on Moral Philosophy and Metaphysics recommended or in use at Cambridge in 1730" which is reproduced by Wordsworth in his Scholae Academicae,[18] so Norris's metaphysical writings did not fall into complete oblivion.

If we turn from the list of Norris's works which were available after his death to the question of their influence, there is no doubt that a high place amongst his admirers must be given to John Wesley. Norris's influence on Wesley was largely on his personal life. In his book The Young Mr. Wesley V. H. H. Green reproduces the list of books which Wesley noted in his journal that he had read during his years at Oxford between 1725 and 1734. During this time no year passed without his reading at least one of Norris's works, while the Treatise concerning Christian Prudence figures on the list four times.[19] Later in life Wesley continued to cite Norris as an authority. Writing on 14 March 1756 to one of his followers, named Samuel Farly, Wesley wrote: "You are sick of ... that evil disease which Marcus Antoninus complains of - the dipsan biblion. That you are far gone in the latter plainly appears from your not loving and admiring that masterpiece of reason and religion, the Reflections on the Conduct of Human Life, with Regard to Knowledge and Learning, every paragraph of which must stand unshaken (with or without the Bible) till we are no longer mortal."[20] Coming from one who was as devoted to the Bible as was Wesley, this is high praise indeed. And on 16 April 1756 he wrote again to the same correspondent, who had suggested in his reply that Norris's Reflections did not agree with Wesley's own Address to the Clergy, "There is no disagreement at all between the Reflections and the Address to the Clergy. I have followed Mr. Norris's advice these thirty years, and so must every man that is well in his senses."[21]

Wesley's greatest admiration went to Reflections upon the Conduct of Human Life and to A Treatise concerning Christian Prudence, both of which he republished in a shortened form. What attracted him above all was Norris's insistence that the attainment of heaven must be the principal aim of every reasonable man. But it is also interesting to observe that when he founded his school at Kingswood, Bristol, its teaching followed the lines suggested by Norris in Reflections upon the Conduct of Human Life. On strictly philosophical questions Wesley, who of course shared Norris's dislike of Calvinism and of schism, did not follow Norris so closely. He did not agree with Norris's theory of the Ideal World and of human knowledge, and he accepted Locke's refutation of innate ideas. On the other hand he followed Norris, and thus Malebranche, in explaining the union of the soul and the body in occasionalist terms. He also agreed with Norris in identifying the substance with the essence or essential attribute of each thing, and was thus able to reject Locke's theory that thought might be an attribute of a material being. He did not however accept one of the consequences which the Cartesians derived from this doctrine: far from regarding animals as machines, he considered that they were endowed with perception and with some degree of intelligence, and he did not exclude them from the possibility of immortality. On the love of God, finally, Wesley followed Norris closely. He warned his followers against any desire of creatures. Like Norris he agreed that one could, in a broad sense, love creatures, but he insisted that all one's desires, in the strict sense, should be reserved for God alone. In essence, Wesley admired Norris's combination of reasonableness with fervour. It is clear that Norris's writings exercised a considerable influence on him during his formative years at Oxford, and that through him some of Norris's ideas, though not the more abstruse ones, were later widely disseminated amongst a popular audience.[22]

Friends and admirers of Norris such as Mary Astell, Lady Mary Chudleigh, and Henry Needler have been mentioned earlier in this book. But Norris's influence on more generally known philosophers is less easy to identify. This is partly due to the fact that Norris's metaphysics and theory of knowledge were never widely accepted; but it is also partly due to their similarity to the theories of Malebranche. It is clear, for example, that Malebranche's philosophy played a considerable part in the formation of Berkeley's immaterialism, but it appears that it was Malebranche's own writings rather than those of Norris which influenced him.[23]

Norris's writings anticipate those of Joseph Butler on several points. An argument from analogy similar to Butler's is adumbrated in Norris's Account of Reason and Faith, while the Treatise concerning Christian Prudence declares, as Butler was later to do, that even the possibility of the truth of the Christian teaching on life after death makes it a vital consideration for any reasonable man. Further, Butler agrees with Norris in holding that the soul alone is the real person and that it has no necessary connection with the body or with any other created substance. Again, Norris in several places anticipates the popular eighteenth century argument for the existence of God from the evidence of design in nature, an argument which was to receive its classical formulation from Paley. It is impossible to say whether these anticipations point to any direct dependence of these authors on Norris. What is certain, however, is that he contributed towards the movement of ideas which they expressed.

Although Hume's philosophy was of course fundamentally opposed to that of Norris, there are indications that Hume knew Norris's writings and had them in view in certain passages of his Dialogues concerning Natural Religion.[24] In this work, Hume argues against the view that the order or organisation of the natural world presupposes the existence of an intelligent creator who knew in advance what he was going to make.

"If reason ... be not alike mute with regard to all questions concerning cause and effect; this sentence at least it will venture to pronounce, that a mental world or universe of ideas requires a cause as much as does a material world or universe of objects; and if similar in its arrangement must require a similar cause ... How therefore shall we satisfy ourselves concerning the Cause of that Being, whom you suppose the Author of Nature, or according to your system of anthropomorphism, the Ideal World, into which you trace the material? Have we not the same reason to trace that ideal world into another ideal world, or new intelligent principle? But if we stop, and go no further: why go so far? Why not stop at this material world? ... To say that the different ideas, which compose the reason of the Supreme Being, fall into order of themselves, and by their own nature, is really to talk without any precise meaning. If it has a meaning, I would fain know why it is not as good sense to say, that the parts of the material

world fall into order of themselves, and by their own nature?
Can the one opinion be intelligible, while the other is not so?"[25]
In Hume's view, the world of bodies is as well organised as is the
world of ideas, so that there is no ground for explaining the former in terms of the latter. Hume's criticism certainly seems to
be directed at the first of the arguments proposed by Norris, in
the First Part of The Theory of the Ideal ... World, to establish
the existence of the Ideal World, and the impression that he had
Norris in mind is strengthened by his speaking explicitly of "that
Being, whom you suppose the Author of Nature, or according to
your system of anthropomorphism, the Ideal World".[26] It is clear,
however, that Hume's criticism takes no account of Norris's explanation of the relationship of the Ideas to the divine essence.
Hume does not recognise the rôle of reason as principle and source
of order. His argument against Norris is valid only if his own negative judgement on the capacities of the intellect is accepted.

If Norris's writings contributed to the spread of Malebranche's ideas, which provoked the reflections of the young Berkeley;
if some of his ideas anticipated those of Butler, while others were
taken by Hume as typical of the views of Christian or theist philosophers, there was nevertheless only one thinker for whom Norris's
works provided the main starting point in his own thinking. This was
Arthur Collier (1680-1732), a philosopher who was little known
even in his own lifetime, but who is interesting for having, independently of Berkeley, denied the existence of the material world.
Collier was born on 12 October 1680 at Steeple Langford, Wiltshire, like Norris the son of a clergyman. Educated at Salisbury
and Oxford, he was ordained a priest in 1704, and was immediately
presented by his mother to the family living, remaining rector of
Steeple Langford till his death. As a young man he was a solitary

student, his favourite authors being Descartes, Malebranche, and Norris, and he probably knew Norris personally.[27] He seems to have begun to formulate his own theories in about 1703, and the first draft of his principal work seems to have been completed by 1708. This work, Clavis Universalis: or, a New Enquiry after Truth, was finally published in 1713.

Clavis Universalis is divided into two parts, in the first of which Collier argues that the visible world, the world that is known by means of the senses, is within our own souls. As all Cartesians admit, colours and other sensible qualities exist only in the minds of those who see or feel them; there is no reason to suppose that extension is any different. Everything that we see, accordingly, is within the soul; if matter or extension is supposed to exist outside our souls, it will be strictly invisible.

In the second part of his book, Collier goes further. Not only would an external world be invisible, he argues, but it does not and cannot exist. Such a world would be a creature, so that it could be known only a posteriori; but the sensible world is within our souls, and the supposed external world is entirely unknown to us. Such an invisible and unknown world would be entirely useless, so that God, who always acts with wisdom, could not have created it. Collier however was not content with this more general argument. He also brought more detailed arguments, which in some ways anticipate Kant's antinomies, to prove that the conception of an external world is a contradictory and impossible one.

Collier affirms that one can prove both that the material world is of infinite extent and that it is finite. Most philosophers, he declares, agree that this is so, and even those who think that they can prove one side of the dilemma never succeed in refuting the arguments of their adversaries. Again, he continues, it can

306

be proved both that real matter must be infinitely divisible and
that it can be divided only to a finite extent. But a world of which
such contradictory propositions can be proved cannot exist. Collier realised that these contradictions were generally taken merely
for signs of the limited power of human intelligence. This was the
view taken by Norris, by Boyle, and by the authors of the Logic
of Port Royal, but Collier replied to them that "'Tis a sign indeed that our understandings are very <u>weak</u> and shallow, when
such stuff as this shall pass not only for common sense, but even
look like argument." [28] To refuse to admit that an object of which
two contradictory assertions can be proved does not exist is not
to reason but to refuse to reason. It is not intellectual humility,
but scepticism. Finite and infinite are mutually exclusive, and a
concept of which both are necessarily affirmed is contradictory in
itself and can correspond to nothing real. Accordingly an external
world cannot exist.

 After further arguing that, in a supposed external world,
movement would be at once possible and impossible, Collier then
replies to three objections which he envisages being made against
his conclusion. The Bible, he declares, does not teach the existence of a world external to the soul; it teaches that the world which
we see and know was created by God, which Collier in no way denies. Again, we have no natural inclination to believe that an invisible world exists outside the soul, and it has already been proved
that the visible world is not external. As a third objection, Collier
considers Norris's position. "The late judicious Mr. <u>Norris</u>, who
purposely considered this question of an external world, was yet
so far from concluding as I have here done, that he declares it to
be no other than arrant <u>scepticism</u> to make a serious doubt or
question of its existence."[29] Collier explains that he has put the

307

objection in this form in order to seem to defend his own view rather than to attack that of Norris, "for whose writings and memory I have a great esteem."[30] But if one considers, not Norris's authority and explicit opinion, but the tendency of his arguments, one finds, in Collier's view, that the whole of Norris's reasoning tends to prove that no solid argument can be found to establish the existence of a real external world. Norris casts doubt on all the arguments for the real existence of an external world, even on those which were accepted by Descartes and Malebranche. In the face of his own arguments, Norris's affirmation of the real existence of the world is valueless.

From this short summary of Collier's argument it is apparent that the theories of Malebranche and Norris formed the starting-point of his thought. As has been seen, Locke argued that Malebranche and Norris's theory of knowledge rendered the external world unknowable. He regarded this as a sign of the absurdity of their system. Collier on the other hand accepted their system, and carried it on to what he regarded as its logical conclusion in immaterialism.

Norris's philosophy, then, formed a principal starting point of Collier's reflections. It seems probable, too, that it was from Norris's writings that Collier drew his version of the antinomies of the infinite extension and divisibility of the material world. Collier's presentation of these paradoxes closely follows that of Norris in Reflections upon the Conduct of Human Life. Norris seems to have derived his view of these problems, which he repeated in An Account of Reason and Faith, mainly from Glanvil and Boyle.[31] Collier may also have been influenced by Pierre Bayle. But if, as Lovejoy writes in his article "Kant and the English Platonists", "the paradoxes about infinite extension and

308

infinite divisibility are, in themselves, of course, a very ancient heritage of European philosophy, going back at all events to Zeno of Elea, .. Collier appears to have been the first modern to whom it occurred to use them as a decisive argument against physical realism in precisely the Kantian manner."[32] It is not known whether Kant was influenced by Collier's argument, though it is certain that he could have known the Clavis Universalis. [33] In any case it is clear that Collier anticipated Kant's reasoning on this matter in an interesting way. Norris would not have accepted the conclusions which Collier drew from his premises; but Collier's immaterialism is interesting as showing one way in which his metaphysics could be developed and transformed.

Norris's life spanned an important period in the history of English thought. A somewhat isolated and highly individual figure, he was not by any means without significance. He carried forward the Platonic tradition in a modernised form, incorporating important elements from Descartes and Malebranche. He was one of the few who criticised Locke from a genuinely philosophical standpoint rather than for theological reasons. In different ways his work looks forward to the classical apologetics of the Age of Reason, to Wesley, to the idealism of Collier, and even, in his poetic outlook, to the beginnings of romanticism.[34] Yet his work had a unity of its own. He was a man who made the highest claims for reason, but who was also a fervent and consistent Christian, for he was convinced that reason is by nature in touch with God.

Yet Norris is not only of interest as a transitional figure in the history of thought; he is also interesting in himself. He was not a philosopher of the first rank; few of his theories were peculiar to himself, and many of his views can hardly be regarded as satisfactorily defensible in the form that he gave them. But, as is often the case in the history of philosophy, his fundamental insights are perhaps of more permanent value than are his detailed opinions. In this sense, perhaps, Norris still speaks to us today, calling philosophy to concern itself with the fundamental problems of human knowledge and life, calling theology and religion not to turn their backs on reason, and calling each individual person to seek truth for himself by assiduous and independent reflection.

NOTES

CHAPTER I:

1) Baptismal register of Collingbourne Kingston. The register gives the year as 1656, just as that of Bemerton gives the date of his burial as 5 February 1711; but according to our reckoning, with the year taken as beginning on 1 January, these dates would be 1657 and 1712 respectively.

2) F.J. Powicke, in his Dissertation on John Norris of Bemerton, (London, 1894), writes concerning the elder Norris (p. 4-5): "After his removal from office, he still lived on at Collingbourne - not one or two years, but many: for his son John entered Winchester School in 1671, and the school register shows that his home at the time was still Collingbourne. But the long years of suspension would seem to have brought the father to another mind as regards nonconformity. This is suggested by the fact that he died Rector of Aldbourne in the same county of Wilts ..." But this is a mistake, - cf. Sir Thomas Phillips, Institutiones Clericorum in Comitatu Wiltoniae, (Middle Hill, 1825), and the parish records of Aldbourne, which also record his burial on 22 March 1681/2. From his Will, preserved in the Wiltshire County Record Office, Trowbridge, it appears that the elder Norris had the following children: Samuel, Mary, John, and James. Samuel entered Exeter College, Oxford, in April 1661, aged 17, and was a Fellow of the college from 1663 till 1682. In 1681 he became rector of Tilehurst, Berkshire, and in 1708 vicar of Englefield in the same county. James lived at Collingbourne Kingston until his death, which occured in 1730. Members of the Norris family are to be found in the parish registers of Collingbourne Kingston until 1802. The elder Norris also had a daughter Hannah, born in 1655, who died in 1658.

3) Cf. Tractatus adversus Reprobationis Absolutae Decretum (1683), in the preface to which our Norris writes: "Ab ineunte aetate, et quasi cum materno lacte, praedestinariae doctrinae principia incautus hauseram."

4) I am indebted to the Warden and Fellows of Winchester College for permission to publish this letter.

5) Cf. A. K. Cook, About Winchester College, (London, 1917).

6) Cf. Frequent references esp. in Essay towards the Theory of the Ideal or Intelligible World (1701-4). Francis Burgersdictus (Burgersdijk), 1590-1629, Dutch logician and philosopher, was a professor successively at Saumur and Leiden, and author of Institutiones Logicae, (Leiden, 1635 etc.) Christoph Scheibler, 1589-1653, was a scholastic philosopher and Lutheran theologian In philosophy he was greatly influenced by Suarez. Successively professor at Giessen and superintendant at Dortmund, his principal work was his Opus Metaphysicum, (Giessen, 1617).

7) Cf. C. Wordsworth, Scholae Academicae, (Cambridge, 1877).

8) Bodleian Library, MS. Rawl. D. 912, fol. 230.
   Also in the Bodleian is an exercise in Latin verse on the theme
   "   sero medicina paratur
   Quum mala per longas convaluere moras."
   This exercise is signed "Johannes Norris e Coll Exon.", and the following note is appended: "This exercise was made in half an hour's time, and was imposed only upon Norris who had formerly spoke verses in the Theater but proposed to all who had a faculty that way." (MS. Tanner 466, fol. 74).

9) Practical Discourses, vol. 2, p. 131-4.

10) This sermon was followed by an important correspondence with Henry More. The sermon and correspondence are examined in ch. 3 of this book.

312

11) <u>Collections</u>, xv, 18 October 1707.

12) <u>Athenae Oxonienses</u>, iv, col. 584-6.

13) The article on John Norris in the D. N. B. attributes only two
sons and a daughter to him, but his Will, dated 4 May 1706
and preserved in the Wiltshire County Record Office, Trowbridge, names the four children mentioned in the text. John
Norris the younger entered University College, Oxford, on
27 March 1708, aged 16; he became B. A. in 1711, and M. A.
at Sidney Sussex College, Cambridge, in 1723. In 1719 he became vicar of Little Langford, Wilts. , where he was thus the
neighbour of Arthur Collier the metaphysician, rector of Steeple
Langford. Edward Norris entered Hart Hall, Oxford, on 18
March 1711/2, aged 19, a month after his father's death. In
1717 he became vicar of Stow-on-the Wold, Glos. Elizabeth
Norris married Thomas Bowyer, vicar of Martock, Somerset.

14) On Joseph Langton and the history of Newton St. Loe, cf. <u>The
Story of Newton St. Loe Manor</u>, (Newton Park Training College,
1953).

15) Cf. ch. 10, sect. 1.

16) Cf. ch. 10, sect. 2.

17) Cf. ch. 10, sect. 1.

18) <u>Pylades and Corinna</u>, ed. Sir Edward Northey (Vol. 2, London 1732)
p. 250.

19) Biographies of Lady Chudleigh, Lady Masham, and Mary Astell
may be found in George Ballard, <u>Memoirs of Several Ladies of
Great Britain, who have been celebrated for their Writings or
Skill in the Learned Languages, Arts, and Sciences</u>, (Oxford,
1752).

20) In an interesting letter dated 9 April 1707, to Dr. Charlett, Master
of University College, Oxford, Norris wrote: "The B. of S.

(Bishop of Salisbury) I find, and am also so informed from
those who well know his mind in that matter, is absolutely
resolved I shall never have anything here. And fata, you know,
non sunt demulcenda." (Letters written by Eminent Persons
in the 17th and 18th Centuries, (London, 1813), p. 156-8.)

In a conversation reported by J. B. Nichols in his Literary
Anecdotes of the Eighteenth Century (1812), vol. I, p. 639-40,
an account is given of a visit paid to Norris at Bemerton by a
certain Thomas Colburne, then a young man: "Mr. Norris treated
him very civilly; and, either before or after dinner, took him
out into his garden, from whence they had a full view of the city
and cathedral. "What a magnificent structure", said young Colburne, "is that great cathedral! You are happy, Sir, in this
delightful prospect." "Yes," said Mr. Norris, "it is all the
prospect that I have with respect to that cathedral"; meaning
that he had no expectation of preferment in it under the present
bishop."

21) Cf. the letter to Charlett quoted above. In the course of this
letter Norris sought Charlett's favour for his son John, who
was then nearly ready to go up to Oxford. And in fact the young
John Norris entered University College on 27 March 1708.

22) She informed him in particular that "the generality of readers
cannot prevail with themselves to allow that brutes are mere
machines. Though at the same time they grant you have set the
matter in a clearer light than any have done before, and con- ⸲
firmed it with arguments they are not able to answer". (Pylades
and Corinna, vol. 2, p. 206.) Five letters between Norris and
"Corinna" were published in 1727 in the second volume of Whartoniana: Letters to the Lady Wharton and several other Persons
of Distinction, a fact which led Powicke to the false conclusion

that Corinna was Lady Wharton (F. J. Powicke, <u>A Dissertation</u> <u>on John Norris of Bemerton</u>, p. 206f.); these were republished with four further letters in the second volume of <u>Pylades and</u> <u>Corinna</u> (1732), edited by Sir Edward Northey. (Pylades was a certain Richard Gwynnett, Corinna was Elizabeth Thomas). It seems certain that Northey published these letters in the wrong order.

23) <u>An Essay towards the Theory of the Intelligible World. In-</u> <u>tuitively Considered. Designed for Forty-Nine Parts. Part III.</u> <u>Consisting of a Preface, a Post-Script, and a little something</u> <u>between</u>, (London 1705) by "Gabriel John" who seems to have been the comic author and Whig pamphleteer Thomas d' Urfey "Gabriel John" took off Norris's addiction to long prefaces, to post-scripts, to long lists of errata, and to a sometimes unduly solemn style. In the course of the same work he also satirised other philosophers, particularly Hobbes.

24) "There are, I believe, very few systems of so abstract and metaphysical a nature that can vie with it, either in respect of the number or clearness of the arguments on which it is built." (<u>Works of Mr. Henry Needler</u>, ed. W. Duncombe, 2nd edition, London, 1728, p. 206). "Mr. Norris's <u>Theory of the Ideal World</u>, (how extravagant and enthusiastic soever his notions may appear to those who have not been conservant in <u>metaphysical</u> enquiries), is really an admirable performance, as being in respect either of the certainty, usefulness, or dignity of the subject scarce in- ferior to any other. His thoughts are great and sublime, yet easy and perspicuous; his fancy is beautiful and entertaining; and his way of reasoning for the most part just and exact." (Ibid. , p. 210-1).

25) Burnet announced the appearance of the First Part of Norris's

315

Theory to Leibniz in a letter dated 22 August 1701 (Niedersächsische Landesbibliothek, Hannover, Leibniz-Burnet Correspondence, Stück 110-1): later in the same year he wrote
from Paris, in his curious French: "Je fus ravi de plaisir alla lecture de quelques chapitres de ce nouveau livre de Monsieur Norris intitulé Theory of the Ideal or Intelligible World
et partic (particulièrement?) dans le chapitre qui a pour titre
Que l'existence du monde intellectuelle comme il l'appelle est
plus certain que du monde même sensible et naturelle, avec une
histoire de la certitude comparative della foi et de la raison
mise en ballance. Il y a des pensées spirituelles, métaphysiques, brodées des fleurs de l'éloquence et embelés de raptures
d'une âme véritablement zélé consacrant sa philosophie alla
piété. Ce n'était pas moi seul qui a gouté du plaisir, l'ingéni-
eux auteur même della Théorie de la Terre, de mon nom et sur-
nom, professait qu'il n'avait rien lu plus touchant que sa rhé-
torique philosophique et même naturelle dans la dernière chapitre qui traite della beauté du monde intellectuelle, et du bon-
heur de ceux qui y s'entretient avec quelques reflexions sur
les avantages qui se trouvent dans une vie contemplative et
solitaire. La lecture de cet article est un plaisir qui me man-
que encore." (Ibid., Stück 117-8).

26) "Je suis quasi du sentiment de M. Norris, dont vous me dites,
Monsieur, qu'il soutient que le monde intellectuel est plus certain que le monde sensible: mais je ne say si nous l'entendons
l'un comme l'autre." (Ibid., Stück 119-24; published in Gerhardt, Philosophische Schriften von G. W. Leibniz, vol 3, p. 285).

27) Acta Eruditorum, April 1708, p. 166-71. The author of this review was Christian Wolff. The Acta had already published a
favourable review of Norris's Account of Reason and Faith in

their October 1697 number, p. 442-9, written by G. Olearius.
I owe the details of the authorship of these reviews to the
kindness of the University Library, Leipzig.

28) Cf. ch. 9.

29) 1712 by our reckoning, when the new year begins on 1 January.

30) John Dunton was the editor of the Athenian Gazette, which published Le Clerc's unfavourable review of Norris's Cursory
Reflections. On Norris's relations with him, cf. our ch. 10,
note 29. Norris is frequently mentioned in Dunton's Life and
Errors, that interesting medley of autobiographical and literary
gossip, generally in terms which show considerable respect.

31) In 1683, it seems, he published A Murnival of Knaves, a burlesque poem attacking the Whigs, and particularly Shaftesbury
and Titus Oates. And cf. the dedication of the Miscellanies to
Finch, James II's nominee as Warden of All Souls.

32) In his letters to Melmoth, Norris based this view purely on the
New Testament. In practice such a view was very similar to
that taught, from an entirely different theoretical basis, by
Hobbes.

33) Norris's view on the source of the obligation to obey a law was
derived from Robert Sanderson's De Legum Humanarum Obligatione in Conscientia; his theory of law thus had a considerable
similarity to that proposed in Locke's Essays on the Law of
Nature.

34) The Charge of Schism Discharged, p. 35.

35) Ibid., p. 44.

36) The Distinction of High Church and Low Church, p. 22-3.

37) Ibid., p. 29.

38) A Treatise concerning Christian Prudence, p. 336.

39) In The Christian Religion as professed by a Daughter of the
Church of England, paras. 54-7, Mary Astell pictures herself
as an African, converted to Christianity by a Christian slave
in Barbary. Coming to Europe in order to follow her conscience,
she rejects successively the Roman Church and that of Geneva,
and finally joins herself to the Church of England, which alone,
she declares, combines biblical faith with the primitive and
traditional form of Church government. Mary Astell's book
dates from 1705, and thus precedes Norris's Treatise concerning Christian Prudence by five years. In The Life of Corinna, by Her Self (in vol. I of Pylades and Corinna, 1731), Elizabeth Thomas (Corinna) claims to have followed Norris's precepts
in this matter and to have become an Anglican after an objective
study of this sort.

CHAPTER II:

1) The suggestion is made by Anne B. Larner in her Manchester M.A. thesis The Ingenious Mr. Norris (Sept. 1965).

2) Hierocles upon the Golden Verses of the Pythagoreans, p. 2.

3) Ibid., p. 3.

4) Ibid., p. 4.

5) Ibid., p. 147.

6) Ibid., p. 151.

7) Ibid., Preface (unnumbered).

9) Athenae Oxonienses, iv, col. 584-6. Wood's remark was omitted from subsequent editions by the editor, Bishop Tanner.

10) It was doubtless this conception of "infused virtues" which made Norris reject all infused virtue as "a great paradox" in An Idea of Happiness, 1683.

11) It was no doubt from the addition of this address that the Tractatus adversus Reprobationis Absolutae Decretum, published anonymously, was immediately recognised as Norris's work. Powicke is in error when he declares (Dissertation on John Norris of Bemerton, p. 157) that the Bodleian copy of the Tractatus does not have this appendix. He used the present copy (8. S. 68. Art.), for he quotes a Latin note written in it in ink by a contemporary hand, and it seems that he must have been misled by the fact that the appendix is printed without a separate heading.

12) Miscellanies (1st edition), p. 397.

13) Ibid., p. 415.

14) Norris notes that some authors call this "divine virtue", and he does not object to this term provided it is not supposed that, while moral virtues are acquired by practice, "divine virtue" is infused. "Infused virtue seemed ever to me as great a para-

dox in divinity, as occult qualities in philosophy." (Miscellanies, p. 419-20). As is clear from his Tractatus adversus Reprobationis Absolutae Decretum, the "infused virtue" to which Norris objected was the idea of a virtue that would owe nothing to man's cooperation.

15) Miscellanies, p. 421.
16) See Chap. 4, sect. 2.
17) Miscellanies, p. 288-9.
18) Ibid., p. 289.
19) Ibid., p. 436-7.
20) Ibid., p. 440-1.
21) Ibid., p. 444.

CHAPTER III:

1) A Discourse concerning the Pretended Religious Assembling in Private Conventicles, wherein the Unlawfulness and Unreasonableness of it is fully evinced by several Arguments. By John Norris, M.A., and late Rector of Aldbourne in the County of Wilts., published posthumously by his son, John Norris, of All Souls College, (London, James Norris, 1685).

2) For More's views on these subjects, see A. Koyré, From the Closed World to the Infinite Universe, (Baltimore, 1957), esp. ch. vi.

3) The Theory and Regulation of Love, p. 146.

4) Miscellanies, (1st edition), p. 338-9.

5) Theory and Regulation of Love, Appendix.

6) Miscellanies, (1st edition), p. 341.

7) Cf. Recherche de la Vérité I, I, 2, (Oeuvres complètes I, p. 47); Eclaircissement I, (O.C. III, p. 19); Méditations Chrétiennes 6, 20, (O.C. X, p. 67); Entretiens sur la Métaphysique 12, 10, (O.C. XII-XIII, p. 289-90).

8) Cf. A. Robinet, Système et Existence dans l'oeuvre de Malebranche, (Paris, 1965) p. 351-2. Robinet quotes a number of passages in this sense which Malebranche added to the sixth edition of La Recherche ..., 1712.

9) Malebranche also, in his later years, came to consider that this question was a mere matter of words. Cf. La Recherche I, 2, 2, (O.C. I, p. 53-4) - a passage added to the sixth edition, 1712.

10) Miscellanies, (1st edition), p. 343.

11) Theory and Regulation of Love, p. 181.

12) Ibid., p. 203-4.

13) Ibid., p.232.

14) Ibid., p.228-9.

15) Ibid., p.235.

CHAPTER IV:

1) Note by the editor to a letter from Norris to Charlett, printed in Letters written by Eminent Persons in the Seventeenth and Eighteenth Centuries, (London, 1813).

2) Robert Watt, M.D., in Bibliotheca Britannica, (London, 1824).

3) Norris considered that it was particularly in theology that ambiguity of terms bedevilled controversy. In support of this view he referred to what Louis Le Blanc, the French Protestant theologian and professor at the Academy of Sedan, had written to this effect in the preface of his Theses Theologicae, (London, 1675).

4) Miscellanies (1st edition), p.151.

5) Ibid., p.198.

6) For the proof of this real identity, Norris refers back to his Letter of Ideas. In the fourth (revised) edition of the Miscellanies (1706), he omitted this reflection, realising that it was not essential to the progress of his argument.

7) Miscellanies (1st edition), p.303.

8) Ibid., p.204.

9) Ibid., p.205.

10) Ibid., p.205.

11) Ibid., p.206.

12) Norris's argument is to be found in De Mente Humana, p.17.

13) Entretiens sur la Métaphysique I, 10, (O.C. XII-XIII, p.45).

14) Theory and Regulation of Love, p.108.

15) Cf. S.Theol. I, II, q.26, a.4: "Sic ergo motus amoris in duo tendit, scilicet in bonum quod quis vult alicui, vel sibi vel alii, et in illud cui vult bonum. Ad illud ergo bonum quod quis vult alteri, habetur amor concupiscentiae; ad illud autem cui aliquis vult bonum, habetur amor amicitiae."

16) Miscellanies (4th edition), p. 367.

17) Méditations Chrétiennes 4, 14, (O. C. X, p. 42-3).

18) Miscellanies (4th edition), p. 367-8.

23) Miscellanies (1st edition), p. 307.

25) Ibid. , p. 367.

26) Ibid. , p. 369.

27) Ibid. , p. 367.

28) Miscellanies (4th edition), p. 297-8.

29) Miscellanies (1st edition), p. 379.

30) This post-script was the object of a misrepresentation by Jean Le Clerc in the course of his review of Norris's Cursory Reflections in the Bibliothèque Choisie for January, 1691. See our Chapter 10, note 29.

31) Miscellanies (1st edition), p. 211.

32) Ibid. , p. 230.

33) Ibid. , p. 232.

34) Ibid. , p. 233.

35) Ibid. , p. 176-7.

36) Ibid. , p. 456.

37) Ibid. , p. 173.

38) Ibid. , p. 168.

39) Cf. Maren-Sophie Røstvig, The Happy Man. Studies in the Metamorphoses of a Classical Ideal, (Oslo, 1954-58); H. N. Fairchild, Religious Trends in English Poetry, (New York, 1939 ss.); John Hoyles, The Waning of the Renaissance. (The Hague, 1971); J. Hoyles, The Fringes of Augustanism (The Hague, 1972). Anne B. Larner's Manchester M. A. thesis on The Ingenious Mr. Norris, (Sept. 1965), which, it is to be hoped, will in due course be published, is also mainly concerned with Norris as a poet and literary figure.

40) <u>Theory of the Ideal or Intelligible World</u>, Part I, p.174-5:

"Lay down Proud Heart thy rebel arms,

And own thy Conqueror Divine ...." (Cf.Ch. 5, n. 8)

<u>Theory ...</u>, Part 2, p.561:

"Sing then ye blest attendants on his throne,

Hymns as immortal as your joys above;

The fountain of your bliss and knowledge own,

And as you shine with light, so burn with love.

Praise the great Author of your brighter day,

To us below a star, to you a sun:

With never silent harps this tribute pay,

And Halleluyas that are still begun.

You see the rising springs of life and light,

Which with a double tide your breasts o'erflow,

Oh praise the beatific object of your sight,

Whose good's your life, and by whose light you know.

You need not fear the exhausting of your lays,

While you in song exalt your heavenly King;

He has a boundless theme to employ your praise,

As you a whole eternity to sing. (Cf.Ch. 5, n. 96)

41) Cf. <u>The Copy of a Letter written to my Friend F. B. concerning the Death of my Dear Niece M.C.</u> , in <u>Miscellanies</u>, (1st edition), p.456.

42) <u>Epod. Carm.</u> 2: "Beatus ille qui procul negotiis ...".

43) Cf. the Preface to <u>Theory of the Ideal or Intelligible World</u>, Part 2.

44) Cf. Røstvig, op.cit., p. 367-73.

45) Cf. Henri Gouhier, <u>Les premières pensées de Descartes</u>, contribution à l'histoire de l'anti-renaissance, (Paris, 1958).

46) In his <u>The Waning of the Renaissance</u>, 1640-1740, John Hoyles

further points out the way in which Norris, as the last of the Metaphysical poets, points forward across the Eighteenth Century to the beginnings of Romanticism.

47) The Theory and Regulation of Love (1688) contains Norris's first references to Malebranche. Reason and Religion (1689) is strongly influenced by Malebranche.

CHAPTER V:

1) <u>Reason and Religion</u>, p. 13.

2) Ibid., p. 18.

3) Cf. F. I. Mackinnon, <u>The Philosophy of John Norris of Bemer-ton</u>, p. 50; J. Muirhead, <u>The Platonic Tradition in Anglo-Saxon Philosophy</u>, p. 105.

4) <u>Reason and Religion</u>, p. 20.

5) Ibid., p. 55.

6) Preface to <u>Theory</u>, Pt. I, p. i-ii.

7) <u>Theory of the Ideal ... World</u>, Pt. I, p. 4. On Malebranche's lack of a clear theory of the Ideas in themselves, cf. F. Alquié, <u>Le Cartésianisme de Malebranche</u>, p. 212-33.

8) Lay down, proud heart, thy rebel arms,
And own thy Conqueror divine,
In vain thou dost resist such charms,
In vain the arrows of his love decline.

There is no dealing with this potent fair,
I must, my God, I must love thee.
Thy charms but too victorious are,
They leave me not my native liberty.

A holy force spreads through my soul,
And ravishes my heart away.
The world its motion does control
In vain, the happy captive will not stay.

No more does she her wonted freedom boast,
More proud of thy celestial chain,
Free-will itself were better lost
Than ever to revolt from thee again.

Sun of my soul, what shall I do
Thy beauties to resist or bear?
They bless, and yet they pain me too,
I feel thy heat too strong, thy light too clear.

327

I faint, I languish, I almost expire,
My panting heart dissolving lies,
Thou must shine less, or I retire,
Shade thou thy light, I cannot turn my eyes.

Theory, Pt. I, p. 174-5.

9) Theory, Pt. I, p. 240.

10) Cf. esp. Malebranche, Traité de la Nature et de la Grâce,
O. C. V.

11) Theory, Pt. I, p. 292-3, referring to Suarez, Disputationes
Metaphysicae, disp. 23, sect. 10, n. II.

12) Theory, Pt. I, p. 330, referring to Suarez, Disp. Met. , disp.
47, sect. 2, n. 22.

13) Theory, Pt. I, p. 407: title of chap. 7.

14) Ibid.

15) On the various Scholastic theories, cf. Suarez, Disp. Met. , disp.
31; John of St. Thomas, Cursus Philosophicus, I, q. 7, n. 4; Pedr
Descoqs, S. J. , Praelectiones Theologiae Naturalis, p. 531-68;
Dictionnaire de Théologie Catholique, art. Essence.

16) Theory, Pt. I, p. 232, et passim.

17) Cf. ch. 9.

18) Reason and Religion, p. 110.

19) Cf. ch. 7.

20) Cf. p. 53 ff.

21) Recherche de la Vérité I, ch. 2; O. C. I, p. 49 ff.

22) Reason and Religion, p. 108-9.

23) Theory of the Ideal ... World, Pt. 2, p. 483-4.

24) Reflections upon the Conduct of Human Life, p. 215-6.

25) Cf. ch. 6.

26) Discourse concerning the Measure of Divine Love (Practical
Discourses Vol. 3), p. 21.

27) Ibid. , p. 34.

328

28) Ibid. , p. 40-1.

29) This radical individualism, which holds that no substance has any necessary connection with any other substance other than God, marks the distance which separates Norris from the vitalist type of thinking characteristic of the Cambridge Platonists. Cf. ch. 11.

30) Norris in fact inclined to think that the occasionalist account of causality could be generalised in accordance with Malebranche's views: cf. Letters concerning the Love of God, p. 309, where he refers approvingly to Malebranche's 15th Eclaircissement to La Recherche de la Vérité (O. C. III, p. 211 ff.) But he never argued ex professo in this sense.

31) Theory of the Ideal . . . World, Pt. 2, p. 358.

32) Cf. ch. 10, sect. 1.

33) Cf. ch. 11, sect. 3.

34) Theory of the Ideal . . . World, Pt. I, p. 190. Malebranche went on to argue from the bible considered as appearance to the reality of the material world: cf. 6th Eclaircissement to La Recherche de la Vérité, (O. C. III, p. 64-5); Norris did not follow Malebranche's reasoning on this point, though there was nothing in his principles to prevent him from doing so.

35) Theory of the Ideal World, Pt. I, p. 200.

36) Ibid. , p. 203-4.

37) Cf. ch. 11, sect. 3.

38) Cf. esp. 10th Eclaircissement to La Recherche de la Vérité (O. C. III, p. 127 ff.); Méditations Chrétiennes (OC. X); Entretiens sur la Métaphysique (O. C. XII-XIII). Cf. ch. 4, note 13.

39) Reason and Religion, p. 110.

40) Reason and Religion, p. 110-9. La Recherche de la Vérité III, II, ch. I-6, O. C. II, p. 413-447.

41) Reason and Religion, p. 111.

42) Ibid., p. 111.

43) Ibid., p. 120.

44) Ibid., p. 126-7.

45) E. g. in Norris's controversies with Locke and especially with the Quakers. Cf. ch. 10.

46) Cf. ch. 9.

47) Que les objets matériels n' envoyent point d' espéces qui leur ressemblent. Title of Recherche III, II, ch. 2.

48) Title of Theory of the Ideal World, Pt. 2, ch. 7.

49) Theory, Pt. 2, p. 349.

50) Ibid., p. 356.

51) In 1896 the American psychologist Stratton did the experiment of wearing for several weeks glasses which reversed the images in his eyes. At first he saw things upside down, but then in due course he saw them the right way up again. When he gave up wearing these glasses, the experience was repeated. This experiment would have pleased Norris, since it proved that the images on the retina are not the immediate object of vision. See L' année psychologique (1896), p. 382.

52) Theory, Pt. 2, p. 367.

53) Ibid., p. 371.

54) Ibid., p. 517.

55) Ibid., p. 369.

56) Title of Theory, Pt. 2, ch. 8.

57) Theory, Pt. 2, p. 381-2.

58) Title of Theory, Pt. 2, ch. 9.

59) Theory, Pt. 2, p. 400.

60) Ibid., p. 400. It is characteristic of the scrupulous honesty of Norris in his later writings that he mentions that the source of

his knowledge of Arnauld's theory was Malebranche's reply to it.

61) Que nous voyons toutes choses en Dieu. Title of Recherche III, II, ch. 6.

62) Title of Theory, Pt. 2, ch. II.

63) Title of Theory, Pt. 2, ch. 12.

64) Norris did not think it necessary to add the Platonic doctrine of reminiscence as a further alternative, although in his earlier writings he had treated its presupposition - the preexistence of the soul - as a real possibility. Norris was convinced that the Ideas, far from being merely remembered, imposed themselves on the mind as actually present.

65) Theory, Pt. 2, p. 426.

66) Norris had already advanced this argument in Reflections upon the Conduct of Human Life. Cf. ch. 7.

67) Theory, Pt. 2, p. 435.

68) Ibid., p. 444-5.

69) Ibid., p. 445.

70) Ibid., p. 453.

71) Ibid., p. 491 ff.

72) Malebranche himself implied this in a very relevant passage which Norris quoted from Entretiens sur la Métaphysique, Entr. II, sect. 5; O. C. XII-XIII, p. 53-4.

73) Theory, Pt. 2, p. 496.

74) Ibid., p. 511-2.

75) Ibid., p. 512.

76) Ibid., p. 514.

77) Contemplation and Love, in Miscellanies (1st ed.), p. 295. The passage was reprinted unchanged in the revised 4th edition of 1706, (on p. 234).

78) Theory, Pt. 2, p. 187.

79) In his Reflections on Locke's Essay, Norris distinguished between pure intellect and imagination in terms of whether the ideas which were known represented objects in a material or an immaterial way. "As our Ideas are all of them immaterial as to their essence and substance, so many, perhaps most, of them are also immaterial as to their representation, that is, they represent after an immaterial manner, as the ideas of truth, virtue, and the like; which Cartesius makes to be the difference between imagination and pure intellection, and whereof he gives an instance in the example of a chiliagon, whose angles we cannot represent in a distinct view, but may clearly understand it." (Cursory Reflections, p. 27). The language of this passage is very close to that of the Second Part of the Theory, but in Cursory Reflections Norris clearly teaches that Ideas of pure intellect can represent material things (e. g. a chiliagon) in an immaterial manner, whereas in the Second Part of the Theory he derives the distinction purely from the material or immaterial nature of the object that is represented.

80) Theory, Pt. 2, p. 193-4.

81) Ibid., p. 199.

82) Ibid., p. 192-3.

83) Theory, Pt. 1, p. 53. Flora Mackinnon in fact criticises Norris in a very similar way: "One of the arguments for the existence of the Ideal World is that, in comparing sensible objects with the ideas, we find the shapes of the sensible things less accurate than the "ideal" figures. How the comparison is possible if the ideal figures are really the only ones we can see, Norris does not explain." (Philosophy of John Norris of Bemerton, p. 92).

84) Cf. Entretiens sur la Métaphysique, Entr. V, sect. 5; O. C. XII-XIII, p. 115-6.

85) Ainsi lorsque je vois le soleil, je vois l'idée du cercle en
Dieu, et j'ai en moi le sentiment de lumière qui me marque
que cette idée représente quelque chose de créé et d'actuelle-
ment existant. (Conversations Chrétiennes, Entr. III; O. C. IV,
p. 67. Quoted by Norris in Theory, Pt. 2, p. 495).

86) Cf. Réponse au Livre des Vraies et des Fausses Idées, ch. 17,
O. C. VI-VII, p. 126; Entretiens sur la Métaphysique, Entr. I,
O. C. XII-XIII, p. 46.

87) Cf. Entretiens sur la Métaphysique, Entr. I, O. C. XII-XIII, p. 46.

88) Cf. Réponse au Livre des Vraies et des Fausses Idées, ch. 9,
O. C. VI-VII, p. 78: Il faut que l'esprit ait l'idée de l'étendue,
afin qu'il y attache, pour ainsi dire, le sentiment de couleur:
de même qu'il faut une toile à un peintre, afin qu'il y applique
les couleurs. And cf. Réponse à Régis, O. C. XVII-I, p. 281 ff.,
and Entretiens sur la Mort, Entr. II, O. C. XII-XIII, p. 407-8.

89) On the ambiguity latent in Malebranche's idea of intelligible
extension, cf. F. Alquié, Le Cartésianisme de Malebranche, p.
506-7.

90) Cf. F. Alquié, Le Cartésianisme de Malebranche, p. 218-26.

91) Reason and Religion, p. 125.

92) Theory, Pt. 2, p. 483-4.

93) Cursory Reflections, p. 34-5.

94) Theory, Pt. 2, p. 267.

95) It follows from this view that, while mathematics are a priori,
the natural sciences must follow an a posteriori method. In
Spiritual Counsel Norris commended "the experiemental philosophy", though he never practised it himself.

96) Norris ends his book by evoking the moral and religious consequences of his theory, which shows that God is the only good of
man, the only source of his light. Reflection on this theme leads

him to praise of God, culminating in the last poem that he
wrote:

Sing then ye blest attendants on his throne,
Hymns as immortal as your joys above;
The fountain of your bliss and knowledge own,
And as you shine with light, so burn with love.

Praise the great Author of your brighter day,
To us below a star, to you a sun:
With never silent harps this tribute pay,
And Halleluyas that are still begun.

You see the rising springs of life and light,
Which with a double tide your brests o'erflow,
Oh praise the beatific object of your sight,
Whose good's your life, and by whose light you know.

You need not fear the exhausting of your lays,
While you in song exalt your heavenly King;
He has a boundless theme to employ your praise,
As you a whole eternity to sing.

CHAPTER VI:

1) Faciunt civitates duas amores duo. Hierusalem facit amor
   Dei; Babylonem amor saeculi. Interroget ergo se quisque quid
   amet, et inveniet unde sit civis. De Civitate Dei, 1. 14, cap.28

2) Theory and Regulation of Love, p. 4.

3) Ibid. , p. 10.

4) Ibid. , p. 17-18.

5) Ibid. , p. 14.

6) Ibid. , p. 31.

7) Norris thought that he differed from Malebranche on this point.
   Referring to the latter's Traité de la Nature et de la Grâce,
   III, 3, (O. C. V, p. 118-19), he wrote: "Indeed the excellent
   Monsieur Malebranche in his Treatise of Nature and Grace
   asserts this non determination of our love to particular goods
   in more large and unlimited terms, when he tells us that
   The natural motion of the soul to good in general is not invin-
   cible in respect of any particular good. And in this non invin-
   cibility he places our liberty or free will. But in my judgement",
   Norris continued, "this proposition of his must either be corrected or better explained." (Theory and Regulation of Love,
   p. 34-5). Norris recognised, however, that it was possible
   that Malebranche did not really differ from his own view, and
   this was in fact the case. The first Eclaircissement to La
   Recherche de la Vérité (O. C. III, p. 31-32) makes it clear that
   Malebranche's view was identical with Norris's.

8) Theory and Regulation of Love, p. 54.

9) Ibid. , p. 56-7.

10) Practical Discourses, Vol. 2, p. 214-5.

11) For Aquinas's teaching, see e. g. Summa Theologica Ia IIae, q. 27.

12) Theory and Regulation of Love, p. 65.

13) Ibid. , p. 69-70

14) Ibid. , p. 76-7.

15) Cf. R. Cumberland, Treatise of the Law of Nature (tr. John Maxwell, London, 1727), p. 44. Marsilio Ficino, Théologie Platonicienne (ed. Raymond Marcel, Paris, 1964), p. 108-9: "Cum igitur mirabilis ordo mundi casu ordinis experte constare non possit, necesse est in opificis ipsius intelligentia formam esse, ad cuius similitudinem sit effectus. Et quoniam Dei proposito universi ordo potissimus est, principalis penes illum idea est idea ordinis universi" (quoted in Theory of the Ideal World, Pt. I, p. 179). Cf. also Ficino, op. cit. , p. 102: "Si igitur Deus aliam ullam cognoscit rem nobilem, quod tu non negas, maxime ordinem universi cognoscet. Ordo huiusmodi non aliter intelligi potest quam si pretiosiora quaelibet et viliora inter se discernantur, in quorum intervallis proportionibusque totius ordo consistit".

16) Theory and Regulation of Love, p. 92.

17) In this matter, Norris keeps to the position to which his correspondence with Henry More had led him.

18) Ibid. , p. 114.

19) Ibid. , p. 120-1. These seems no reason to think, with Powicke (Dissertation on John Norris of Bemerton, p. 11), that this passage represents a veiled request on Norris's part that Lady Masham, to whom the book was dedicated, should find

him a benefice, and that she was bound to be offended by it. An ecclesiastical benefice would be, for Norris, an obvious example of an office involving the common good. And it is certain that Lady Masham did not take offence at this time: she remained on good terms with Norris for several years more, and was instrumental in obtaining for him the benefice of Bemerton in 1691-2.

20) Theory and Regulation of Love, p. 125.

21) L'Idéalisme en Angleterre au 18e siècle, (Paris, 1888), p. 193.

22) Malebranche's views on the divisions of love are expressed chiefly in his Traité de Morale and Traité de l'amour de Dieu. They are well summarised in Y. de Montcheuil, Malebranche et le quiétisme (Paris, 1946), p. 132-6.

23) In the dedicatory letter to the Traité de Morale, Malebranche writes: "N'ayant point une idée claire de l'âme ... c'est une nécéssité que la pluspart des termes de Morale n'expriment que des sentiments confus." (O.C. XI, p. 3).

24) "I found it necessary sometimes to use new terms, and such as would raise more clear and distinct ideas than those which had before obtained ..." (Introductory Letter to the Reader, Theory and Regulation of Love).

25) Theory and Regulation of Love, p. 10.

26) Practical Discourses, vol. 2, p. 118-9.

27) Ibid., p. 120.

28) A Discourse concerning the Measure of Divine Love is the first Discourse of the Third Volume of Practical Discourses.

29) Practical Discourses, vol. 3, p. 10.

30) Ibid., p. 19.

31) Practical Discourses, vol. 3, p. 70-1.

32) Ibid. , p. 71-2.

33) Ibid. , p. 73-4.

34) Mary Astell (1668-1731) was the daughter of a merchant of
Newcastle-upon-Tyne. Educated by a clerical relative, she
became a literary figure of considerable interest. In her
Proposal to the Ladies (1694) she called for the establishment of a house which would have been something between
an Anglican convent and a university college for women: a
house to which ladies could retire, without vows or the obligation to remain indefinitely, in order to give themselves
to study and prayer. This interesting project encountered
the opposition of Gilbert Burnet, the same Bishop of Salisbury who was hostile to Norris, who thought that it savoured
of Popery, and was never realised. A decided tory and supporter of the High Church party, Mary Astell was a friend of
Francis Atterbury. She defended Norris's teaching on a number of subjects in her later book The Christian Religion as
professed by a Daughter of the Church of England (1705). Cf.
George Ballard: Memoirs of Several Ladies of Great Britain,
who have been celebrated for their Writings or skill in the
Learned Languages, Arts, and Sciences (Oxford, 1752).

35) Cf. Traité de Morale II, ch. 2, sect. 3; O. C. XI, p. 158-9.

36) The Discourse concerning the Love of God was originally
taken for Locke's work by Thomas Burnet, the correspondent
of Leibniz, and hence by Leibniz himself. It was only when
Pierre Coste published a translation of Lady Masham's book
(Discours de la'amour divin, Amsterdam, 1705) and sent him
a copy that Leibniz learned that she was the author.

37) <u>Discourse concerning the Love of God</u>, p. 18.

38) In the forth edition of the <u>Miscellanies</u> (1706), Norris made certain changes in his <u>Letter concerning Platonic Love</u> and <u>Treatise of Heroic Piety</u>, thus perhaps taking account of Whitby's criticisms.

39) <u>Practical Discourses</u>, vol. 4, p. 407-8.

40) Ibid. , p. 419-20.

41) <u>The Christian Religion</u> . . . , p. 136.

42) A particular example of such misunderstanding became current on the continent. In a letter of 4 May 1697 Thomas Burnet wrote to Leibniz about the dispute on the love of God "que Monsieur Norris veut qui soit des la complaisance ou delectation en Dieu pour lui-même, sans raport à nous ou l'amour qu'il apelle de desir", adding that "Mademoiselle Ash (= Astell) une jeune fille de 20 ans a merveilleusement bien ecrit sur cet sujet en lettres à Monsieur Norris." (Niedersächsiche Landesbibliothek, Hannover, Correspondence Leibniz-Burnet, Stück 54). This was of course the reverse of the truth, since Norris insisted that our love for God could only be one of desire. Burnet also wrote to the same effect to the Electress Sophia (Ibid. , Stück 58). Basing himself on this erroneous information, Leibniz wrote to his French correspondents Nicaise and Morell that the French dispute on disinterested love had passed "par contagion" to England, where Norris contended that our love for God ought to be disinterested and free from any admixture of desire. (To Nicaise, 28 May 1697, printed in Gerhardt, <u>Philosophische Schriften von G. W. Leibniz</u>, vol. 2, p. 569; to Morell, 31 May 1697, printed in Grua, <u>Leibniz: Textes Inédits</u>, vol. 1, p. 108). It was only in 1705,

when he read Pierre Coste's translation of Lady Masham's
Discourse concerning the Love of God, that Leibniz understood what Norris's teaching on the love of God really was.
He then wrote on 4 July 1706 to Coste that "Il y a quelque
chose de joli dans cette expression de M. Norris, que Dieu
ne peut estre aimé d'un amour de bienveuillance, et que la
créature ne doit pas estre aimée d'un amour de desir; et on
la peut rendre bonne en expliquant la bienveuillance par la
volonté de procurer du bien à quelcun, et le desir par une
volonté portée à l'objet sans limitation ou reserve, au lieu
que les biens temporels ne doivent estre demandés qu'avec
modification. Mais il faut avouer que cette explication des
termes n'est pas assez conforme à l'usage ... Cependant
je crois qu'il faut pardonner aux auteurs les expressions
eloignées de l'usage ordinaire, quand elles servent d'ail-
leurs à insinuer quelque bonne pensée, parceque souvent nous
manquons de termes appropriés". (In Gerhardt, Philosophische Schriften von G. W. Leibniz, vol. 3, p. 382-6; Robinet,
Malebranche et Leibniz, p. 389-90).

43) This post-script does not immediately follow the Discourse
concerning the Measure of Divine Love, the first of the seven
which comprise the third volume of Practical Discourses, but
is printed at the end of the volume. It was presumably added
after Norris had completed the composition of all the sermons
in the volume, but before this had been printed.

44) Practical Discourses, vol. 3, p. 342.

45) Cf. Traité de Morale I.

CHAPTER VII:

1) The first volume was originally published under the title of Christian Blessedness: or, Discourses upon the Beatitudes. Later editions were entitled Practical Discourses upon the Beatitudes. The other three volumes were always entitled Practical Discourses upon several Divine Subjects.

2) The first edition is not now easily obtainable, and the author is grateful to the Librarian of Christ Church, Oxford, for allowing him to use that library's copy of this book, which is not to be found in the Bodleian.

   For Norris's misunderstanding regarding the supposed blindness of Lady Masham, which was reflected in the first edition of Reflections upon the Conduct of Human Life and corrected in the second edition, see chap. 10, sect. 1.

3) See chap. 11, sect. 3.

4) Reflections upon the Conduct of Human Life, p. 173.

5) This was the first occasion on which Norris used the term "omniformity", which he derived from Marsilio Ficino and Henry More.

6) When "Corinna" (Mrs. Elizabeth Thomas) wrote to ask Norris's advice for the direction of her studies, he replied by urging her to learn French. "It is the most commanding, and therefore most useful language at present, and Malebranche alone will abundantly reward all the pains you shall take in it, which need not be great neither, if omitting the tedious way of learning the grammar, you only read over twice or thrice the particles, next the verbs, and then proceed to go over the Dialogues, and after that any plain book with a translation, by

341

which way you may be mistress of French so far, as to read
a book by the help of a dictionary, in a month's time. I speak
upon experience, and would have you try". (Pylades and Corinna, vol. II, p. 204-5). Norris later corrected French exercises for her, and in her autobiography she claimed to have
learnt French, following his instructions, in less than two
months. For what Norris advised her to read, cf. our chap.
II, sect. 1.

7) Reflections upon the Conduct of Human Life, p. 186.

8) Ibid. , p. 188.

9) The Works of Mr. Henry Needler. Consisting of Original Poems,
Translations, Essays, and Letters ... Published by Mr. Duncombe (Second Edition, London, 1728), p. 112-3.

10) Cf. chap. 10, sect. 2.

11) La Recherche de la Vérité, VI, II, ch. I; O. C. II, p. 295 ff.

12) Reflections upon the Conduct of Human Life, p. 208-9.

13) Ibid. , p. 222.

14) Cf. chap. II, sect. 3. Norris's view of these paradoxes seems
to have been derived chiefly from J. Glanvil: The Vanity of
Dogmatizing.

15) Reflections upon the Conduct of Human Life, p. 234.

16) Ibid. , p. 240.

17) Ibid. , p. 253.

18) Ibid. , p. 254.

19) F. I. Mackinnon, The Philosophy of John Norris of Bemerton,
p. 78.

20) E. Elys, <u>Reflections upon some Passages in a Book entitled</u> <u>Reflections upon the Conduct of Human Life</u> (no date). Cf. chap. 10, sect. 2.

21) <u>Reflections upon the Conduct of Human Life</u>, p. 258.

22) Cf. especially Malebranche's Preface to <u>La Recherche de la</u> <u>Vérité.</u>

23) This thought of how easily manuscripts might be lost may reflect the position in Norris's home with children in the house; perhaps it accounts for the fact that he seems to have hurried to print everything that he wrote.

24) <u>Spiritual Counsel</u> attained its 17th edition in 1733. "Corinna" sent Norris a French translation of it, the work of Charles, Marquis of Worcester, when aged 8. Norris replied to her that "I greatly admire the performance of the child (if it be really his)". It seems afterwards to have been printed under the title <u>Conseil Spirituel, ou Avis d'un Père à ses Enfans.</u> <u>Traduit de l'Anglois en Francois par un jeune Milord, âgé</u> <u>de huit ans</u>, 8°, 1698. Cf. <u>Pylades and Corinna</u>, vol. II, p. 212.

25) <u>Spiritual Counsel</u>, p. 472.

26) Ibid., p. 473.

27) Ibid., p. 490-1.

28) Ibid., p. 499.

29) Ibid., p. 503.

30) Cf. chap. 6 for references to the teaching of <u>A Discourse concerning the Excellency of Praise and Thanksgiving</u> (from <u>Practical Discourses</u>, vol. 2) and for an analysis of <u>A Discourse</u> <u>concerning the Measure of Divine Love</u> (from vol. 3).

31) <u>A Discourse concerning Religious Singularity</u>, in <u>Practical</u> <u>Discourses</u>, vol. 2, p. 105.

32) A Discourse of the Honour due to Good Men, in Practical Discourses, vol. 3, p. 275.

33) Ibid.

34) This was particularly true of A Murnival of Knaves, and to a lesser degree of Tractatus adversus Reprobationis Absolutae Decretum.

35) In Practical Discourses, vol. 4, p. 157 ff.

36) A Discourse concerning Charity to the Poor, in Practical Discourses, vol. 4, p. 301-2.

37) A Discourse concerning the Right Use of the World, in Practical Discourses, vol. 4, p. 332.

38) Cf. chap. 9.

39) Practical Treatise concerning Humility, p. 4.

40) Ibid. , p. 158.

41) Ibid. , p. 159.

42) Nolunt homines facere quod justum est, sive quia latet an justum sit, sive quia non delectat (Augustine, De Peccatorum Meritis et Remissione, quoted in Malebranche, Traité de la Nature et de la Grâce, II, 2, O. C. V, p. 100).

43) Treatise concerning Christian Prudence, p. 70. Prudence in general is "a practical knowledge of good and evil, actually directive of the will in the choice of that which is good and refusal of that which is evil", (Ibid. , p. 69).

44) Ibid. , p. 90-1.

45) Ibid. , p. 92.

46) Cf. J. Butler, The Analogy of Religion, Pt. 2, chap. 6.

47) Treatise concerning Christian Prudence, p. 230.

48) Wesley read Norris's <u>Treatise concerning Christian Prudence</u> to a girl who was ill on the ship carrying him to Georgia in 1735. He himself had read it at least four times while at Oxford. That the discussion of "half-Christians" was his favourite part of the book is clear both from his own explicit statements and also from the fact that he reproduced it almost in full in his otherwise greatly shortened edition of the book.

49) <u>Treatise concerning Christian Prudence</u>, p. 237.

50) Cf. the conclusion of John Hoyles: "Both his religion and his poetry belong to the tradition of the Caroline divines and lyricists. But Norris appears so late in time that his religious spirit seems to be transmitting these Caroline insights forward into the age of pietism and Evangelicalism. If the echo and the intimation constitute two strands in Norris's religious thought, they are defined and regulated by the pressures of a third; for his commendation of experimental religion is not untinged with the prudent spirit of Enlightenment orthodoxy. Norris thus not only points back to Herbert and forward to Wesley, but also qualifies the sweetness of his spirit with the cold touch of Butler's argument from analogy and probability. In registering simultaneously these three strands of the religious spirit, Norris pinpoints the metamorphosis from Renaissance to modern in a unique if eclectic way." (<u>The Waning of the Renaissance, 1640-1740</u>, The Hague, 1971, p. 120-1). With this judgement we would largely agree, while emphasising the unity of Norris's thought in itself.

CHAPTER VIII:

1) An Account of Reason and Faith: Preface.

2) An Account of Reason and Faith, p. 54.

3) Ibid. , p. 79.

4) Cf. Reflections upon a Theological Distinction, according to which it is said that some Articles of Faith are Above Reason, but not Against Reason, published by Boyle as an appendix to his Christian Virtuoso (London, 1690-1).

5) An Account of Reason and Faith, p. 116-7.

6) Ibid. , p. 124.

7) Cf. the Post-script to An Account of Reason and Faith, in which Norris praises the attempt of William Whiston, in A New Theory of the Earth (London, 1696), to account for the biblical Flood in terms of Newtonian physics.

8) An Account of Reason and Faith, p. 171.

9) Norris mentions N. Malebranche, Traité de la Nature et de la Grâce, and Pierre Poiret, Economie Divine, as the two most important attempts to explain the working of divine providence, but declares that not even they throw light on its essential mystery.

10) An Account of Reason and Faith, p. 240-1.

11) In Principes de la Philosophie, Pt. I, art. 76, Descartes writes: "Surtout, nous tiendrons pour règle infaillable, que ce que Dieu a révélé est incomparablement plus certain que le reste; afin que, si quelque étincelle de raison semblait nous suggérer quelque chose au contraire, nous soyons tou-jours prêts à soumettre notre jugement à ce qui vient de sa part. Mais, pour ce qui est des vérités dont la théologie ne se mêle point, il n'y aurait pas d'apparence qu'un homme

qui veut être philosophe reçut pour vrai ce qu'il n'a point connu être tel, et qu'il aimât mieux se fier à ses sens, c'est-à-dire aux jugements inconsidérés de son enfance, qu'à sa raison, lorsqu'il est en état de la bien conduire."

12) La Recherche de la Vérité, I, ch. 3, sect. 2, (O. C. I, p. 62): "Il faut se soumettre également à la foi et à l'évidence: mais dans les choses de la foi il ne faut point en chercher l'évidence avant que de les croire; comme dans celles de la nature il ne faut point s'arrêter à la foi, c'est-à-dire à l'autorité des philosophes. En un mot, pour être fidèle il faut croire aveuglément, mais pour être philosophe il faut voir évidemment."

13) An Account of Reason and Faith, p. 280-1.

14) See note 12 above.

15) Entretiens sur la Métaphysique, Ent. 14, sect. 3; (O. C. XII-XIII, p. 336). Malebranche goes on to uphold the reasonableness of believing in the infallibility of the Church, a principle which Norris did not accept.

16) In Norris's view, for example, the Calvinist doctrine of predestination contradicted the known attributes of God, and must be rejected for this reason.

17) An Account of Reason and Faith, p. 287.

18) Ibid., p. 300-1.

19) In the Miscellanies. See ch. 4, p. 91-2.

20) An Account of Reason and Faith, p. 319.

21) Norris never encountered Unitarianism as an interpretation of the New Testament. He was concerned only with the philosophical Socinianism of Toland, which was in fact a thinly veiled from of deism.

22) An Account of Reason and Faith, p. 64.

23) Theory of the Ideal ... World, Pt. I, p. 219.

24) Norris suggests that such a special illumination may have been given to "the inspired writers, prophets, and apostles"; but noone now, he declares, would claim such a thing except "those that plead for inward revelation and immediate inspiration".

25) Ibid., p. 219-20. Norris had already earlier examined moral certainty in A Discourse concerning Righteous and Unrighteous Judgement, in Practical Discourses, vol. 2.

26) Theory of the Ideal World, Pt. I, p. 221.

27) Ibid.

28) Daniel Waterland commends the study of An Account of Reason and Faith, together with that of Norris's Practical Discourses and his works on Humility and Prudence, in his Advice to a Student (1729). H. Croft, as has been seen, commended its study to the Unitarian Joseph Priestley in the introductory letter to his edition of it. Bishop van Mildert describes Norris as "having treated the subject (of the nature of faith) with peculiar accuracy.", in his Boyle Lectures, 4th ed., Vol. 2, p. 133.

CHAPTER IX:

1) Title of the first chapter of <u>Theory</u> . . . , Pt. II.

2) <u>Theory</u> . . . , Pt. II, p. 3.

3) See ch. 10, part 1.

4) <u>Theory</u> . . . , Pt. II, p. 24.

5) <u>Letter to Mr. Dodwell</u> . . . , p. 150-1.

6) <u>Theory</u> . . . , Pt. II, p. 38.

7) Cf. <u>Conversations Chrétiennes</u>, Entr. III, (O. C. IV, p. 68-9).

8) <u>Theory</u> . . . , Pt. II, p. 48.

9) Locke to Collins, 21 March 1703/4; in <u>A Collection of Several</u> <u>Pieces of Mr. John Locke</u> (London, 1720), p. 300.

10) <u>Remarks on what Mr. Norris hath said</u> . . . , p. 179.

11) Ibid. , p. 193.

12) "The general idea of substance being the same everywhere, the modification of thinking, or the power of thinking joined to it, makes it a spirit . . . . As on the other side, substance that has the modification of solidity is matter whether it has the modification of thinking or no." Locke, <u>First Letter to the Bishop</u> <u>of Worcester</u>, in <u>Works</u> (London, 1824), vol. 3, p. 33.

13) <u>The Christian Religion</u> . . . , p. 256-7.

14) Locke, <u>Essay concerning Human Understanding</u>, Bk. IV, ch. 3, no. 6.

15) <u>Letter to Mr. Dodwell</u> . . . , p. III.

16) It is interesting to note that Leibniz corresponded with Lady Masham on this same subject. Their letters are reproduced in Gerhardt, <u>Philosophische Schriften von G. W. Leibniz</u>, vol. 3, p. 336-63. In a letter of 30 June 1704 Leibniz expressed his view in terms very similar to Norris. "Ce serait . . . par un miracle continuel que la matière perscroit, rien estant

dans la matière elle même, c'est à dire dans l'étendue et impénétrabilité, d'où la pensée pourroit estre déduite, ou sur quoy elle pourroit estre fondée ... Or je dis que Dieu, dans ce cas là de la matière pensante, devroit non seulement donner la capacité de penser à la matière, mais encor l'y entretenir continuellement par le même miracle, puis qu'elle n'y a point de racine, à moins que Dieu y adjoute une nouvelle nature. Mais si l'on disoit que Dieu donne à la matière cette nouvelle nature ou la force de penser radicale, qui depuis s'y entretienne d'elle-même, ce seroit justement l'âme pensante qu'il luy auroit donnée, ou bien ce qui n'en differeroit que de nom; et cette force radicale n'estant pas proprement une modification de la matière, ... elle seroit independante de la matière". (Ibid., p. 355-6). Lady Masham replied on 8 August 1704 from a strictly Lockean standpoint (Locke was of course at Oates at the time): "Solidity and thought being both of them but attributes of some unknown substance, and I see not why it may not be one and the same which is the common support of both these; there appearing to me no contradiction in a co-existence of thought and solidity in the same substance. Neither can (I) apprehend it to be more inexplicable that God should give thought to a substance which I know not, but whereof I know some of its attributes, than to another, supposed, substance, of whose very being I have no conception at all." (Ibid., p. 359-60). The exact date of Leibniz's reply to this letter is unknown, but it was written in September of the same year. In this letter Leibniz confined himself to saying "Je ne say, Madame, comment on pourroit discerner une faculté naturelle primitive de penser, d'un principe substantiel de la pensée joint à la matière." But in an immediately following

350

passage of his draft, which appears not to have been included in the letter as sent, Leibniz continued: "A proprement parler, l'étendu solide sans âme n'est qu'un resultat de plusieurs substances, et nullement une vraye substance. Ainsi la matière qui pense sans ame ne peut estre qu'une fiction impossible, ou tout au plus un miracle dans mon systeme; il est vray de dire qu'il y a une substance qui a de la pensée et de l'étendu en même temps, si par la substance on entend le composé de l'ame et du corps, par exemple l'homme; mais si l'on entend la substance simple, il est manifeste qu'elle ne saurait avoir de l'étendue en elle, car tout étendu est composé." (Ibid., p. 363). This passage shows how fundamentally Leibniz's view on this matter differed from that of Norris and Malebranche, despite the superficial similarity of their expressions. The views of Locke, Norris, and Leibniz on what it is that thinks in man reflect their three different views on the nature of substance.

17) Theory ..., Pt. II, p. 63.

18) Ibid., p. 86; Norris derived this example from the Physics of the Cartesian Pierre-Sylvain Régis.

19) Ibid, p. 91.

20) Ibid., p. 94.

21) "Quamvis autem pro demonstrato habeam, probari non posse aliquam esse in brutis cogitationem, non ideo puto posse demonstrari nullam esse, quia mens humana illorum corda non pervadit." Descartes to More, 5 February 1649; in Descartes: Correspondance avec Arnauld et Morus, ed. Geneviève Lewis (Paris 1953), p. 124.

22) Theory ..., p. 99-100.

23) Cf. N. Kemp Smith's Introduction to his edition of D. Hume:

<u>Dialogues concerning Natural Religion</u>, (Oxford, 1935).

24) Having said in <u>Theory ...</u>, Pt. II, p.10, that he did not accuse all those who suggested that matter might have the power of thinking of any desire to prejudice the doctrine of immortality, he added in a note: "I say <u>all</u>, because I think there is a certain late author, who by his Second Thoughts of Human Soul (a book which shows that second thoughts are not always the wisest) has given us but too just an occasion that we should except him." The author of <u>Second Thoughts concerning Human Soul</u> was William Coward.

25) <u>A Philosophical Discourse concerning the Natural Immortality of the Soul</u>, p. 33-4.

26) Ibid., p. 37.

27) Ibid., p. 38.

28) That conservation in existence amounted to a continuous creation was the teaching of Descartes and also, in a somewhat different sense, of Scholastics such as Suarez.

29) The works in question were: Edmund Chishall, <u>A Charge of Heresy maintained against Mr. Dodwell's late Epistolary Discourse concerning the Mortality of the Soul of Man</u>, (London, 1706), and Samuel Clarke, <u>A Fourth Defence of an Argument made use of in a Letter to Mr. Dodwell to prove the Immateriality and Natural Immortality of the Soul</u> (London, 1708). At the end of his <u>Expostulation</u> Dodwell adjures Chishall and Clarke "to imitate the more <u>gentle</u>, as well as <u>Christian</u>, example of Mr. <u>Norris</u>" (p. 157).

CHAPTER X:

1) Dedicatory Letter or Preface of the 1st edition of <u>Reflections upon the Conduct of Human Life</u>.

2) <u>Some Familiar Letters between Mr. Locke and Several of his Friends</u>, (London, 1708) p. 182 (Letter of 22 Feb. 1696/4).

3) <u>Cursory Reflections upon a Book called an Essay concerning Human Understanding</u>, p. 7-8.

4) Ibid., p. 9.

5) Ibid., p. 11.

6) <u>Essay</u>, Book IV, ch. 3, sect. 18; quoted by Norris, <u>Cursory Reflections</u>, p. 15.

7) In a letter to Locke dated 15 March 1703/4, (Bodleian, MS Locke c. 7, fol. 26-8), Anthony Collins suggested "That there can be nothing advanced contradictorily to the design of the <u>Essay of Human Und.</u> but on the principle of Innate Ideas, in that sense they are refuted by the Author in the 1st Book." In his reply, dated 21 March 1703/4, and published in Des Maiseaux's <u>Collection of Several Pieces of Mr. John Locke</u>, (London, 1720), p. 296-302, Locke agreed that "all that do not argue against it (the <u>Essay</u>) from innate ideas, in the sense I speak of innate ideas, tho' they make a noise against me, yet at last they so draw and twist their improper ways of speaking, which have the appearance and sound of contradiction to me, as to leave no contradiction in it to my <u>Essay</u>".

8) <u>Cursory Reflections</u>, p. 20.

9) Ibid., p. 21.

10) <u>Essay</u>, Book II, ch. 8, sect. 8; quoted by Norris, <u>Cursory Reflections</u>, p. 22.

11) "Ainsi, par ce mot <u>idée</u>, je n'entends ici autre chose, que ce

qui est l'objet immédiat, ou le plus proche de l'esprit, quand il appercoit quelque chose." Recherche de la Vérité III, II, ch. I, sect. 1; O. C. I, p. 414. (From the 5th edition the end of the text was altered to read "... quelque objet").

12) Cursory Reflections, p. 22.

13) Ibid. , p. 29.

14) This was one of Norris's two references in 1690 to his projected work on the Ideal World, which did not appear, of course, till 1701-4.

15) Cursory Reflections, p. 35. Locke of course also accepted the existence of real essence, though he held that they are unknown to us.

16) Essay, Book IV, ch. 3, sect. 2; quoted by Norris, Cursory Reflections, p. 37.

17) Ibid. , p. 38.

18) Essay, Book IV, ch. II, sect. 14; quoted by Norris, Cursory Reflections, p. 39.

19) Cursory Reflections, p. 39.

20) Ibid. , p. 41-3.

21) Cf. Gabriel Bonno, Lettres Inédites de Le Clerc à Locke, (Berkeley and Los Angeles, 1959), p. 44.

22) A Brief Consideration of the Remarks made upon the foregoing Reflections ..., whose title was abbreviated by Norris to Remarks upon the Athenian Society, was reprinted with all subsequent editions of Cursory Reflections. It is wrongly identified in Gilbert D. McEwen's introduction to the Augustan Reprint Society's edition of Cursory Reflections (no. 93, 1961) with the post-script which Norris added to the first edition of Cursory Reflections retracting what he had previously written on the positive nature of sin. This post-script was not

354

printed in later editions of <u>Cursory Reflections</u>, since it became superfluous after the amendment of <u>Considerations upon the Nature of Sin</u> in the fourth edition of the <u>Miscellanies</u> (1706). On this post-script, see note 29 to this chapter. The Augustan Reprint Society's edition of <u>Cursory Reflections</u> includes this post-script but does not include <u>Remarks upon the Athenian Society</u>.

23) Supplement to the Third Volume of the <u>Athenian Gazette</u>, p. 2.

24) Ibid., p. 3.

25) <u>A Brief Consideration of the Remarks made upon the foregoing Reflections by the Gentlemen of the Athenian Society</u> (Remarks upon the Athenian Society), p. 59.

26) Cf. R.I. Aaron, <u>John Locke</u>, p. 108-9.

27) Cf. Locke's Letter quoted in note 7.

28) <u>Remarks upon the Athenian Society</u>, p. 61-2.

29) Ibid., p. 64.

30) At the end of his review, Le Clerc referred to the post-script that Norris had appended to <u>Cursory Reflections</u>, retracting what he had written in <u>Considerations upon the Nature of Sin</u> (in his <u>Miscellanies</u>) regarding the positive nature of sin. Le Clerc wrote laconically that "we find furthermore at the end of the book an Addition where the Author retracts having maintained, in an English book, that sin was a real thing; he declares now that he believes 'tis mere nothing". It is hardly possible to excuse Le Clerc of deliberate misrepresentation on this point, and Norris was rightly angry: "This is a gross misrepresentation that savours neither of the justice nor of the civility of the press ... .. does it follow that, because I disown the positiveness of sin, that therefore I hold 'tis a <u>mere nothing</u>?

Suppose I should say that these gentlemen's ignorance in philosophy and the common principles of metaphysics were not of a positive nature, do I thereby say it is nothing? Must sin be either positive or nothing? Is there no medium? What, did these gentlemen never hear of a privation? But this 'tis, when nature is not followed, when science is usurped, and when a sort of men whose talent was never known to lie much towards philosophy will needs turn a conventicle into a Port Royal, and set up for virtuosos." (Remarks upon the Athenian Society, p. 64-5.)

In view of this vigorous attack on the Athenian Society, whom Norris took for the authors of the review, it is surprising to note that a number of authorities speak of Norris himself as a member of this society. It is true that John Dunton, the moving spirit of the Athenian Society, speaks of Norris in his memoirs with respect, and that the publication of Le Clerc's review was doubtless not meant as a personal attack on him, since the Athenian Gazette reproduced all those reviews from the Bibliothèque Choisie which could interest English readers; but nevertheless the publication of this review, together with the tone of Norris reply to it, which was reprinted with all subsequent editions of Cursory Reflections, seem to exclude the possibility of Norris's membership. The idea that John Norris was a member of the Athenian Society seems to have originated with John Bowyer Nicholls in his 1817 edition of The Life and Errors of John Dunton. Nicholls wrongly identified John Norris, to whom Dunton always referred as "Mr. Norris", with the "Dr. Norris", a physician (probably to be identified with Dr. Edward Norris, fifth son of Thomas Norris of Speke, Lancs., and younger brother of Sir William

Norris the envoy to India), who was indeed, along with Dunton, Samuel Wesley, and Richard Sault, a regular contributor to the Athenian Gazette. Nicholls's false identification of the two Norrises was repeated by Luke Tyerman in his Life and Times of the Revd. Samuel Wesley (1866), and by the Dictionary of National Biography.

31) Bodleian Library, MS. Locke, c. 16, fol. 163.

32) MS. Locke, c. 16, fol. 165.

33) MS. Locke, c. 16, fol. 167.

34) JL Answer to Mr. Norris's Reflections 92
The first exception is at those words p. I § The understanding like the eye whilst it makes us see and perceive other things takes no notice of itself. But if it be not the privilege of a Cursory Reflector to take notice of or pass by what he pleases the very next words would have told him what the author intended and I suppose readers versed in civil conversation and who think it no prejudice to truth the world and their own ingenuity to be willing to understand what the author intends will not find it hard by reading those words contained in the same sentence viz And it requires art and pains to set it at a distance and make it its own object. But whatever be the difficulty etc.: to find by the help of a little charity that I meant this for an apology for myself and an excuse for my failings in treating a subject which had as I apprehended some peculiar difficulty and had not that I knew been much considered. And I would desire the Reflector for his own sake as well as mine to make a little more allowance for the future to poor authors if he and I may take that title for if the spirit of criticism should once be so rampant as to bring to a rigid examen all that is to be found in books, and should observe what is amiss

in expression, in method in argument in decorum in dedication etc.: it would be a hard time for those who set pen to paper especially if they have any fondness for their own conceptions and think the world injured if they are not presently showed in print. I for my part have always thought if a writer were not guilty either of great disingenuity or great mistakes whereby truth and good manners were like to be injured his other marks of human frailty might be forgiven him and with me the obligation I had to him for what he taught or seemed sincerely to intend to teach me compounded for those slips which perhaps I thought I met with in him. At least I think this is due to everyone that his words should be understood in the most favourable and most consistent meaning (which) could be put upon them. If the Reflector had been in this of my mind a good deal of precious ink and paper might have been spared and he might have allowed more time to others to be better employed in reading his other writing. For what need the world be troubled with it if he could not make any consistent sense in a sentence of mine which whether true or false sense or nonsense was nothing to the main design of my treatise or what is his reader edified by a whole page spent in finding fault with my method in not beginning with the definition of the word idea, which I believe scarce anyone who reads my book doubts what I mean by, or if he did he might be satisfied before he came to the end of this first chapter where I tell him that it is a term which I think stands best to stand for whatsoever is the object of the understanding when a man thinks or whatever the mind can be employed about in thinking, p. 4 § 8, and so I suppose the Reflector might have spared blaming me for not having stated the meaning of the word idea before I proceeded to the origination of ideas which I conclude upon a review he will find I have done.

Indeed he condemns me in this same p. 3, that I have not given him an account of the nature of ideas. If a Cursory Reflector were not excused from remembering anything he reads he might have prevented this exception by taking in good part what I say c. I, § 2 That I shall not meddle with the physical consideration of the mind or trouble myself to examine wherein its essence consists or by what motions of our spirits or alterations of our bodies we come to have any sensation by our organs or any ideas in our understandings and whether those ideas do in their formation any or all of them depend on matter or no these are speculations however curious and entertaining I shall decline as being out of my way in the design I am now upon etc. This a hard case that this man of Reflections will not suffer a poor neighbour of his to know his own design in writing, or pursue that design according to his own fashion and abilities. Perhaps I was lazy and thought the plain historical method I had proposed to myself was enough for me perhaps I had other business and could afford no more of my time to these speculations, nay possibly I found that discovery beyond my reach and being one of those that do not pretend to know all things am not ashamed to confess my ignorance in this and a great many other and therefore shall acknowledge it as a great favour from the Reflector to instruct me better in the nature of ideas which he so magisterially accuses me for having against the laws of all method omitted. This rankness of criticism which prescribes to others what they shall and what they shall not treat of and makes me answer for what I have not as well as what I have written is owing undoubtedly

359

to the richness of the soil. There are some happy genuises who think they either are not or ought not to be ignorant of anything. The unlimited possessions which these sons of light by the luckiness of their birth enjoy in the intellectual world justly deserve our admiration and I readily vail (=bow) to them but yet for all that tis troublesome living near those great potentates for they always expect that their poor neighbours who have not the good fortune to be born to so large inheritances should never the less treat them with the same plenty. If you once mention ideas you must be presently called to an account what kind of things you make these same ideas to be though perhaps you have no design to consider them any further than as the immediate objects of perception or if you have you find they are a sort of sullen things which will only show them what but will not tell you whence they came nor whither they go nor what they are made of and yet you must be examined to all those particulars 1° whether they be real beings or no, in the next place whether they be substances or modifications of substances and further whether they are material or immaterial substances and then upon their being material you must answer to an hundred solid questions. I must confess it a mark of my poverty not to be provided with ragousts to entertain him according to his relish on all these subjects for there is not I perceive a leg or a wing of any of those dotterel (=stupid) ideas that imitate everything whether you would hash them up as material effluvias or serve immaterial as to their substance or immaterial as to their representation but managed by good cookery might make (make - repeated) a considerable dish, as you may see p. 21-31 where out of his abundant liberality and in consideration of my unprovided kitchen has

360

furnished out to himself (has furnished out to himself - repeated) a large entertainment according to his own palate and
thither I send anyone who has a mind to feast himself upon
ideas. (I am indebted to the Keeper of the Western Manuscripts,
Bodleian Library, Oxford, for permission to publish this text).

35) In its manuscript form this was entitled <u>JL Of Seeing all things
in God 1693.</u>

36) In manuscript this was entitled <u>Some other loose thoughts which
I set down as they came in my way in a hasty perusal of some
of Mr. Norris's writings, to be better digested when I shall have
leisure to make an end of this argument</u>

37) Charlotte Johnston, <u>Locke's "Examination of Malebranche" and
John Norris,</u> in <u>Journal of the History of Ideas</u> (1958), p. 551-8.

38) MS. Locke, d. 4, § 4.

39) Ibid. , § 3.

40) Ibid. , § 5.

41) Cf. <u>Letters concerning the Love of God,</u> "Two Letters by way
of Review".

42) Cf. ch. II, sect. 3.

43) MS Locke, d. 4, § 5 (not in published version).

44) <u>Remarks upon some of Mr. Norris's Books,</u> § 15, p. 255.

45) Ibid. , § 16, p. 255-6.

46) <u>A Discourse concerning the Love of God.</u>

47) "C'est donc le Créateur de ton âme qui te donne tes idées;
mais, comme il a laissé à ton coeur la liberté, il donne à
ton esprit les idées que ton coeur mérite; tu vis dans Dieu,
tu agis, tu penses dans Dieu; tu n'as donc qu'à ouvrir les
yeux à cette lumière qui éclaire tous les hommes; alors tu
verras la vérité, et la feras voir. - Eh! voilà le père Malebranche tout pur! m'écriai-je.   Je connais ton Malebranche,
dit-il; il était un peu quaker, mais il ne l'était pas assez".

English translation from <u>Letters concerning the English Nation,</u> with introduction by Charles Whibley, (London, 1926).

48) Bodleian Library, Ballard MSS. XXX, 24.

49) Taylor published translations of <u>La Recherche de la Vérité</u> and of the <u>Traité de la Nature et de la Grâce</u> in 1694. In 1700 he added a translation of Malebranche's <u>Discours sur la Lumière et les Couleurs,</u> which had then not yet been published in French but which became the <u>16e Eclaircissement</u> to <u>La Recherche de la Vérité.</u> When publishing this <u>Eclaircissement</u> himself, Malebranche complained that the English translation was based on a defective copy of his text.

50) <u>Reflections upon the Conduct of Human Life,</u> p. 202.

51) Post-script to the second and subsequent editions of <u>Reflections upon the Conduct of Human Life;</u> in <u>Treatises upon Several Subjects,</u> p. 260-2.

52) <u>A Just Reprehension</u> ..., p. 15.

53) <u>Two Treatises concerning the Divine Light,</u> p. 353.

54) Ibid., p. 452-3. Norris finds Barclay an adversary worthy of more respect than the most famous Roman Catholic apologists.

55) George Keith, <u>The Way to the City of God,</u> p. 130; quoted by Norris, op. cit., p. 440.

56) Robert Barclay, <u>Apology for the True Christian Divinity,</u> p. 87; quoted by Norris, op. cit., p. 437.

57) More's <u>Brief Discourse of the Real Presence</u> was published anonymously in 1686, a year before his death. He did not try seriously to preserve his anonymity. More had mutual friends with the early Quakers in Lady Conway and her doctor F. M. van Helmont, the Cabbalist.

58) <u>Truth and Innocency Defended; being a Sober Reply to some Excesses in a Treatise written by John Norris concerning the</u>

Divine Light: wherein his Personal Reflections and Misrepre-
sentations of the Quakers about their Principle of the Light
are further considered, (London, 1693).

59) Of Whitehead the Dictionary of National Biography writes:
"It is almost impossible to overestimate Whitehead's share
in the foundation of the Society of Friends."

60) It would be interesting to know whether Elys's refusal of the
oath of allegiance to William and Mary was motivated by a
non-juring allegiance to James II or by the Quaker objection
to oaths as such.

CHAPTER XI:

1) Glanvil was of course an Oxford man.

2) Cf. F.J.Powicke, The Cambridge Platonists; a Study, Preface.

3) Cf. Maren-Sophie Røstvig, The Happy Man. Studies in the Metamorphoses of a Classical Ideal, p.372.

4) Spiritual Counsel, p.499-500.

5) On this matter the influence of the Scholastics and of Henry More enabled Norris to propound a more satisfactory theory of the Ideas than Malebranche.

6) The title of John K.Ryan's article, "John Norris: a Seventeenth Century English Thomist", (in The New Scholasticism (14), April 1940, p.109-45), is highly misleading.

7) He also recommends in passing "the experimental philosophy", while commenting on the wealth that is required for its pursuit.

8) Pylades and Corinna, (ed.Sir Edward Northey, London,1732), vol.II, p.203.

9) F.J.Powicke, Dissertation on John Norris of Bemerton, p.147.

10) Cf. F.Alquié, Le Cartésianisme de Malebranche, passim.

11) E.g. to John Byrom and the young William Law. Cf. A.Keith Walker, William Law, his Life and Thought, London, 1973, and J.Hoyles, The Fringes of Augustanism, The Hague, 1972.

12) Cf. my article "Malebranche and his Heirs" in Journal of the History of Ideas (1977), p.673-6.

13) Norris was not, of course, a Latitudinarian in the party sense.

14) A Treatise concerning Christian Prudence: or, The Principles of Practical Wisdom, fitted to the Use of Human Life, and designed for the better Regulation of it. In Octavo. The 7th Edition. Price 3s. 6d. in Calf.

Treatises upon several Curious Subjects formerly printed single, now collected into two Volumes. Price 5s.

The Theory and Regulation of Love. A Moral Essay, in two
Parts. With some Motives to the Study and Practice of Regular Love by way of Consideration. To which are added
Letters Philosophical and Moral to Dr. Henry Moore (sic),
with the Doctor's Answers. As is also by way of Appendix
An Hypothesis concerning the Root of Liberty; formerly printed by itself and dedicated to the Doctor, and treated of in one
of his said Letters. The Seventh Edition. Price 2s. in Calf.
A Collection of Miscellanies, consisting of Poems, Essays,
Discourses, and Letters. Carefully revised, corrected, and
improved by the Author. The 8th Edition. Price 3s. in Calf.
A Philosophical Discourse concerning the Natural Immortality
of the Soul. Wherein the great Question of the Soul's Immor-
tality is endeavoured to be rightly Stated and fully Cleared.
In two Parts. In 8vo. The 4th Edition.
A Letter to Mr. Dodwell concerning the Immortality of the
Soul of Man, in Answer to one from him relating to the same
matter. In 8vo. The 4th Edition.
A Practical Treatise concerning Humility, Designed for the
Furtherance and Improvement of that Virtue, both in the Lives
and Minds of Men. In Octavo. The Fifth Edition. Price 4s.
in Calf.
Christian Blessedness: Or, Practical Discourses upon the
Beatitudes of our Lord and Saviour Jesus Christ. The 10th
Edition. Price 3s. in Calf.
Reason and Religion, Or the Grounds and Measures of Devotion,
considered from the Nature of God and the Nature of Man, in
several Contemplations, with Exercises of Devotion applied
to every Contemplation. The Seventh Edition. Price 2s. in
Calf.

Reflections upon the Conduct of Human Life, with Reference
to the Studx of Learning and Knowledge. To which is annexed
a Visitation Sermon. The 5th Edition. Price 2s. in Calf.
Practical Discourses in Four Volumes. In Octavo. Price 10s.
An Account of Reason and Faith: In Relation to the Mysteries
of Christianity. The Twelfth Edition.
Letters Philosophical, Moral, and Divine to the Reverend
Mr. John Norris, with his Answers. OR, Letters concerning
the Love of God; between the Author of the Proposal to the
Ladies and Mr. John Norris; wherein his late Discourse,
showing that it ought to be entire and exclusive of all other
loves is further cleared and justified. The Second Edition
corrected by the Authors, with some few things added.
An Essay towards the Theory of the Ideal or Intelligible World,
in Two Parts. The first considering it absolutely in itself.
The Second being the Relative Part of it, with relation to Human Understanding. In 8vo. The 3rd Edition. Price 10s.
Two Treatises concerning the Divine Light, the first being an
Answer to a Letter of a Learned Quaker. The Second being a
Discourse concerning the Grossness of the Quaker's Notion
of the Light within, with their Confusion and Inconsistency in
explaining it. The Second Edition.
The Charge of Schism Continued; being a Justification of the
Author of Christian Blessedness, for his charging the Separa-
tists with Schism, with a Postscript concerning Moderation.
The Seventh Edition.
Spiritual Counsel, Or, the Father's Advice to his Children.
The 16th Edition.
Of Religious Discourse in Common Conversation. In Three
Parts. The Ninth Edition.

A Discourse concerning Worldly and Divine Wisdom. The
Sixteenth Edition.

The Importance of a Religious Life considered from the Happy
Conclusion of it. The Ninth Edition.

Religious Singularity Displayed: Showing the Necessity of
Practising that great Christian Virtue. The Ninth Edition.

The last four of these are single sermons from Practical
Discourses.

15) In 1733 the same works were on sale, except that The Importance of a Religious Life was no longer available, its place
being taken by An Effectual Remedy against the Fear of Death.

16) Advice to a Young Student, p. 27.

17) Historical View of the Rise and Progress of Infidelity, vol. II,
p. 133 and 192.

18) Scholae Academicae, p. 131.

19) The following is the list of works by Norris and related authors
which Wesley read during these years:

1725: J. Norris: Practical Discourses upon Several Divine Subjects.

1726: Unspecified works by Norris.

1727-8: These years are missing from Wesley's Journal.

1729: Norris: Of Human Understanding; Theory of the Ideal
World.

1730: Norris: Of Humility; Of Christian Prudence.

1731: Norris: On Human Understanding; On Christian Prudence.
Mary Astell: Serious Proposal to the Ladies.

1732: Norris: On Schism (read twice during the year); On
Christian Prudence.

1733: Norris: Spiritual Counsel; Miscellany.
Mary Astell: Serious Proposal to the Ladies.

Malebranche: Recherches.

1734: Norris: On Christian Prudence.

Malebranche: Recherches.

The titles are here given in the abbreviated form used by Wesley. Norris's work On Human Understanding is presumably his Cursory Reflections upon a Book called, An Essay concerning Human Understanding.

20) The Letters of John Wesley (Standard Edition, London, 1931), vol. III, p. 173.

21) Ibid. , p. 175.

22) In this summary of some of Wesley's philosophical ideas, the following works have been consulted in addition to the Journals and the Letters: Thoughts on Christian Perfection (1759); Further Thoughts on Christian Perfection (1762); A Survey of the Wisdom of God in the Creation: or a Compendium of Natural Philosophy (1763); and The Arminian Magazine.

23) For Malebranche's influence on Berkeley, see the works of A. A. Luce.

24) Dialogues concerning Natural Religion, 4th Part, (ed. N. Kemp Smith, Oxford, 1935, p. 197-201), and 8th Part (ibid. , p. 229-30). My attention was drawn to these passages by Dr. L. J. Beck.

25) Ibid. , p. 198-200.

26) Ibid.

27) Steeple Langford is situated less than ten miles from Bemerton.

28) Clavis Universalis (Edinburgh, 1836, edition), p. 81.

29) Ibid. , p. 123.

30) Ibid.

31) Joseph Glanvil, Scepsis Scientifica: or, Confessed Ignorance the Way to Science; in an Essay on the Vanity of Dogmatizing, and Confident Opinion (London, 1665).

Robert Boyle, Reflections upon a Theological Distinction, according to which it is said that some Articles of Faith are above Reason, but not against Reason, published as an Appendix to The Christian Virtuoso (London, 1690-1).

32) "Kant and the English Platonists", in Essays Philosophical and Psychological in honour of William James (New York, 1908), p. 289.

33) Clavis Universalis was translated into German, together with Berkeley's Dialogues, and published in Eschenbach, Sammlung der vornehmsten Schriftsteller, die die Wirklichkeit ihres eignen Körpers und der ganzen Körperwelt leugnen, (1757). This was the only German version of Berkeley that Kant could have known; he may well, therefore, have read Collier too. Cf. L. Robinson, "Le "cogito" cartésien et l'origine de l'idéalisme moderne", in Descartes; Recueil publié par la "Revue Philosophique" à l'occasion du troisième centenaire du "Discours de la Méthode", (Paris, 1937). But see also the more negative conclusion of H. J. de Vleeshauwer, "Les antinomies kantiennes et la Clavis Universalis d'Arthur Collier", in Mind (N. S.), 1938, p. 303-20.

34) The literary significance of Norris's poetry has not been examined in this book. But see John Hoyles, The Waning of the Renaissance, 1640-1740 (The Hague, 1971), p. 75-139.

BIBLIOGRAPHY

I. NORRIS'S WORKS

The following, it is hoped, is a complete list of Norris's writings; it is not, however, a complete list of the editions of these works. In cases where different editions vary in their text or pagination, the edition from which quotations are taken and to which page references in this book refer (except where another edition is specifically mentioned) is indicated by + thus:

+ 1687 (1). This means that references and quotations are from the first edition of the work in question, published in 1687.

(a) <u>Works by Norris published in his lifetime</u>
1) Effigies Amoris in English. 1682 (1), 1701 (2), 1744 (4).
2) A Meditation upon Life and Death. 1682.
3) Hierocles upon the Golden Verses of the Pythagoreans. 1682.
4) Tractatus adversus Reprobationis Absolutae Decretum. 1683.
5) A Murnival of Knaves. 1683.
6) An Idea of Happiness, in a Letter to a Friend. 1683 (1). Reprint in 7 and 9 below. Our references are to + 9.
7) Poems and Discourses occasionally written. 1684. Reprinted in + 9.
8) Sermon on Romans XII, 3, ("The Root of Liberty"). 1685. Reprint in + 9.
9) A Collection of Miscellanies. + 1687 (1), 1692 (2), 1699 (3), 1706 (4, revised), 1710 (5), 1717 (6), 1722 (7), 1723 (8), 1730 (9).
10) The Theory and Regulation of Love. + 1688 (1), 1694 (2), 1723 (7).

11) Reason and Religion. 1689 (1), 1693 (2), 1724 (7). Reprinted in + 24.

12) Visitation Sermon on John XXI, 15. 1689. Reprinted in + 24.

13) Reflections upon the Conduct of Human Life, with reference to the Study of Learning and Knowledge. 1690 (1), 1691 (2), 1723 (5). Reprinted in + 24.

14) Christian Blessedness, or Discourses upon the Beatitudes. 1690 (1), + 1692 (2), 1694 (3), 1699 (4), 1707 (5), 1713 (6), 1724 (10), 1728 (15). (The third edition, with several subsequent ones, is entitled Practical Discourses upon the Beatitudes).

15) Cursory Reflections upon a Book called, An Essay concerning Human Understanding. 1690 (1), + 1692 (2), etc. (Always printed with 14 above. Cursory Reflections has been reprinted by Gilbert D. McEwen (Augustan Reprint Society, n. 93), - cf. our ch. 10, note 22).

16) A Brief Consideration of the Remarks made upon the foregoing Reflections by the Gentlemen of the Athenian Society, ("Remarks upon the Athenian Society"). + 1692 (1). (Always printed with 14 and 15 above as from the second edition).

17) Practical Discourses upon several Divine Subjects, Vol. II. (Vol. 1 is 14 above). + 1691 (1), 1693 (2), 1697 (3), 1707 (5), 1716 (8), 1728 (15).

18) Practical Discourses upon several Divine Subjects, Vol. III. + 1693 (1), 1711 (3), 1722 (8), 1728 (15).

19) Practical Discourses upon several Divine Subjects, Vol. IV. + 1698 (1), 1707 (2), 1722 (8), 1728 (15).

20) The Charge of Schism continued. 1691 (1), 1703 (2). Reprinted in + 24.

21) Two Treatises concerning the Divine Light. 1692. Reprinted in + 24.

371

22) Spiritual Counsel: or, The Father's Advice to his Children. 1694 (1), 1722 (16), 1733 (17). Reprinted in + 24.

23) Letters concerning the Love of God, between the Author of the Proposal to the Ladies and Mr. John Norris. + 1695 (1), 1705 (2), 1730 (3). (This work is also called Letters Philosophical, Moral, and Divine to the Reverend Mr. John Norris, with his Answers.)

24) Treatises upon Several Subjects. 1697 (1), 1698 (2). (Contains nos. 11, 12, 13, 20, 21, and 22, reprinted in a single volume. Our references to these works are to this edition.)

25) An Account of Reason and Faith, in relation to the Mysteries of Christianity. 1697 (1), 1724 (12), 1728 (13), 1790 (14).

26) An Essay towards the Theory of the Ideal or Intelligible World, Part I. 1701 (1). (A third edition was on sale in 1722.)

27) An Essay towards the Theory of the Ideal or Intelligible World, Part II. 1704 (1). (A third edition was on sale in 1722.)

28) The Distinction of High Church and Low Church, distinctly considered and fairly stated. 1705.

29) A Practical Treatise concerning Humility. 1707 (1), 1722 (5), 1730 (6).

30) A Philosophical Discourse concerning the Natural Immortality of the Soul. 1708 (1), + 1722 (4), 1732 (5).

31) A Letter to Mr. Dodwell concerning the Immortality of the Soul of Man. 1709 (1), + 1722 (4), 1732 (5). (After the first edition this work was printed as the second part of 30 above.)

32) A Treatise concerning Christian Prudence. 1710 (1), 1722 (7).

Apart from these complete works, the following sermons (from Practical Discourses upon several Divine Subjects) were reprinted separately as pamphlets in the course of the eighteenth century.

372

A Discourse concerning Religious Singularity (from Practical Discourses, Vol. II).

A Discourse concerning Wordly and Divine Wisdom (from Vol. II).

The Importance of a Religious Life, considered from the Happy Conclusion of it (from Vol. II).

Of Religious Discourse in Common Conversation (from Vol. IV).

A Discourse of the Fear of Death (from Vol. IV).

The Successive Vanity of Human Life (from Vol. IV).

(b) Other books containing some of Norris's writings

1) A Discourse concerning the Pretended Religious Assembling in Private Conventicles, by John Norris (senior), published by our Norris in 1685.

2) The Institution and Life of Cyrus the Great, translated from the Greek of Xenophon, the first four books by Francis Digby, the four last by John Norris, 1685.

3) An Essay on Poetry, by John Sheffield, Duke of Buckinghamshire, with a translation into English Verse by John Norris, 1691.

4) Letters to the Lady Wharton, and several other persons of distinction (Vol. II of Whartoniana), 1727. Contains five letters from Norris to "Corinna" (Mrs. Elizabeth Thomas).

5) Pylades and Corinna, edited by Sir Edward Northey, 1731-2. Vol. I contains the Life of Corinna, written by herself; Vol. II contains the same five letters of Norris to Corinna as 4 above, together with four others, and one from her to him.

6) Reflections upon the Conduct of Human Life, extracted from Mr. Norris by John Wesley. 4th edition 1776.

7) A Treatise concerning Christian Prudence, extracted from Mr. Norris by John Wesley. 3rd edition 1749.

8) The Scholar armed against the Errors of the Time (Vol. II), 1795 (1), 1800 (2). Contains the last chapter and post-script of <u>An Account of Reason and Faith.</u>

9) Memoirs of a Late Distinguished Advocate, by William Melmoth (junior), 1796. Contains Norris's correspondence with William Melmoth (senior).

10) Letters written by Eminent Persons in the Seventeenth and Eighteenth Centuries, 1813. Contains the letter written by Norris to Dr. Charlett of University College, Oxford, in 1707.

Individual poems by Norris are to be found in many anthologies of English verse. Larger selections are to be found in the following.

A Collection of Divine Hymns and Poems on Several Occasions, by the Earl of Roscommon, Mr. Dryden, Mr. Dennis, Mr. Norris, Mrs. Kath. Phillips, Philomela, and others, 1709.

The Christian Poet, or Divine Poems on the Four Last Things, written by Mr. Pomfret, the Earl of Roscommon, Mr. Norris, and others, 1735.

Miscellanies of the Fuller's Worthies' Library: the Poems of John Norris, for the first time collected and edited after the original texts, with Memorial-Introduction by A. B. Grosart, 1877. This rare volume contains all the poems of Norris's <u>Miscellanies.</u>

Thomas Traherne: Selected Poems; Thomas Vaughan: English Verse Remains; John Norris: Selected Poems; edited by W. C. Hall, Pembroke Booklets, no. 2, 1905.

(c) <u>Manuscripts of Norris</u>

Very few manuscripts of Norris remain. The following are in the Bodleian Library.

374

MS. Rawlinson D. 912, fol. 230: Latin exercise on the theme "Ferrum tuetur principem melius fides".

MS. Tanner 466, fol. 74: Latin verse exercise on the theme
"sero medicina paratur
Quum mala per longas convaluere moras".

MS. Tanner 41, fol. 148: Latin letter from Norris to Archbishop Sancroft thanking him for his nomination as Fellow of All Souls.

MS. Locke c. 16, fol. 163: Letter from Norris to Locke thanking him for his share in Norris's presentation to the benefice of Bemerton. Locke's reply is in MS. Locke c. 24, fol. 204.

MS. Locke c. 16, fol. 165; ibid. fol. 167: Two letters from Norris to Locke defending himself against the latter's complaints. A letter from Locke to Norris is to be found in MS. Locke c. 24, fol. 205.

II. OTHER SOURCES

(a) Biographical Sources

1) John Dunton: John Dunton's Life and Errors, London, 1705, re-edited by J. B. Nichols, London, 1817.

2) Thomas Hearne: Remarks and Collections (1705-35), Oxford, 1885-98.

3) J. B. Nichols: Literary Anecdotes of the Eighteenth Century (Vol. I), London, 1812.

4) Anthony à Wood: Athenae Oxonienses (1691 etc.), London, 1813-20.

Manuscripts concerning Norris are to be found in the archives of Winchester College, Hampshire, and in the Wiltshire County Record Office, Trowbridge, Wiltshire.

(b) Works of Controversy and Contemporary Comment

1) Mary Astell: The Christian Religion as Professed by a Daughter of the Church of England (London, 1705).

2) Samuel Bold (or Bolde): Remarks on what Mr. Norris hath said in his First Chapter of the Theory of the Ideal World, Part 2, to demonstrate the Immortality of the Soul, (1704). (Published as an appendix to the same author's Discourse concerning the Resurrection of the Same Body, London, 1705).

3) Gabriel Bonno: Lettres inédites de Le Clerc à Locke, (Berkeley and Los Angeles, 1959).

4) Simon Browne: The Charge of Schism against the Dissenters Discharged, (London, 1710).

5) Henry Dodwell: A Letter to the Reverend Mr. John Norris of Bemerton. (Published as an appendix to the same author's Explication of a Famous Passage in the Dialogue of St. Justin Martyr with Tryphon, concerning the Immortality of Human Souls, London, 1708).

6) Edmund Elys: A Vindication of some Sentiments of Robert Barclay against the Arguments of a Book entituled Anti-barclaius (London, 1693).

7) Edmund Elys: A Letter from Edmund Ellis, a Minister of the Church of England, to John Norris, another Minister of the same Church, in vindication of the Quakers from the Charge of being Socinians (1693, no place of printing given).

8) Edmund Elys: Reflections upon some Passages in a Book entitled Reflections upon the Conduct of Human Life, with reference to the study of Learning and Knowledge (no place or date).

9) "Gabriel John" (pseudonym for Thomas d'Urfey?): An Essay

376

towards the Theory on the Intelligible World. Intuitively Considered. Designed for Forty-nine Parts. Part III. Consisting of a Preface, a Post-Script, and a Little Something between, (London, 1705).

10) John Locke: Some Familiar Letters between Mr. Locke and several of his Friends (London, 1708).

11) John Locke: An Examination of P. Malebranche's Opinion of Seeing All Things in God (in The Posthumous Works of Mr. John Locke, London, 1708).

12) John Locke: Remarks upon some of Mr. Norris's Books, wherein he asserts P. Malebranche's Opinion of our Seeing All Things in God (in A Collection of Several Pieces of Mr. John Locke, ed. P. Des Maiseaux, London, 1720).

13) Lady Damaris Masham: A Discourse concerning the Love of God (London, 1696).

14) William Tong: A Defence of Mr. M. H.'s Brief Enquiry into the Nature of Schism and the Vindication of it (London, 1693).

15) Richard Vickris: A Just Reprehension to John Norris of Newton St. Loe for his Unjust Reflection on the Quakers, in his Book entitled, Reflections upon the Conduct of Human Life, etc., (London, 1692).

16) Richard Vickris: Truth and Innocency Defended: Being a Sober Reply to some Excesses in a Treatise written by John Norris concerning the Divine Light (London, 1693).

17) George Whitehead: The Divine Light of Christ in Man, and his Mediation, truly confessed by the People called Quakers (London, 1693).

18) Daniel Whitby: A Discourse of the Love of God (London, 1697).

(c) Manuscripts

Amongst Locke's manuscripts in the Bodleian Library are several which are concerned with Norris.

MS. Locke c. 28, fol. 107-11: JL Answer to Mr. Norris's Reflections 92. The manuscript is also marked JL to Mr. Norris, and was first published in The Locke Newsletter, no. 2, Summer 1971. It is reproduced in our chap. X, note 34.

MS. Locke d. 3, fol. 1-122: JL Of Seeing all things in God 1693. This manuscript was printed, with omissions, as II above.

MS. Locke d. 3, fol. 123-34: Some other loose thoughts which I set down as they came in my way in a hasty perusal of some of Mr. Norris's writings, to be better digested when I shall have leisure to make an end of this Argument. This manuscript was printed, with slight alterations, as 12 above.

MS. Locke c. 7, fol. 26-8: Manuscript letter of Anthony Collins to Locke, in which Collins examines and comments on those passages of the Second Part of Norris's Theory of the Ideal ... World which refer to Locke. Locke's reply was printed in 10 above.

In the Niedersächsische Landesbibliothek, Hannover, are several manuscript letters of Thomas Burnet of Kemney to Leibniz which refer to Norris. The letters in question are: Correspondance Leibniz-Burnet, Stücke 54, 58, 110-1, 117-8. See our chap. VI, note 42, and chap. I, note 25.

(d) Periodicals

Bibliothèque Choisie (of Jean Le Clerc, Amsterdam), no. 20, Jan. 1691, p. 65-72: critical review of Norris's Cursory Reflections on Locke's Essay.

Athenian Gazette (London), Supplement to the Third Volume, 1691,

p. 2-3: English translation of the review in the Bibliothèque Choisie.

Acta Eruditorum (Leipzig), October, 1697, p. 442-9: review of An Account of Reason and Faith, by G. Olearius

Acta Eruditorum (Leipzig), April, 1708, p. 167-71: review of the Second Part of the Theory of the Ideal ... World, by Christian Wolff.

III. LITERATURE

(a) Before 1830

1) St. Thomas Aquinas: Opera Omnia (Rome, 1882 ss.)

2) Mary Astell: A Proposal to the Ladies (London, 1694).

3) A. Arnauld: Livre des vraies et des fausses idées (Cologne, 1683).

4) St. Augustine: Opera Omnia (ed. Migne, Patres Latini, Vol. 32-47, Paris, 1845 ss.)

5) George Ballard: Momoirs of Several Ladies of Great Britain, who have been celebrated for their Writings or Skill in the Learned Languages, Arts, and Sciences (Oxford, 1752).

6) Robert Barclay: Apology for the True Christian Divinity (Aberdeen and London, 1678).

7) Robert Baron (Baronius): Metaphysica Generalis (London, 1657).

8) Pierre Bayle: Dictionnaire, art. Zénon (Rotterdam, 1697).

9) Francois Bernier: Abrégé de la philosophie de M. Gassendi (Paris, 1674).

10) Robert Boyle: The Christian Virtuoso; with Reflections upon a Theological Distinction, according to which it is said that some Articles of Faith are Above Reason, but not Against Reason (London, 1690-1).

11) F. Burgersdijk (Burgersdictus): Institutiones Logicae (Leyden, 1635 etc.)

12) Thomas Burnet: Telluris Theoria Sacra (London, 1681).

13) Joseph Butler: Works (ed. W. E. Gladstone, Oxford, 1896).

14) Alexander Chalmers: General Biographical Dictionary (London, 1815).

15) Edmund Chishall: A Charge of Heresy, maintained against Mr. Dodwell's late Epistolary Discourse, concerning the Mortality of the Soul (London, 1706).

16) Lady Mary Chudleigh: Essays upon Several Subjects (London, 1710).

17) Samuel Clarke: A Letter to Mr. Dodwell, wherein all the Arguments of his Epistolary Discourse against the Immortality of the Soul are particularly answered, and the Judgement of the Fathers concerning that Matter truly represented (London, 1706).

18) Samuel Clarke: A Defence of the Argument made use of in the above-mentioned Letter to Mr. Dodwell, ... in Four Letters to the Author of "Some Remarks..." (= A. Collins) (London, 1731).

19) Arthur Collier: Clavis Universalis, or a New Enquiry after Truth (London, 1713).

20) Arthur Collier: A Specimen of True Philosophy, in a Discourse on Genesis I, 1 (Salisbury, 1730).

21) Arthur Collier: Logology, or a Treatise on the Logos or Word of God (London, 1732).

22) Anthony Collins: A Letter to the Learned Mr. Henry Dodwell, containing some Remarks upon a (pretended) Demonstration of the Immateriality and Natural Immortality of the Soul, in Mr. Clark's Answer to his late Epistolary Discourse (London, 1709).

23) Anthony Collins: A Discourse on Free Thinking (London, 1713).

24) Anthony Collins: A Philosophical Enquiry concerning Human

Liberty (London, 1715-17).

25) Anthony Collins: A Dissertation on Liberty and Necessity (London, 1729).

26) William Coward: Second Thoughts concerning Human Soul (London, 1702).

27) John Craig: Theologiae Christianae Principia Mathematica (London, 1699).

28) Ralph Cudworth: True Intellectual System of the Universe (London, 1678).

29) Richard Cumberland: De Legibus Naturae (London, 1672); (translated by John Maxwell, Treatise of the Law of Nature, London, 1727).

30) Etienne de Courcelles (Curcelleus): Institutio Religionis Christianae (in Opera Theologica, ed. Ph. van Limborch) (Amsterdam, 1675).

31) Gabriel Daniel, S.J.: Voyage au Monde de Descartes (Paris, 1690).

32) René Descartes: Oeuvres (ed. Adam et Tannery, Paris, 1897-1909).

33) René Descartes: Correspondance avec Arnauld et Morus (ed. G. Lewis, Paris, 1953).

34) Henry Dodwell: An Epistolary Discourse proving from the Scriptures and the first Fathers, that the Soul is a Principle naturally Mortal, but immortalised actually by the pleasure of God ... by its union with the Divine Baptismal Spirit (London, 1706).

35) Jean-Baptiste Du Hamel: De Consensu Veteris et Novae Philosophiae (Paris, 1663).

36) Jean-Baptiste Du Hamel: De Mente Humana (Paris, 1672).

37) Jean-Baptiste Du Hamel: Philosophia Vetus et Nova, ad usum

scholae accomodata, in Regia Burgundia olim pertractata
(= La Philosophie Bourguignonne) (Paris, 1684).

38) John Duns Scotus: Opera Omnia (Lyons, 1639).

39) Marsilius Ficinus: Opera Omnia (Basel, 1576).

40) Marsilius Ficinus: Théologie platonicienne de l'immortalité des âmes (trans. Raymond Marcel, Paris, 1964).

41) Pierre Gassendi: Exercitationes Paradoxicae (Grenoble, 1624).

42) Joseph Glanvil: Lux Orientalis (London, 1662; republished by H. More in Two Choice and Useful Treatises .., London, 1682).

43) Joseph Glanvil: Scepsis Scientifica, or Confessed Ignorance the Way to Science: in an Essay on the Vanity of Dogmatizing, and Confident Opinion (London, 1665).

44) Francis Glisson: De Natura Substantiae Energetica (London, 1672).

45) Sir Richard Colt Hoare: History of Modern Wiltshire (Hundred of Branch and Dole) (London, 1825).

46) David Hume: Dialogues concerning Natural Religion (ed. N. Kemp Smith, Oxford, 1935).

47) George Keith: The Way to the City of God (Aberdeen, 1678).

48) Francois Lamy: De la connaissance de soi-même (Paris, 1694-8).

49) Louis Le Blanc de Beaulieu: Theses Theologicae, variis temporibus in Academia Sedanensi editae ... (London, 1675).

50) Henry Lee: Anti-Scepticism, or Notes upon each Chapter of Mr. Locke's Essay (London, 1702).

51) G. W. Leibniz: Philosophische Schriften (ed. Gerhardt, Berlin, 1875-90).

52) G. W. Leibniz: Leibniz: Textes inédits (ed. Grua, Paris, 1948).

53) G. W. Leibniz: Kleine Schriften zur Philosophie (ed. Hans Heinz Holz, Frankfurt am Main, 1965).

54) John Locke: Works (10th edition, London, 1801).

55) John Locke: Essays on the Law of Nature (ed. W. von Leyden, Oxford, 1954).

56) John Locke: Essay concerning Human Understanding (ed. J. W. Yolton, London, 1961).

57) John Locke: Epistola de Tolerantia: A Letter on Toleration; Latin Text edited by R. Klibansky; English Translation by J. W. Gough (Oxford, 1968).

58) J. Lowde: Discourse concerning the Nature of Man (London, 1694).

59) J. Lowde: Moral Essays (London, 1699).

60) P. Magelhaens (Magellaneus): Tractatus Theologicus de Scientia Dei (Lisbon, 1666).

61) Nicolas Malebranche: Oeuvres Complètes (ed. A. Robinet, Paris, 1958 ss.)

62) Henry More: Opera Omnia (ed. S. Hutin, Hildesheim, 1966).

63) Henry More: Two Choice and Useful Treatises... (London, 1682).

64) Henry More: An Illustration of those two Abstruse Books ... the Book of Daniel and the Revelation of St. John (London, 1685).

65) Henry More: A Brief Discourse of the Real Presence of the Body and Blood of Christ (London, 1686).

66) Pierre du Moulin: Anatome Arminianismi (Leyden, 1619).

67) Henry Needler: The Works of Mr. Henry Needler, consisting of Original Poems, Translations, Essays, and Letters, Published by Mr. Duncombe (2nd ed., London, 1728).

68) P. Nicole and A. Arnauld: La logique, ou l'art de penser (ed. Clair et Girbal, Paris, 1965).

69) J. Overall: Bishop Overall's Convocation Book (ed. Sancroft, London, 1690).

70) Sir Thomas Phillips: Institutiones Clericorum in Comitatu Wiltoniae (Middle Hill, 1825).

71) Jean de la Placette: Nouveaux Essais de Morale (Amsterdam, 1697).

72) Jean de la Placette: Traité de la Foi Divine (Amsterdam, 1697)

73) Pierre Poiret: Cogitationes Rationales de Deo (Amsterdam, 1677).

74) Pierre Poiret: L'oeconomie divine (Amsterdam, 1687).

75) Timothy Puller: The Moderation of the Church of England (London, 1679).

76) Pierre-Sylvain Régis: Métaphysique (in Système de Philosophie, Lyons, 1690).

77) Samuel Richardson: Clarissa (ed. Leslie Stephan, London, 1883).

78) Jacques Rohault: Entretiens sur la Philosophie (Paris, 1671).

79) George Rust: A Discourse of Truth (ed. H. More, Two Choice and Useful Treatises, London, 1682).

80) John of St. Thomas: Cursus Philosophicus (Paris, 1883).

81) Robert Sanderson: De Legum Humanarum Obligatione in Conscientia (London, 1660).

82) C. Scheibler: Opus Metaphysicum (Gießen, 1617).

83) C. Scheibler: Opus Philosophicum (Frankfurt am Main, 1665).

84) W. Sherlock: The Case of Allegiance (London, 1691).

85) F. Suarez: Opera Omnia (ed. André, Paris, 1856 ss.)

86) Jeremy Taylor: The Rule and Exercises of Holy Living (London, 1650).

87) Jeremy Taylor: The Rule and Exercises of Holy Dying (London, 1651).

88) Thomas Taylor: A Sermon on Providence (London, 1697).

89) Thomas Taylor: The Two Covenants of God with Mankind (London, 1704).

384

(Taylor also translated the following French works: Daniel:
Voyage au Monde de Descartes; Malebranche: La Recherche
de la Vérité; Traité de la Nature et de la Grâce; Discours
sur la Lumière et les Couleurs).

90) John Toland: Christianity not Mysterious (London, 1696).

91) John Toland: Amyntor (London, 1699).

92) John Toland: Letters to Serena (London, 1704).

95) John Toland: Nazarenus (London, 1718).

97) John Toland: Pantheisticon (London, 1720).

98) William Van Mildert: An Historical View of the Progress of
Infidelity (Boyle Lectures, 1802-05) (London, 1806).

99) Francois-Marie Arouet de Voltaire: Lettres Philosophiques
(London, 1734);(English translation, with introduction by C.
Whibley, Letters concerning the English Nation, London,
1926).

100) Francois-Marie Arouet de Voltaire: Grâce (article in the
Encyclopédie of Diderot and d'Alembert, Paris, 1751-65).

101) Daniel Waterland: Advice to a Young Student (London, 1730).

102) Robert Watt: Bibliotheca Britannica (London, 1824).

103) John Wesley: A Survey of the Wisdom of God in the Creation:
or, a Compendium of Natural Philosophy (Bristol, 1763).

104) John Wesley: Journal (London, 1909-16).

105) John Wesley: Letters (London, 1931).

106) John Wesley: A Plain Account of Christian Perfection (London,
1952).

107) John Wesley: The Arminian Magazine (London, 1778 ss.)

108) William Whiston: A New Theory of the Earth (London, 1696).

Anonymous

109) The Whole Duty of Man (London, 1658).

Amongst Classical authors cited by Norris may be mentioned
Plato, Aristotle, Cicero, Lucretius, and Horace, in addition to
those whose works he translated.

(b) <u>After 1830</u>

1) Richard I Aaron: John Locke (2nd ed., Oxford, 1955).

2) Ferdinand Alquié: La Découverte métaphysique de l'homme
chez Descartes (Paris, 1950).

3) Ferdinand Alquié: Le Cartésianisme de Malebranche (Paris,
1974).

4) L. J. Beck: The Metaphysics of Descartes (Oxford, 1965).

5) Robert Benson: Memoirs of the Life and Writings of the Revd.
Arthur Collier (London, 1837).

6) William J. Bouwsma: Concordia Mundi: the Career and Thought
of Guillaume Postel (1510-1581) (Cambridge (Mass.), 1957).

7) A. Clark: The Colleges of Oxford (London, 1891).

8) A. K. Cook: About Winchester College (London, 1917).

9) M. Cranston: John Locke: A Biography (London, 1957).

10) Pedro Descoqs, S. J.: Praelectiones Theologiae Naturalis
(Paris, 1935).

11) H. N. Fairchild: Religious Trends in English Poetry (New
York, 1939).

12) Henri Gouhier: La Philosophie de Malebranche et son expérience
religieuse (2nd ed., Paris, 1948).

13) Henri Gouhier: La Pensée métaphysique de Descartes (Paris,
1962)

14) V. H. H. Green: The Young Mr. Wesley (London, 1961).

15) C. Grua: La Justice humaine selon Leibniz (Paris, 1956).

16) Martial Gueroult: Malebranche (Paris, 1955 ss.)

17) Johannes Hessen: Augustins Metaphysik der Erkenntnis (2nd
ed., Leyden, 1960).

18) J. Hoyles: The Waning of the Renaissance, 1640-1740 (The
Hague, 1971).

19) J. Hoyles: The Frings of Augustanism (The Hague, 1972).

20) Serge Hutin: Henry More (Hildesheim, 1966).

21) Alexandre Koyré: From the Closed World to the Infinite Universe (Baltimore, 1957).

22) P. O. Kristeller: The Philosophy of Marsilio Ficino (New
York, 1953).

23) A. O. Lovejoy: Kant and the English Platonists (in Essays Philosophical and Psychological in honour of William James,
New York, 1908).

24) A. O. Lovejoy: The Great Chain of Being (Cambridge, Mass.,
1936).

25) A. A. Luce: Berkeley and Malebranche (London, 1934).

26) A. A. Luce: Malebranche et le Trinity College de Dublin
(in Malebranche: Recueil publié par la Revue Philosophique,
Paris, 1938).

27) A. A. Luce: The Dialectic of Immaterialism (London, 1963).

28) Georges Lyon: L'Idéalisme en Angleterre au 18e siècle
(Paris, 1888).

29) F. I. Mackinnon: The Philosophy of John Norris of Bemerton
(Philosophical Monographs, Psychological Review Publications, Vol. I, no. 2, Baltimore, 1910).

30) Y. de Montcheuil, S. J.: Malebranche et le quiétisme (Paris,
1946).

31) J. Muirhead: The Platonic Tradition in Anglo-Saxon Philosophy
(London, 1931).

32) P. Petersen: Geschichte der aristotelischen Philosophie im
protestantischen Deutschland (Leipzig, 1921).

33) F. J. Powicke: A Dissertation on John Norris of Bemerton
(London, 1894).

34) F.J. Powicke: The Cambridge Platonists: A Study (London, 1926).

35) Carl-Heinz Ratschow: Lutherische Dogmatik zwischen Reformation und Aufklärung (Gütersloh, 1968).

36) André Robinet: Malebranche et Leibniz: Relations personnelles (Paris, 1955).

37) André Robinet: Système et existence dans l'oeuvre de Malebranche (Paris, 1965).

38) L. Robinson: Le "Cogito" cartésien et l'origine de l'idéalisme moderne (in Descartes: Recueil publié par la Revue Philosophique, Paris, 1937).

39) Geneviève Rodis-Lewis: Nicolas Malebranche (Paris, 1963).

40) Maren-Sophie Røstvig: The Happy Man: Studies in the Metamorphoses of a Classical Ideal (Oslo, 1954-8).

41) A.D. Sertillanges, O.P.: S. Thomas d'Aquin (Paris, 1910).

42) J.J. Simon: John Wesley and the Religious Societies (London, 1921).

43) Norman Kemp Smith: Studies in the Cartesian Philosophy (London and New York, 1902).

44) P.E. Spaulding: Richard Cumberland als Begründer der englischen Ethik (Leipzig, 1894).

45) Luke Tyerman: Life and Times of the Reverend Samuel Wesley, M.A., Rector of Epworth (London, 1866).

46) C. Wordsworth: Scholae Academicae: Some Account of the Studies in the English Universities in the Eighteenth Century (Cambridge, 1877).

47) M. Wundt: Die Deutsche Schulmetaphysik des 17en Jahrhunderts (Tübingen, 1939).

Anonymous

48) The Story of Newton St. Loe Manor (Essay published for the annual celebration of Newton Park Training College, Newton St. Loe, Bath, 1953).

Periodicals

The Downside Review (1957): God and Human Knowledge in St. Augustine, by Richard Acworth, (p. 207-14).

Journal of the History of Ideas (1958): Locke's "Examination of Malebranche" and John Norris, by Charlotte Johnston, (p. 551-8).

Journal of the History of Ideas (1977): Malebranche and his Heirs, by Richard Acworth (p. 673-6).

Mind (N. S.) (1938): Les antinomies kantiennes et la Clavis Universalis d'Arthur Collier, by H. J. de Vleeshauwer, (p. 303-20).

The New Scholasticism (1940): John Norris, a Seventeenth Century English Thomist, by John K. Ryan (p. 109-45).

Manuscript Study

Anne B. Larner: The Ingenious Mr. Norris (M. A. Thesis presented to the University of Manchester, September 1969).

The fullest account of Norris's writings is contained in Richard Acworth: La Philosophie de John Norris (1657-1712), a thesis presented to the Sorbonne in 1970 and published in 1975 by the University of Lille III (Service de Reproduction des Thèses).

Since the above list was compiled, the following works have been reprinted by Garland Publishing Inc., New York, in their series "British Philosophers and Theologians of the 17th and 18th Centuries":

A Collection of Miscellanies. 1687 (I).
Christian Blessedness..., with Reflections upon a Late Essay concerning Human Understanding. 1690 (I).
Treatises upon Several Subjects. 1698 (2).
An Essay towards the Theory of the Ideal or Intelligible World. 2 Vols., 1701, 1704 (I).